Memory, Space, Sound

Memory, Space, Sound

Edited by
Johannes Brusila, Bruce Johnson and John Richardson

intellect Bristol, UK / Chicago, USA

First published in the UK in 2016 by
Intellect, The Mill, Parnall Road, Fishponds, Bristol, BS16 3JG, UK

First published in the USA in 2016 by
Intellect, The University of Chicago Press, 1427 E. 60th Street,
Chicago, IL 60637, USA

A catalogue record for this book is available from the
British Library.

Cover designer: Emily Dann
Copy-editor: MPS Technologies
Production editor: Tim Mitchell and Mareike Wehner
Typesetting: Contentra Technologies

Print ISBN: 978-1-78320-602-5
ePDF ISBN: 978-1-78320-603-2
ePUB ISBN: 978-1-78320-604-9

Part of the Studies on Popular Culture series
Series ISSN: 2041-6725
Electronic ISSN: 2042-8227

Printed and bound by Gomer, UK

This is a peer-reviewed publication.

Contents

Chapter 1

Introduction

Johannes Brusila, Bruce Johnson and John Richardson

ultural researchers over the past couple of decades have increasingly grappled with the conundrum of how sound, and music in particular, becomes meaningful, regardless of background and disciplinary affiliation. The answer for many has been to situate sounds and their corresponding social and cultural activities within the contexts of space and memory. This triangular relationship has become a key issue in many fields of music research, promising to open up neglected areas of inquiry as well as creating linkages between interests that might previously have been regarded as unconnected; for example, acoustics, film music studies, soundscape studies, sociological theories of space, heritage and memory studies.

Technological developments have made formerly temporally and spatially distant sonic phenomena a part of our present culture in unforeseen ways, many of which are explored in this collection. Technology impinges on our subject in other ways, too. Not only are digital technologies transforming the landscape of our everyday social interactions when it comes to sound and music (Castells 1996; Bull 2000; Richardson and Gorbman 2013; Vernallis, Herzog and Richardson 2013), but they also offer increasingly sophisticated tools for understanding how sound, far from being easily separable from the surrounding physical and discursive world, is closely interconnected with it. There is no such thing as a *neutral* acoustic environment – one that is not conditioned in some way by an enveloping physical space, which in turn exists by dint of social actions and interactions. How we listen to sounds, with reference to the framing environment or bracketing it out, is thus a matter of choice – one made either unwittingly or with conscious reference to the social norms and conventions that inform the actions and responses we consider appropriate and meaningful. Once we couple sounds and their intrinsic situation-dependency with the memories of those who produce, perceive and respond to them, the plot thickens considerably. These relationships are the ones we choose to navigate, with a view to offering, in the totality of this collection, new insights on a range of topics related to these core themes.

In this book we present a multidisciplinary approach to studying how sound becomes meaningful in relation to time and place. Collectively, the essays endeavour to show how sounds, most frequently their musical forms, are located in actual and symbolic auditory spaces and how they are encoded as part of our cultural and social memory. We highlight relevant theoretical and empirical issues with a particular focus on cultural and social memory, space and place. Drawing on musicology and ethnomusicology, popular music studies, cultural history, media and cultural studies and other relevant approaches, the themes are explored through analyses of a wide range of examples, including performances, audiovisual material and the Internet. This enquiry in relation to both space and memory produces a synthesis of the synchronic and diachronic dimensions of cultural analysis.

Memory

According to an old axiom attributed to the influential Italian philosopher Benedetto Croce, 'all history is contemporary history'. This is certainly true when it comes to cultural studies of memory over the past few decades, during which there has been a growing historiographical and sociological interest in how the past is understood. Memories are not only individual, but collective, cultural and social (Halbwachs 1992; Assmann 1995, 2011). The past is present in various sites of memory, where cultural memories are crystallized (Boym 2001; Nora 1989). From a musicological perspective, it is interesting to study how our personal musical memories and culturally institutionalized memories construct our ideas of the past. After all, music has a unique power in acts of memory, to bring to consciousness events we had forgotten, to reclaim the past, to activate collective memory, and in doing so regenerate the most powerful sense of community and to laminate more firmly the present over the past.

Research on memory accomplishes much the same thing by sidelining the fictionalizing or reconstructive narratives of traditional histories in favour of the alternative, often more close-up-oriented stories that have emerged in writing on historiography, Foucault's archaeological and genealogical approaches to discourses, microhistory (e.g. Ginzburg 1980, 1983), critical studies of social groups (including the history of women and postcolonial history), research on autobiography, material culture and 'the social life of things' (e.g. Appadurai 1988) and archaeology in the traditional sense (as in Assmann's writing). Writing on collective memory and cultural memory has more in common with all of the above areas of inquiry than traditional historical research. While a common misapprehension is that memories are fleeting and inconsequential, in contrast to the assumed hard facts of historical textbooks, research in these fields provides compelling evidence that the reverse might be the case: the first-hand accounts of cultural actors – which we find in documents, recollections and personal reflections – often convey more direct and reliable information about experiences across and *of* history than official accounts. Memories are often, moreover, closely bound up to the world of material objects and social spaces. These are not peripheral by-products of history but affectively loaded crystallizations that offer windows onto the past and the present.

Memory is implicated also with a wide range of contemporary practices where music is circulated in material and immaterial forms. For a long period of time, music was understood to be an abstract art and the material dimensions of music were largely neglected; but during the past couple of decades, musicologists have also become interested in the relationship between the material culture of music and its cultural meanings (e.g. Brusila 2009). Equally important insights into music have been gained by viewing it as a creative activity, so new research is revealing the various ways in which it can be approached in terms of its distinctive 'thingness' – as something that can be preserved, owned, exchanged and appropriated. Questions have been raised about how music is preserved as sonic phenomena, material objects and individual and social memories. Music has often been archived as scores for aesthetic, functional and symbolic reasons, but simultaneously it has continued to exist as emotional memories, creative practices and social activities. Now, there is a growing interest for studying the ways in which music is preserved both at public or institutional museums and archives and at the private or individual level in, for example, private collections and recollections (see, e.g., Cohen et al. 2014, and the Australian project *Popular Music and Cultural Memory*). An interest in the past has also become more important for the music industry, which, as a part of the current 'retromania' (Reynolds 2011), invests in nostalgia, revivals and reissues of previous decades. The development of digital technology has made musics of the past present in today's media, not least the Internet, in both material and immaterial forms that to a growing extent break old physical boundaries.

Space

The questioning of the idea of 'autonomous music' and the increasing recognition that 'context' is as important as 'text' have brought forward the recognition that, far from being 'inherent', musical meanings are largely discursively constructed in dynamic interaction with musical sounds situated in physically concrete places and culturally constructed framing spaces. The notion of 'framing' has been around for some time, in Gregory Bateson's ecological view of human (and non-human) thought systems and interactions (Bateson 1972:183–198), Erving Goffman's theory of 'frame analysis' (1974), Derrida's deconstruction and, more recently, Mieke Bal's (2002) ideas about how cultural frames of reference shape our experiences of art. Broadly speaking, what unites these theories is the conviction that frames are understood as 'determining the type of "sense" that will be accorded everything within the frame' (Goffman 1961:20). Derrida and Bal add to this accumulation of knowledge the provocative idea that frames connect with general systems of knowledge that define also what falls *outside* the frame of reference (see also Richardson 2015). Where we experience music is crucial in several ways. It largely conditions the 'semiotics' of the music: the meanings and values we conventionally attach to it. Music made in one place simply has a different valorization from the same music made in another space.

Music has often been contextualized according to locality: in music history often according to nations; in ethnomusicology based on small-scale social groupings that live in a certain place or region; in popular music studies in relation to, for example, certain urban areas. Influences from, for example, cultural studies and cultural geography have also made music researchers question simplified notions of locality; for example, separation of physical place from socially constructed space (Giddens 1990), and the increasing scope and intensity of global and transnational processes, which has led to a 'time-space compression' (Harvey 1989:240). Simultaneously, technological development has changed the ways in which music is produced, disseminated and consumed spatially and geographically. Digital technology and Internet have created new ways of territorializing, deterritorializing and reterritorializing local communities through musical practices (e.g. Brusila 2010). However, sound technologies have not simply provided new conduits for music; they have of course also changed it (e.g. Katz 2010). The infinite reproducibility of music that can be achieved by digitization and the portability afforded by various forms of personal sound systems mean that music may now be experienced by millions in completely different spaces, each of which will be a crucial factor in forming its meanings.

While much of the research on popular music genres in particular has focused on urban spaces and geographies (e.g. Krims 2007), one cannot take for granted that theorizations of urban spaces are the only relevant models. This might explain why researchers working in more sparsely populated regions have taken such a keen interest in fields like soundscape studies and ecomusicology. Some of the defining questions in ecocritical research on music in fact come back to issues of spatial mapping, both within music and beyond its boundaries. Generally speaking, ecocritical research correlates an environmental or non-human frame of reference with a human and cultural one, thereby allowing the emergence of a more expansive perspective on familiar issues (Richardson 2015).

Space is routinely assumed to be something we experience visually, but of course information about space and place is communicated also in sounds. Since the invention of the phonograph, sound recordings have captured and mediated sonic spaces. Research on music technology is now beginning to take this sort of information just as seriously as aspects of music such as structure, form and melody were taken in the past. Musicologists (e.g. Tagg 2000; Richardson 2011: 219–223; Moore 2012:29–44) have asked how the relative positioning of elements in the mix – what Allan Moore calls the 'soundbox' – inflects our perceptions of performers and the 'messages' they put across – about intimate or distanced, interactional or individualistic modes of performance and so on. Readings of this kind can provide valuable insights into the social functions and *position* (in a broader sense) of performers and their listeners when combined with other analytical means. Just as sonically delineated space frames and configures experiences of ethnic and racialized space, so it is also a factor in social categories like class, language, age, generation and gender. Moving across ethnic and social spaces requires sensitivity to the notions of authenticity within the different audience cultures. For example, Third World musicians who enter the world music market must apply to their new audience's sonic ideas of 'the West and the Rest' and of world music as 'local music, not from here' (Brusila 2003).

Sound

The emergence of the systematic study of sound as a cultural phenomenon rather than as an object of scientific interest may be traced back to the work of R. Murray Schafer's benchmark study *The Tuning of the World* (Schafer 1977). His foundational work in the 1960s was conducted with the World Soundscape Project, which included Hildegard Westerkamp, and Barry Truax who authored the *Handbook of Acoustic Ecology* (Truax 1978/1999). One of the earliest collections outside the World Soundscape Project was the 1994 *Soundscapes: Essays on Vroom and Moo* (Järviluoma 1994), edited by Finnish scholar Helmi Järviluoma who, with Greg Wagstaff, also published the book *Soundscape Studies and Their Methods* (Järviluoma and Wagstaff 2002). Järviluoma has built on the foundations set down by the World Soundscape Project and Schafer, the results published as *Acoustic Environments in Change* (Järviluoma et al. 2009). Other work in the field confirms its interdisciplinary range, including, for example, that of cultural historian Alain Corbin (1999), ethnomusicologist Steven Feld (2012), science historian Jonathan Sterne (2013) and literary historian John Picker (2013). Significant institutionalizations of sound studies include the founding of the World Forum for Acoustic Ecology in 1993, which now has its own journal and annual conferences; and the establishment of CRESSON sound research centre in Grenobles, France, in 1998.

In the twenty-first century, the status of sound studies has increasingly been validated by 'handbook' or 'encyclopaedia' compilations that proclaim the interdisciplinary compass of the field. These include *The Auditory Culture Reader* (Bull and Back 2003), *Aural Cultures* (Drobnick 2004), *Hearing Cultures* (Erlmann 2004), *The Sound Studies Reader* (Sterne 2012), *Sound Studies* (Bull 2013), as well as more specialized texts as *The Soundscape of Modernity: Architectural Acoustics and the Culture of Listening in America, 1900–1933* (Thompson 2004), *Hearing History* (Smith 2010), *Sound: A Reader in Theatrical Practice* (Brown 2010) and *The Sound Handbook* (Crook 2012) (for an overview of the state and directions of sound studies, see Johnson forthcoming).

One pattern gradually emerging in this literature is an appreciation of the convergence of the intellectual and the material in auditory cognition, as exemplified in one of the most recent collections, *The Oxford Handbook of Sound Studies* (Finch and Bijsterveld 2012), with contributions ranging through cognitive studies, acoustic engineering, physiology, ecology, geography and neuroscience. This research has also been one of the most powerful drivers in problematizing the separation between music and sound, and by extension, music and social practice. Sonic phenomena in general are now recognized to be important elements in our understanding of not only aesthetic objects as such, but also art, our environment and the connections between human beings and technology.

As in the case of this collection, a substantial section of that field deals with music, perhaps the most semiotically complex form of anthropogenic sound. Indeed, it is the overlap between soundscape studies and music that has helped to problematize the latter term. For the more conservative branches of musicology, at least until the late 1980s, the idea of 'music' was often taken as a given, and studied with a focus on musical works and the study of classical scores. For a great many reasons associated with influences from, for example, ethnomusicology and general changes in intellectual and material culture, the perspectives have widened within music research, leading to a more generous and instructive understanding of the importance of context in addition to text, and raising ontological and epistemological questions regarding the nature and function of music. Resituating music within the larger sonic environment, for example, enlarges our understanding of its social role, as well as the importance of the senses, theories of cognition and technology (see, e.g., Birdsall and Enns 2008). Indeed, the very opposition of text and context is also increasingly problematized in general in recent humanities research, which interrogates the underlying assumptions and corresponding social practices that hold these and other concepts in place rather than taking them as something given or natural (see Bal 2002; Richardson 2015).

Musicology and ethnomusicology are therefore expanding to include ear-opening new perspectives, while interdisciplinary collaborations and mixed methods approaches to the study of music cultures have brought valuable new insights on music and its relations to surrounding cultural forms and practices. A notable example is the emergence of audiovisual studies, among which film studies are of special significance. Studies of film music have expanded understanding of musical meaning and affect and how they operate, in particular helping to conceptually resituate music within contexts as disparate as narratology, cultural theory, sound engineering and semiotics (see, e.g., Chion 2009; Tagg 2012). Much of the recent research on film music and other audiovisual uses of music – in gaming, music videos and live performances, for example – is robustly interdisciplinary (e.g. Richardson, Gorbman and Vernallis 2013). A notable shift has been towards an approach in which sounds and corresponding affects carry as much weight as the traditional means of narrative exposition. This shift has gone hand in hand with a corresponding interest in the sensory aspects of the subject. Recent research is beginning to unpack the implications of what some have called a new 'cinema of the senses' (Marks 2000; Elsaesser and Hagener 2010; Richardson 2011; Chion 2013), with reference to disciplinary standpoints including sound design, acoustics, phenomenology and aesthetics and the psychology of listening. These insights are helping researchers to situate experiences of music more convincingly in a multisensory field defined ultimately by the coordinates and capabilities of the human body. Understanding film sound as rooted in the spatialized experiences of embodied human agents augments one of the principal concerns of film music studies, which is to situate sounds against spatial coordinates in the filmed world (or, equally, outside of its bounds).

If awareness of how we experience sounds in the body at one end of the spectrum and as part of the sonic environment at the other end is coming into sharper focus in the light of new research, how we conceptualize and account for the cultural functions and meanings of sounds depends greatly also on points of reference located between these two extremes, many of which connect in some way with ideas about memory or space. All three converge in the following essays.

Contributions, contents of the book

It would be remiss of us to discuss issues of sound and space without acknowledging the salience of social and geographical space in which our soundings about this subject first took shape. This collection brings together work based on presentations given at the international conference *The Cultural Memory of Sound and Space*, organized jointly by the University of Turku and Åbo Academy University in Turku, Finland, 13–15 March 2013. The range of disciplines and regions covered by the contributors gives the collection great breadth both culturally and geographically. The authors and editors have a very wide international personal and professional background (e.g. Australia, Finland, Denmark, Serbia, Sweden, United Kingdom and United States). The case studies presented in the book originate from different parts of the world and in some cases, they also raise questions of intercultural connections and power relations.

The following chapters also reflect the breadth of approaches and methodologies, with a range of platforms including ethnography, musicology, cultural theory, media studies and archaeoacoustics. In aggregate, these chapters embrace the three elements of sound, space and memory, but individually the balances of thematic emphasis are as various as the disciplinary bases. At the same time, they all demonstrate implicitly if not explicitly that we have never been able to construct any one of them without some reference to the other two. All three are implicated in the construction of sonic meaning; arguably even the neonate arrives with a 'memory' of sound and its associations with place, since hearing develops within the womb. No individual can make meaning out of a sound without reference to both space and memory.

The way we have arranged these essays is not at all intended to suggest that the three can be uncoupled. The arrangement reflects a general balance of attention in each essay, but without wishing to suggest the possibility of any absolute quarantine. Detailed synopses of the chapters are provided below, but as an overview, we begin with discussions that on balance lean towards memory: the physical, corporeal construction and preservation of memory in the essays by Heinonen (the proclamation of the Christmas message in Finland), Kaijser (a restaging of a Pink Floyd performance) and the mediated enactment of memory in the essays by Kilpiö (cassette technology) and Long and Collins (music and online heritage). These are followed by examinations of the way in which imaginary and literal space functions to frame memory and sound, beginning with an essay by Cohen on the mapping of musical memories. Gligorijevic explores the literal space that helps to define the meanings of two music festivals, while Michelsen charts the figurative spaces created by radio. In the third section, Andean analyses sound in the particular form of electroacoustic music, Benjamin provides a case study in industrial sound and Gorbman reviews some of the changes in the aesthetics and role of film music that have taken place since her pioneering work in the field. We provide more detailed synopses below.

Opening the collection, Yrjö Heinonen analyses the annual declaration of Christmas peace in Turku, a tradition that is said to have continued virtually unbroken since the 1320s, and is still conducted with thousands of locals filling the square for the 15-minute ceremony and most Finns listening to it on radio or TV (for the TV film of the 2013 event, see *Joulurauhan julistus 2013 – The Declaration of Christmas Peace 2013*). Heinonen explores historical layers traceable in the contemporary form of the ceremony with reference to Raymond Williams' concept 'selective tradition', Jan Assmann's notion of 'cultural memory' and Eric Hobsbawm's ideas of 'invented traditions'. Today, three historical layers can be distinguished in the declaration of Christmas peace: the medieval core, the early modern layer and the layer of nineteenth and early twentieth century nationalism. Thus, the ceremony represents the cultural memory of certain crucial periods of the Finnish past. In his analysis, Heinonen shows how, in its contemporary form, it is an invented tradition fabricated to serve nationalist purposes. It is residual in the same sense as, for example, ceremonies of organized religion or monarchy: functioning to maintain cultural memory in and through the sounds, as well as the physical spaces, that frame the ceremony.

In a participant/observer ethnographic study, also drawing on the scholarly literature, Lars Kaijser uses one event, the so-called *The Pink Floyd Happening*, which was held in Stockholm in May 2011, to explore two of the most debated issues in popular music canon formation and perpetuation: that of authenticity and what Simon Reynolds called 'retromania'. These discourses frame the assessment of covers, tribute acts and museums, in which as in this case, space negotiates with memory in the discussion of how representations, performances or enactments of the past can be apprehended and interpreted. The event was a re-enactment of a Pink Floyd concert, which the band had played in 1967 at the same venue, and it asserted several claims to authenticity. Kaijser explores how the event simultaneously was characterized by eclecticism and an anachronistic bricolage, where irony and play sometimes were more important than memory and context. The happening addressed a certain time-space in music history and its representation held various authenticities. It was to be identified and recognized through iconic images of clothes, instruments and bodies, but also in sounds and artistry. Kaijser emphasizes that the staging of a historical music event in an entrepreneurial setting such as this does not follow ideas of academic rigour or accurate use of historical sources. Instead, it combines various layers of authenticity that work together at the event – not competing, but complementing each other.

Kaarina Kilpiö discusses how Finnish C-cassette users remember constructing their own musical and social practices in the 1970s, 1980s and 1990s through the use of this affordable and low-quality mass listening technology. Her research material consists of Finnish listeners' recollections of the influence and consequences of C-cassette use for their everyday life and music listening in these decades. Kilpiö shows how C-cassette users found the active pursuit of their personal musical identities and the expansion in soundscape control the most important factors in recalling their relationships with the listening technology. The cassettes offered children and young people an opportunity to express their independence and to defy authority. Equally significant is that the format was embedded in both the social practices of the young and in the family life and domestic routines. Thus, the analysis also offers a wider understanding of the meaning of recorded music for users in everyday situations in late twentieth century.

Paul Long and Jez Collins examine how online practices of musical memory-making have proliferated across social media, in blogs, web pages, forums and Facebook groups. They reflect on the manner in which online communities construct memories in such digital *non*-spaces albeit in and around references to geographically and temporally specific sites of music culture. Central is an exploration of how music, its experience, form and meaning, is evoked in order to understand its role in memory-making and its display. Informing this exploration is the idea of affect and the capturing of the emotive, material and physical role of music in memory. The practices raise questions about the nature of memory, the music archive, of history and the heritage recorded in such sites. Long and Collins argue that, alongside the collection and sharing of music and of associated artefacts, the archive is manifest in the nature of such collective memories forged in online interactions, which involves an ongoing assessment of the significance of venues, individuals, bands moments and of course – the music itself – as a resource for personal and shared pasts.

The second section begins with Sara Cohen's report on a recent project exploring the relationship between space, music and autobiographical memory. The emphasis is on memory as a social practice produced through social interaction, grounded in social situations and contexts and informed by social and ideological conventions. This approach draws attention not only to the process of memory-making but also to memory as work, a common way of conceptualizing memory within disciplines such as social anthropology that helps to emphasize the effort of memory-making (recalling, forgetting, inventing, re-inventing, organizing, sharing and so on). The chapter begins by explaining how audiences in England were invited to map and share autobiographical memories of their musical past and moves on to describe how these memories were spatially situated and related to a narrower, more defined sense of place. Reflecting on this process, Cohen considers what it reveals not just about the relationship between music, space and autobiographical memory, but also about the value and significance of music in general.

Jelena Gligorijević asks critical questions about uses of cultural space and memory in connection with Exit festival and the Guča trumpet festival in the historical context of post-Milošević Serbia. Encapsulating the organizers' and participants' idealistic aspirations, the festivals in her view become microcosms of nationhood set against the broader background of the Serbian nation state. Taking as her point of departure commentary that emphasizes schematic binaries (as, e.g., 'East/West'), she argues for more flexible and nuanced modelling incorporating 'a range of other conflictual arenas as well', and a 'more fluid, dynamic pluralistic and outward projected idea of national identification'. Gligorijević thus makes no attempt to oversimplify the complex and overlapping social formations undergirding the festivals' constructions of space. Drawing on Lefebvre's theories (1991/1974), she addresses how the festivals simultaneously become spaces of consumption and aspiration, with Exit festival encouraging alignments with western modernity and hedonistic freedom, a 'counter-space' that challenges the organizational principles of the surrounding nation state. The Guča festival, in turn, evokes identifications along lines of eastern ethnic continuity and nostalgia, a point of view commensurate with the concept of 'organic space'. Both formations are in Gligorijević's argument characterized by a liminality that evades straightforward categorization.

Morten Michelsen takes as his starting point how radio between the two world wars landed like a UFO in the midst of cultures more or less nationally defined all over the world.

It changed fundamentally cultural and political communication as well as the structure and content of the local musical cultures. Michelsen develops his argumentation to a general tri-partite model for discussing spatiality in relation to radio, consisting of radio 'hereness', radio 'thereness' and radio 'between here and there'. These three perspectives cover a trajectory from radio as part of personal and family life, typically in the home, over radio as a mediator between the local and personal on one hand and the global and public on the other, towards radio as a preliminary structuring of the world out there, be it just outside your house or international politics. The examples analysed by Michelsen are mainly taken from interbellum Danish music radio and concern both the uses of music, music listening and music programming.

In the final section, 'the sound is turned up', James Andean approaches questions of sound and space from the perspective of electroacoustic composition, where the spatial dimension of sound has been a preoccupation for decades. Not only is this musical genre concerned with capturing or representing real and symbolic spaces, the spatialization of sound is realized also concretely in acousmatic performance practices, which situate listeners in immersive surround-sound environments that nevertheless remain ontologically distinct from sources, even if they might consciously map or resemble physical spaces in the represented world. This parallels directions in cinema and audiovisual forms over the past few decades, at the experimental margins and arguably also the mainstream, where the more expansive potential of expressive space is increasingly taking priority over a narrowly demarcated and largely taken-for-granted sense of verisimilitudinous place. Through acousmatic music and other means, we are becoming increasingly cognisant of the mutability of the auditory landscape when it comes to evocations of space, and this idealistic trajectory has clear symbolic extensions in the sociocultural sphere. The 'persistence of memory' is also confirmed when sounds summon up specific as well as generic spaces, evocations that can only work by appealing to the memories that give those spaces their identities. And even generic associations require, as the author puts it, 'the listener's own memories and experience to swell up and create meaning'. It is impossible to detach place from memory, even if 'placeness' is the focus.

Jeffrey Benjamin's work draws on writing in archaeoacoustics with a view to posing new questions about our experiences of industrial soundscapes. His readings of the historical accounts of workers in North American industrial communities challenge influential views of industrial sounds as importing solely alienation and negative affect. Apart from reference to other writers who have engaged directly with sonic repetition, including Veblen, Augoyard and Torgue and Attali, Benjamin employs Kierkegaard's 'will to repetition' as a conceptual touchstone, and considers how sonic repetition might instead constitute an important mode of social structuring that resounds with our formative experiences of being in and interacting with objects in the world. This mode of understanding might resonate also with our experiences of repetitive musical forms, which we tend to experience as pleasurable, thereby transforming as much as reiterating the conditions of modernity.

Finally, Claudia Gorbman argues for a reassessment of her seminal theorization of screen sound in the book *Unheard Melodies: Narrative Film Music* (1987) by arguing that there have since been significant changes in the aesthetics of film music composition, and in the kinds of attentiveness to music now expected of film-goers. This invites us to think about the changing role of music in shaping cinematic space both diegetically and extradiegetically. We are watching a flat screen, yet we are constantly aware of three-dimensional spatial relationships between the elements on that screen, and this is constructed by sound as well as image (see also Andean in this volume), especially in the era of stereophonic Dolby. Above all, the predominance of musicalized sounds in Anderson's films, in contrast to the 'vococentric' bias of traditional narrative approaches to the soundtrack, reminds audio-viewers that what they perceive is in fact a 'rendered' sound world, as Michel Chion has called it, rather than an unmediated reflection of some pre-existing extra-cinematic, psychological or social reality. This rendering extends also to questions of space and memory, since audiences in such circumstances are likely to become more cognisant of the physical, phenomenal and historical spaces that surround them, whether it is the collective (anti?)social space of a cinema's auditorium, or the scaled-down and privately experienced audiovisual spaces that are native to contemporary digital culture (when using a computer, handheld tablet or cable television). And as in all discussions of space, memory is implicated both in terms of what we bring to the film (songs that evoke an era) and in binding the narrative, as, for example, in the 'passed-along song'. Gorbman's essay surveys the changes in the way music functions to create cinematic space, both within the cinematic frame and in relation to the film-goer. But there is also the physical and experiential space occupied by the audience: where we feel ourselves physically to be in relation to what we see and hear, but also how we relate to events on the screen as mediated by the soundtrack. Are we engaged, detached, passionate, critical, 'inside' or 'outside' the narrative? In this, it is arguable that music is at least as important as dialogue, and the sonic in general is at least as important as the visual, in creating this space. It is therefore precisely Anderson's uses of pre-existing music, Gorbman argues in her final point, that allows this director to move music from the background to the foreground, and thereby to entice audiences to remember memories that more often than not imply a spatial dimension.

Final words

Self-evident from much of the above is the fact that no single method, approach or discipline holds the key to answering questions related to sound, memory and space. Research in this area benefits greatly from its interdisciplinary scope and methodological plurality. Only by pooling resources and by consciously moving between existing epistemological frames of reference can we hope to adequately theorize the relevance of sound, memory and space to research on music and culture in the years ahead. The various approaches presented in this collection explore some of the possibilities offered by interdisciplinarity.

The themes dealt with in the essays are important not only for scholars and students of musicology and ethnomusicology, popular music studies, cultural history, media and cultural studies, but also within music media and industry, cultural heritage and memory industry. Themes relating to memory are also gaining more and more general attention in society because of demographic factors, and sonic and spatial questions are also important in social planning. Apart from academia, therefore, we hope that this collection will be relevant to individuals and organizations concerned with the formation and implementation of cultural policy-related fields ranging from the built environment to public health.

References

Appadurai, Arjun (ed.) (1988), *The Social Life of Things*, Cambridge: Cambridge University Press.

Assmann, Jan (1995), 'Collective Memory and Cultural Identity', *New German Critique*, 65, Spring–Summer, pp. 125–133.

—— (2011), *Cultural Memory and Early Civilization: Writing, Remembrance, and Political Imagination*, Cambridge: Cambridge University Press.

Augoyard, Jean-François and Henry Torgue (2003), *Sonic Experience: A Guide to Everyday Sounds*, Montreal and Kingston: McGill-Queen's University Press.

Bal, Mieke (2002), *Traveling Concepts in the Humanities: A Rough Guide*, Toronto: University of Toronto Press.

Bateson, Gregory (1972), *Steps to an Ecology of Mind: Collected Essays in Anthropology, Psychiatry, Evolution, and Epistemology*, Northvale: Jason Aronson.

Birdsall, Carolyn and Anthony Enns (eds) (2008), *Sonic Mediations: Body, Sound, Technology*, Newcastle-upon-Tyne: Cambridge Scholars Publishing.

Born, Georgina (2013), *Music, Sound and Space: Transformations of Public and Private Experience*, Cambridge: Cambridge University Press.

Boym, Svetlana (2001), *The Future of Nostalgia*, New York: Basic Books.

Brown, Ross (2010), *Sound: A Reader in Theatrical Practice*, Basingstoke: Palgrave Macmillan.

Brusila, Johannes (2003), '"Local Music, Not from Here" – The Discourse of World Music Examined Through Three Zimbabwean Case Studies: The Bhundu Boys, Virginia Mukwesha and Sunduza', Dissertation, Helsinki: Finnish Society for Ethnomusicology.

—— (2009), 'Musik som ting: Musikens materiella manifestationer i belysning av historiska instrument, fonogram och minnesböcker', *Musiikki*, 39:2, pp. 6–50.

—— (2010), '"Maximum output for minimum input": 1G3B and the reterritorialization of a Finland-Swedish metal identity on the Internet', *IASPM@Journal*, 1:2, http://www.iaspmjournal.net. Accessed 25 November 2015.

Bull, Michael (2000), *Sounding Out the City: Personal Stereos and the Management of Everyday Life*, Oxford: Berg.

Bull, Michael (ed.) (2013), *Sound Studies*, London and New York: Routledge.

Bull, Michael and Les Back (eds) (2003), *The Auditory Culture Reader*, Oxford and New York: Berg.

Castells, Manuel (1996), *The Rise of the Network Society: The Information Age: Economy, Society and Culture*, Vol. I, Oxford: Blackwell.

Chion, Michel (2009), *Film: A Sound Art*, Trans. Claudia Gorbman, New York: Columbia University Press.

———— (2013), 'Sensory Aspects of Contemporary Cinema', in John Richardson, Claudia Gorbman and Carol Vernallis (eds), *The Oxford Handbook of New Audiovisual Aesthetic*, New York and Oxford: Oxford University Press, pp. 325–330.

Cohen, Sara, Robert Knifton, Marion Leonard and Les Roberts (eds) (2014), *Sites of Popular Music Heritage: Memories, Histories, Places*, London and New York: Routledge.

Connell, John and Chris Gibson (2002), *Sound Tracks: Popular Music Identity and Place*, London: Routledge.

Corbin, Alain (1999), *Village Bells: Sound and Meaning in the Nineteenth Century French Countryside*, London: Macmillan.

Crook, Tim (2012), *The Sound Handbook*, New York and Abingdon Oxon: Routledge.

Drobnick, Jim (ed.) (2004), *Aural Cultures*, Banff: YYZ Books.

Elsaesser, Thomas and Malte Hagener (eds) (2010), *Film Theory: An Introduction Through the Senses,* New York: Routledge.

Erlmann, Veit (ed.) (2004), *Hearing Cultures: Essays on Sound, Listening and Modernity*, Oxford and New York: Berg.

Feld, Steven (2012), *Sound and Sentiment: Birds, Weeping, Poetics and Song in Kaluli Expression*, 3rd edition, Durham: Duke University Press.

Finch, Trevor and Karen Bijsterveld (eds) (2012), *The Oxford Handbook of Sound Studies*, Oxford and New York: Oxford University Press.

Giddens, Anthony (1990), *The Consequences of Modernity*, Cambridge: Polity Press.

Ginzburg, Carlo (1980), *The Cheese and the Worms: The Cosmos of a Sixteenth-Century Miller*, Baltimore: The Johns Hopkins University Press.

———— (1983), *The Night Battles: Witchcraft and Agrarian Cults in the Sixteenth and Seventeenth Centuries*, Baltimore: The Johns Hopkins University Press.

Goffman, Erving (1961), *Encounters: Two Studies in the Sociology of Interaction*, Indianapolis: Bobbs-Merrill.

———— (1974), *Frame Analysis: An Essay on the Organisation of Experience*, Boston: Northeastern University Press.

Gorbman, Claudia (1987), *Unheard Melodies: Narrative Film Music*, London: BFI Publishing.

Halbwachs, Maurice (1992), *On Collective Memory*, (trans. and ed.) Lewis A. Coser, Chicago: University of Chicago Press.

Harvey, David (1989), *The Condition of Postmodernity*, Oxford and Cambridge: Blackwell.

Johnson, Bruce (2016), 'Sound Studies Today: Where Are We Going?', in Paula Hamilton and Joy Damousi (eds), *Sound, Memory and the Senses*, London and New York: Routledge.

Järviluoma, Helmi (ed.) (1994), *Soundscapes: Essays on Vroom and Moo*, Tampere and Seinäjoki: Department of Folk Tradition and Institute of Rhythm Music.

Järviluoma, Helmi and Gregg Wagstaff (eds) (2002), *Soundscape Studies and Their Methods*, Helsinki and Turku: Finnish Society of Ethnomusicology and Department of Art, Literature and Music.

Järviluoma, Helmi, Meri Kytö, Barry Truax, Heikki Uimonen and Noora Vikman (eds) (2009), *Acoustic Environments in Change*, Tampere University of Applied Sciences with University of Joensuu, in co-operation with the World Soundscape Project: Simon Fraser University.

Järviluoma, Helmi and Noora Vikman (2013), 'On Soundscape Methods and Audiovisual Sensibility', in John Richardson, Claudia Gorbman and Carol Vernallis (eds), *The Oxford Handbook of New Audiovisual Aesthetics*, New York and Oxford: Oxford University Press, pp. 645–658.

Joulurauhan Julistus (2013), 'The Declaration of Christmas Peace', Finnish Broadcasting Company, Available at http://youtube.com/watch?v=5ZSAnUGLH8g. Accessed 8 August 2015.

Katz, Mark (2010), *Capturing Sound: How Technology Has Changed Music*, Revised edition, Berkeley and Los Angeles: University of California Press.

Krims, Adam (2007), *Music and Urban Geography*, New York: Routledge.

Kytö, Meri (2013), 'Soundscapes of Istanbul in Turkish Film Soundtracks', in John Richardson, Claudia Gorbman and Carol Vernallis (eds), *The Oxford Handbook of New Audiovisual Aesthetics*, New York and Oxford: Oxford University Press, pp. 389–411.

Lefebvre, Henri (1991/1974), *The Production of Space*, Trans. Donald Nicholson-Smith, Oxford: Blackwell.

Marks, Laura (2000), *The Skin of Film: Intercultural Cinema, Embodiment and the Senses*, Durham: Duke University Press.

Moore, Allan F. (2012), *Song Means: Analysing and Interpreting Recorded Popular Song*, Farnham: Ashgate.

Nora, Pierre (1989), 'Between Memory and History: Les Lieux de Mémoire', *Representations*, 26, Spring, pp. 7–25.

Picker, John M. (2003), *Victorian Soundscapes*, Oxford: Oxford University Press.

Pinch, Trevor and Karin Bijsterveld (2012), *The Oxford Book of Sound Studies*, Oxford: Oxford University Press.

Reynolds, Simon (2011), *Retromania: Pop Culture's Addiction to Its Own Past*, London: Faber & Faber.

Richardson, John (2011), *An Eye for Music: Popular Music and the Audiovisual Surreal*, New York and Oxford: Oxford University Press.

—— (2015), 'Closer Reading and Framing in Ecocritical Music Research', in Gerlinde Feller and Birgit Abels (eds), *Music Moves: Exploring Musical Meaning Through Spatiality, Difference, Framing and Transformation*, Göttingen Studies in Music, Vol. 6, Hildesheim: Olms.

Richardson, John and Claudia Gorbman (2013), 'Introduction', in John Richardson, Claudia Gorbman and Carol Vernallis (eds), *The Oxford Handbook of New Audiovisual Aesthetics*, New York and Oxford: Oxford University Press, pp. 3–35.

Richardson, John, Claudia Gorbman and Carol Vernallis (eds) (2013), *The Oxford Handbook of New Audiovisual Aesthetics*, New York and Oxford: Oxford University Press.

Schafer, R. Murray (1977), *The Tuning of the World*, Toronto: McClelland & Stewart.

Smith, Mark (ed.) (2010), *Hearing History: A Reader*, Athens: University of Georgia Press.

Sterne, Jonathan (2003), *The Audible Past: Cultural Origins of Sound Reproduction*, Durham: Duke University Press.

—— (ed.) (2012), *The Sound Studies Reader*, London and New York: Routledge.

Tagg, Philip (2000), 'Analysing Popular Music: Theory, Method, and Practice', in Richard Middleton (ed.), *Reading Pop: Approaches to Textual Analysis in Popular Music*, Oxford: Oxford University Press, pp. 71–103.

—— (2012), *Music's Meanings: A Modern Musicology for Non-Musos*, New York and Huddersfield: Mass Media Music Scholars' Press.

Thompson, Emily (2004), *The Soundscape of Modernity: Architectural Acoustics and the Culture of Listening in America, 1900–1933*, Cambridge, MA and London: MIT Press.

Truax, Barry (ed.) (1978/1999), *Handbook of Acoustic Ecology*, Burnaby, BC: Simon Fraser University and ARC Publications.

Vernallis, Carol, Amy Herzog and John Richardson (eds.) (2013), *The Oxford Handbook of Sound and Image in Digital Media*, New York and Oxford: Oxford University Press.

Part I

Memory

Chapter 2

Cultural Memory of Sound and Space: The Case of the Declaration of Christmas Peace in Turku, Finland

Yrjö Heinonen

The declaration of Christmas peace was originally a European municipal tradition dating back to the thirteenth century. The custom waned during the nineteenth century practically everywhere except in Turku, where it is said to have continued virtually unbroken since the 1320s. The ceremony takes place annually on Christmas Eve at noon in the Old Great Square, near the medieval cathedral. It has been broadcast live on radio since 1935, on television since 1983 and via the Internet since 2006. In Finland, the ceremony is assumed to represent a sense of continuity with certain crucial periods of the Finnish past as reconstructed within the nationalist frame of reference. On a very general level, three layers of the past are distinguished in the current form of the ceremony: the 'medieval core', the 'early modern layer' and the 'nationalist frame'. In the following, I will explore the sense of continuity with the past in the ceremony from the perspectives of tradition and cultural memory, with a special emphasis on the cultural memory of sound and space.

Tradition and cultural memory

During the last two or three decades, traditional rituals and ceremonies have been studied from various intriguing points of view. For the purposes of this chapter at hand, I single out the following three interrelated concepts: selective tradition (Williams 1977), cultural memory (Assmann 1995) and invented traditions (Hobsbawm 2000a), all of which appear to be relevant to the study of such a traditional ceremony as the declaration of Christmas peace in Turku. The relation of sound and space to cultural memory will also be discussed in the present section.

Raymond Williams (1977) approaches tradition as a dynamic process consisting of 'dominant', 'emergent' and 'residual' aspects of culture. 'Dominant' consists of contemporary hegemonic meanings, values and practices maintained by a certain social group or an alliance of such groups (Williams 1977:122; Hebdige 2006:150). Both 'residual' and 'emergent' are defined in relation to the 'dominant'. 'Residual' refers to such meanings, values and practices that have been 'effectively formed in the past' but are 'still active in the cultural process, not only and often not at all as an element of the past, but as an effective element of the present' (Williams 1977:122). 'Emergent', in turn, refers to 'new meanings and values, new practices', which are often 'substantially alternative or opposite' to the dominant order (Williams 1977:123). Residual appears to be particularly relevant as regards the present study.

Residual is sustained by cultural memory. Jan Assmann (1995) and Jörn Rüsen (2007) take cultural memory to represent the core of the historical identity of a community. According to Assmann, cultural memory consists of 'fateful events of the past, whose memory is maintained through cultural formations (texts, rites, monuments) and institutional communication (recitation, practice, observance)' (1995:129). More specifically, for Assmann, cultural memory is an 'archive' of 'reusable texts, images, and rituals specific to each society in each epoch', which each contemporary context reinterprets from its own perspective (1995:130, 132). Rüsen considers cultural memory 'a matter of rituals and highly institutionalized performances', each having 'its own media and a fixed place in the cultural life of a group' (2007:173), whereas Pierre Nora (1996:1) has used the term 'sites of memory' (*lieux de mémoire*) to refer to how certain key texts, images and rituals maintain 'a residual sense of continuity' with the national past. Both Rüsen's 'fixed place' and Nora's 'sites of memory' refer to the specific position or status of cultural products or performances in the life and cultural memory of a certain community.

Raymond Williams (1977:115) maintains that tradition is not just 'a relatively inert, historicized segment [...] of the surviving past' but a dynamic, selective and actively shaping force. Foucault (1972:5), for his part, lays stress on the discontinuity (rupture, break, transformation) of tradition. Related to these is Eric Hobsbawm's notion of 'invented tradition':

'Invented tradition' is taken to mean a set of practices, normally governed by overtly or tacitly accepted rules and of a ritual or symbolic nature, which seek to inculcate certain values and norms of behaviour by repetition, which automatically implies continuity with the past. In fact, where possible, they normally attempt to establish continuity with a suitable historic past.

(Hobsbawm 2000a:1)

The idea of invented tradition has been developed further in recent research on new or revitalized festivals and rituals (Manning 1983:5; Boissevain 2013:202). Revitalization can mean reviving an old ritual as such but it can also refer to the rejection of old elements from and/or incorporation new ones in a dormant or already terminated ritual. In many cases, one can even recognize 'a series of revitalizations in the course of a fairly continuous history' (MacClancy and Parkin 1997:76–77). Revitalization always 'marks a renegotiation of identity' (Boissevain 2013:206); in other words, it can be seen as a sign or expression of an emerging or re-emerging identity.

The concepts of sound and space are understood here as inseparable properties of place. Sound literally *takes place* in a particular physical space. According to Edward T. Relph (1976:61), the identity of place consists of three interrelated components: 'physical features or appearance, observable activities and functions, and meanings or symbols'. Space is related primarily to the physical location and appearance of a place, whereas it is the functions, activities and symbolic meanings that transform a space into a place with a particular identity. In the case of the declaration of Christmas peace in Turku, not only does the physical space (including the Old Great Square and the cathedral) provide the ceremony with a special symbolic meaning but also the ceremony (including the recited declaration, church bells and music) provides the physical space with extra symbolic meanings. Indeed, the declaration is one of the activities that has transformed this particular physical space into the place with the particular identity it has today. The Brinkkala building is a case in point: according to the official website of Turku, the building 'is best known for the traditional proclamation of Christmas peace' from its 'balcony since 1886' (Turku 2014a). The case of the Brinkkala building also aptly illustrates the interrelatedness of sound, space and cultural memory in the declaration ceremony.

The remaining chapter is divided into three sections. The first focuses on the sense of historical layers in the current form of the ceremony. Special attention will be paid to the interrelation of sound and space as contributing to the emergence of the sense of each historic layer. In the second section, the elements present in the ceremony (its 'numbers') are explored as sites of memory having a fixed position in Finnish cultural life, acquired by being associated with certain crucial events and periods in the Finnish past. The concluding section summarizes the analysis and discusses the contemporary functions of the event.

Layers of the past

The history of Finland relevant to the topic of the present chapter can be divided into the following four periods:

- the Middle Ages (ca. 1150–1523);
- the early modern age (1523–1809);
- the age of autonomy (1809–1917);
- the age of independence (since 1917).

From circa 1150–1809, the area of present-day Finland was under the rule of Sweden[1] and during 1809–1917, an autonomous grand duchy of the Russian Empire. Both the site of the ceremony and the ceremony itself received their approximate current forms during Russian rule. In the following, I will explore three layers of the Finnish past recognizable in the current form of the Christmas peace declaration ceremony: the nationalist frame, the early modern layer and the medieval core.

The nationalist frame

Becoming an autonomous grand duchy of the Russian Empire meant neither an abrupt nor complete change in the legal and social systems since Finland was allowed to preserve Swedish law, the Evangelic Lutheran religion and Swedish as its official language (Pulma 2003:374–376). In spite of this, the years 1809–1917 have been considered 'the Russian parenthesis' in the Finnish cultural memory (Kantonen 1951:5). The awakening nationalistic aspirations of the Finns were aptly expressed in the slogan usually ascribed to A. I. Arwidsson: 'Swedes are we no longer, Russians we do not want become, therefore let us be Finns' (cf. Kirby 2006:90; Kantonen 1951:5–6).[2] Obviously, the Pan-Slavist objectives of the Russian nationalistic imperialism of the late nineteenth and early twentieth centuries, expressed in the slogan 'one law, one church, one tongue' (Kantonen 1951:6), were in irreconcilable contradiction with those of the Finnish nationalists. The contradiction culminated during the so-called Russification periods (1899–1905, 1908–1917), also known in Finland as 'the years of oppression'.

After the Great Fire of Turku in 1827, the early modern 'old town' was almost entirely rebuilt. Buildings surviving to the extent that they were considered worth renovating included the cathedral, the town hall, the Brinkkala building, the Old Court House together with its neighbouring building and the Old Academy House, which had been built only in 1802–1815. New buildings included the Hjelt House, the Cajander House and the Trapp House, all of which were built between 1829 and 1833. All new buildings were designed more or less according to the ideals of Empire style, and the facades of the surviving buildings were redesigned to fit the same style. No buildings were raised in the area between the Old Great Square and the cathedral. Instead, the area was transformed into a monumental square consisting of three parks: the Brahe Park, the Porthan Park and the Cathedral Park. The area was further divided by Uudenmaankatu, a major street located between the Brahe Park and Porthan Park. The narrow Convent Street between the Brinkkala House and the newly built Cathedral School remained. In 1863, the quaint Pinella restaurant was built on the southern side of the Porthan Park.[3] Towards the latter half of the nineteenth century, the commercial centre began to be established on the western side of the river, and the cathedral area gradually began to gain a new function as the old or historic centre of Turku (Helin et al. 2008; Sundman 1991:75–76; Figure 1).

The custom of the Christmas peace declaration waned during the nineteenth century in Sweden (Welin 1936) and also in most Finnish towns, but not in Turku where the tradition was revitalized. The present form of the ceremony was fixed in several stages in the spirit of late nineteenth and early twentieth century nationalism. The songs 'Our Land' and 'The March of the Pori Regiment' are the most obvious examples of this nationalist frame of reference. The former is currently the national anthem of Finland and the latter the official march of the Finnish Defence Forces. Both 'Our Land' and 'The Pori March' were already performed in the 1880s, although they became a fixed part of the ceremony only in the 1890s. In fact, the 'medieval core' (cathedral bells, fanfare, declaration) became framed by three of the most popular songs performed in religious-patriotic gatherings during the turn of the century: 'A Mighty Fortress', 'Our Land' and 'The Pori March' (cf. Kurkela 2011:94).

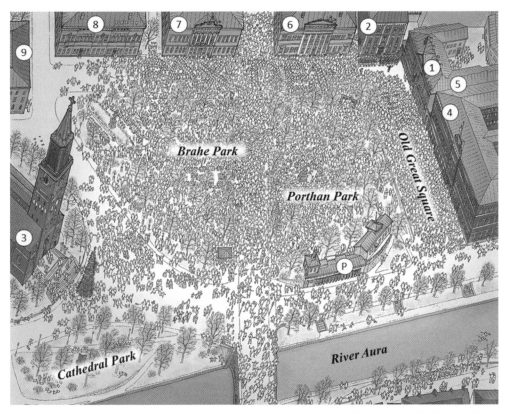

Figure 1: Declaration of Christmas peace at the historical centre of Turku; (1) Brinkkala building; (2) Old Town Hall; (3) Cathedral; (4) Cathedral School; (5) Convent Street (a narrow street between the Brinkkala building and Cathedral School); (6) Hjelt building; (7) Trapp building; (8) Calonius building; (9) Academy building; (P) Pinella restaurant. Source (original drawing): © Erkki Kiiski 2009. Used by permission.

Generally speaking, the ceremony can be said to have been reinvented or revitalized as part of what Hobsbawm (2000b) has called 'the mass production of traditions' in Europe between 1870 and 1914. In its new form, the ceremony clearly established a residual sense of continuity with a suitable historic past – that is, the time of the Swedish rule – by references included in the cathedral bells, the fanfare and declaration (the medieval core) and in 'A Mighty Fortress' (the early modern layer). Any references to the values, norms and practices of the contemporaneous dominant order, Russian rule, were left out of the ceremony. Instead, besides the sense of continuity with the Swedish past, the new form of the ceremony reflected the emergent values, beliefs and practices of the awakening Finnish nationalism (particularly in 'Our Land' and 'The Pori March'). Thus, the revitalization of the Christmas peace tradition was closely connected with the renegotiation of Finnish identity, in which a residual sense of continuity with a suitable historic past was a central aspect.

The early modern layer

In Finland, the early modern period is framed by the election of Gustav Vasa as King of Sweden in 1523 and the beginning of Russian rule in 1809. From the point of view of the present chapter, the epoch is further delineated by the conversion of Sweden to Evangelic Lutheran Protestantism (1527), the reign of the Vasa Dynasty (1523–1654), the so-called Great Power era of Sweden, framed by the peace treaties of Stolbova (1617) and Nystad (1721), and the two short periods of Russian occupation in the eighteenth century referred to in Finnish cultural memory as the 'Great Wrath' (1713–1721) and the 'Lesser Wrath' (1741–1743). According to folk memory, Christmas peace was not declared in Turku during the 'Great Wrath'.

The early modern centre of Turku was markedly different from what it was before the late fifteenth century and from what it became after the Great Fire of Turku in 1827. The cathedral reached approximately its present height and shape between the 1460s and the late 1480s and was surrounded by a wall with two towers and five gates by the 1470s. Moreover, several stone buildings and wooden houses with stone or mortar end walls were built between and in the neighbourhood of the cathedral and the Old Great Square. These included the first stages of both the Brinkkala House, built in the late sixteenth century, and the Old Town Hall, built in 1734–1736. Early modern Turku is represented in several drawings and paintings from the eighteenth and early nineteenth centuries, perhaps most notably in Carl Ludwig Engel's aquarelle from 1814 (Figure 2a). A somewhat idealized representation of the wall can be found in Albert Edelfelt's triptych on the opening ceremony of the Royal Academy of Turku in 1640, painted in 1905 (Figure 3).[4] These and other more or less similar images (Figure 2b) maintain a residual sense of continuity with the early modern Turku, even though this sense is not necessarily active in the current Christmas peace declaration ceremony.

During this epoch, the medieval tradition of the declaration of Christmas peace was revitalized to meet the needs of the renaissance court of the early Vasa Dynasty and particularly the baroque pomp and circumstance of the 'Great Power' era. Especially during the reigns of Queen Christina, the last monarch of the Vasa Dynasty (r. 1644–1654), and the absolute sovereign Charles XI (r. 1672–1697), both the form and contents of the declaration ceremony were regulated by royal ordinances. Traces of Christmas peace ordinances from this time can still be found in the wording of the current declaration text, even though in a thoroughly revised form. Performances of multi-voiced music were added to the 'medieval core' by 1680 at the latest (Dahlström and Salmenhaara 1995:145–146). These might have included Lutheran chorales, ecclesiastical and school songs from the *Piae Cantiones* collection (1582, 1625) and/or some kind of contemporary military music. The residual sense of continuity with the early modern period is most obviously represented in the current ceremony by Martin Luther's chorale 'A Mighty Fortress Is Our God', even though it is not known whether this particular chorale was actually sung at the event before 1903 when it became a fixed part of the ceremony.

Figure 2a–b: Early modern Turku; (a) view from the window of the Brinkkala building (aquarelle by Carl Ludwig Engel, 1814); (b) view from the other side of the river (drawing by O. M. Reuter).
Sources: (a) The National Library of Finland/Doria repository of digital services; (b) O. M. Reuter, *Finland i ord och bild*, Stockholm 1901.

Figure 3: Opening ceremony of the Academy of Turku in 1640. Johannes Gebhard: Turun akatemian vihkiäiskulkue (copy), 1961. Used by permission. Original painting by Albert Edelfelt, 1905.
Photo: Eero Roine/Helsinki University Museum.

The 'medieval core'

In Finland, the Middle Ages are usually considered to comprise the period from mid-twelfth century to 1523; that is, from what later has been called 'the first Catholic crusade' to the election of Gustav Vasa as King of Sweden. Turku was not only the most important town of the medieval Finland but also one of the most important towns in the entire Sweden. A Dominican monastery was founded in 1249, the castle in the 1280s and an early form of the cathedral was consecrated in 1300. After several conflicts between Sweden and Novgorod (nowadays part of Russia), the western and southern parts of the present geographical area of Finland became annexed by Sweden in the peace treaty of Nöteborg (1323). As a consequence, the Swedish legal and social systems began to be established in Finland. The declaration of Christmas peace in Turku emerged as part of these legal and social systems.

The medieval town plan of Turku was based on German-Hanseatic ideals of town planning. It had the cathedral on one side of the centre, the market square with the adjacent town hall on the other and blocks of wooden buildings between the cathedral and the square (Hietala 1999:44). In spite of several destructions and reconstructions, a few remnants – the cathedral, the market square (nowadays called the Old Great Square) and the narrow Convent Street located between the present Brinkkala building and the Cathedral School – still partially suggest a 'sense of the medieval atmosphere' in the old town centre of Turku (Seppänen 2011:476–477; Figure 4). Yet, like the idea of rural community (cf. Williams 1977:122), the idea of medieval old town is residual and based on idealization. The idealized

Figure 4: Medieval Turku: (a) Cathedral from fourteenth century to mid-fifteenth century; (b) Convent Street in early twenty-first century.
Sources: (a) drawing by author, cf. Juhani Rinne, *Turun tuomiokirkko keskiaikana I – Tuomiokirkon rakennushistoria* (Helsinki: Otava, 1941); (b) Wikipedia, Old Great Square (Turku).

European 'old town' is typically built on a river and consists of a church, a town hall, a market square, narrow streets enclosed by buildings – all surrounded by a town wall with towers and gates (Jovinelly and Netelkos 2007:10–12, 29; Braunfels 1990:38).

As for sound and music, the 'medieval core' is most obviously embodied in the bell strikes, the fanfare and the recited declaration itself. No material remnants have survived but the typical soundscape of a medieval Finnish town is assumed to have consisted of chiming church bells, proclamations by trumpet and/or drum, singing minstrels, as well as warnings and announcements of town criers. Trumpet fanfares and drum rolls also appear to have been accompanied the declaration ceremony of Christmas peace already quite early in the tradition (Dahlström and Salmenhaara 1995:61, 149). Like the townscape of the 'old medieval town', also the idea of medieval soundscape is residual and based on idealization: together with the singing minstrel, chanting monk, banquet and riding knight, the church bells and trumpet fanfares or horn calls are among the most important aural signifiers of the Middle Ages in film (Haines 2014: xvi, 45). In any case, together with the few surviving material remnants of the medieval architecture, the strikes of the cathedral bells, the fanfare and the recited declaration maintain a residual sense of continuity with the medieval past even in the present form of the Christmas peace ceremony in Turku.

Elements of the ceremony as sites of memory

In the following, I will explore the six parts of the current ceremony as sites of Finnish cultural memory. In doing so, I apply on the one hand Alan P. Merriam's (1964) distinction between the uses and functions of music; on the other hand, I make use of the notions of genre and intertextuality in the analysis. The use of music is taken to refer to 'the situation in which music is or has been employed', whereas the function of music 'concerns the reasons of its employment and particularly the broader purpose which it serves' (Merriam 1964:210). I will pay particular attention to how each element of the ceremony has functioned and still functions 'as the symbolic expression of the main values, patterns, or themes' of the Finnish culture (Nettl 1983:150; cf. Merriam 1964:223–227). By genre, I mean types or styles of music whose uses and functions are associated with or determined by certain sociocultural institutions (cf. Ratner 1980:9), while I take intertextuality to mean various kinds of references between different texts – musical, literature or otherwise (cf. Korsyn 1999:56; Kramer 1990:9–10).

'A Mighty Fortress'

The declaration ceremony opens with 'A Mighty Fortress Is Our God'. As a chorale, 'A Mighty Fortress' builds a link between the ceremony and the half-millennium-long tradition of Evangelic Lutheran Protestantism in Finland. Besides its use in liturgical and domestic practice, the Protestant chorale has functioned as a confession of faith (Leaver 1992:130–131) and played an important role in creating and defining a Lutheran identity (Loewe 2013:72, 77). Probably the most well-known Protestant hymn internationally, 'A Mighty Fortress', was written by Martin Luther and published for the first time in 1529. The melody appears to be woven out of fragments of a few Gregorian melodies (Schweitzer 1955:16; Wilson 1914:21–31, 68–69). The inspiration for the words came from Psalm 46, particularly from its opening lines 'God is our refuge and strength, a very present help in trouble'. The first stanza reads as follows (translation by Catherine Winkworth):

> A mighty fortress is our God,
> A trusty shield and weapon;
> He helps us free from every need that
> Hath us now o'ertaken.
> The old evil foe now means deadly woe;
> Deep guile and great might
> Are his dread arms in fight;
> On Earth is not his equal.

Of all Luther's hymns, 'A Mighty Fortress' has held a dominant position in all Nordic countries. In Finland, it has become 'almost a second national hymn' by serving as a 'collective consolation and a national identification' in times of war and crises (Hansson 2008:737). Three examples of this kind of use are mentioned here. Firstly, King Gustaf II Adolf of Sweden is said to have asked his forces – a third of them being Finns – to sing 'A Mighty Fortress' before the battle of Lützen on 16 November 1632. In the battle, the Protestant Swedish corps defeated the Catholic forces of the Holy Roman Empire, but at the cost of the life of King Gustaf II Adolf (Tucker 2011:195–197). Secondly, towards the end of the nineteenth century, 'A Mighty Fortress' began to be sung at any major patriotic and religious-political meetings. During the first Russification period (1898–1905), it became 'a symbol of the Finnish national existence and fighting spirit' (Vapaavuori 2008:51). At this time, 'Russian imperialism became the concrete personification of "the old bitter foe"' mentioned in the first stanza of 'A Mighty Fortress' (Kantonen 1951:5). Finally, during the Winter War (1939–1940) and the Continuation War (1941–1944) between Finland and the Soviet Union, the hymn was sung at several official and patriotic occasions, including presidential radio speeches (Vapaavuori 2008:50). By being associated with these and other fateful events or epochs in the Finnish past, 'A Mighty Fortress' has become an important site of the Finnish national memory, acting in the Christmas peace ceremony as a kind of religious-political credo.

Cathedral bells

The performance of 'A Mighty Fortress' is scheduled so that it ends just before the noon strikes of the cathedral bells are sounded from the opposite side of the old town centre.

Generically, by the twelfth century, the sound of the church bells had become 'part of the "short hand" by which Christian identity was signaled' (Arnold and Goodson 2012:112). The noon strikes themselves have both ecclesiastical and civic roots. The ecclesiastical roots can be traced back to the practice called the Angelus prayer, which emerged during the late Middle Ages. The Angelus was observed three times each day: in the morning, at noon and in the evening. During the Ottoman siege of Belgrade in 1456, Pope Calixtus III ordained the noontime Angelus obligatory for the entire church as a prayer against the Turkish threat. In the German-speaking regions of Europe, the noontime Angelus came to be called 'pro pace schlagen' (to ring the peace) or simply 'the peace bells' (Carroll 1989:28, 39–40; Dohrn-van Rossum 1996:204).

The civic roots of the noon strikes date back to the fourteenth century, when the rationalization of trade and work began to require more accurate measurement of time. The solution was the invention of the mechanical clock, also called the striking clock, sometime between 1280 and 1300 (Whitrow 1988:105). Communal belfries were built and church towers were equipped with mechanical clocks to regulate commercial transactions and working hours (Leeuwen 2006:65; Dohrn-van Rossum 1996:204). A strict measurement of time enabled the workers to 'begin and end work at *fixed hours*' (Goff 1982:35–36, original italics). The uniform hour of 60 minutes was adopted, and the hours began to be counted in two sets of 12 from midnight and from noon, respectively (Whitrow 1988:107–108). The noon strikes mark the end of the first cycle of 12 hours.

There are two kinds of bells in the Turku Cathedral: six church bells for ecclesiastical use and two striking bells for civic use. The noon bells are sounded by the two striking bells programmed by the mechanism of the Cathedral clock. The clock itself was erected in the tower of the Cathedral in the fifteenth century at the latest (Heikkilä and Suvikumpu 2011:14). Newspaper reports on the Christmas peace ceremony witness that the declaration has been read at least since the mid-nineteenth century at noon (Anon. 1851:1). The noon strikes received a deeper religious-patriotic meaning during the Second World War, when the Soviet army began a massive offensive against the Finnish forces. On 19 June 1944, the national Finnish broadcasting company began to broadcast the noon strikes of the Turku Cathedral on a daily basis – a tradition that still continues (Kivimäki and Tepora 2012:271). Moreover, Gerda Ryti, the spouse of President Risto Ryti, gave a radio speech on 16 July in which she called on the whole of Finland to collectively pray for the nation:

Throughout the centuries God has revealed Himself to us as One who is powerful to help. The history of our people is living proof of this miracle. We are reminded of this every day when on our radios we hear the clock of Turku Cathedral, our national shrine, striking twelve. It is a symbol of God's [sic] guidance and grace throughout the centuries. Therefore these moments when the bell strikes twelve are a fitting time for prayer for our country. Let then every one of our people at that moment keep silence in prayer before the Almighty. And in these moments we will grow into a united praying people who may believe that they will find God's help.

(Quoted from Paarma 2000, original translation)

The speech and the continuing practice of broadcasting the noon strikes every day on the radio, show noticeable similarity to the practice established by Pope Calixtus III to ring the noontime Angelus as 'peace bells' against the threat of the enemy. They also show the invention of traditions at work: how an originally civic everyday practice is discursively sacralized and eventually etched on the cultural memory as a national symbol.

Fanfare

After the sound of the bells has fallen silent, the Navy Band begins a blaring fanfare. During the Middle Ages and the early modern era, the function of the fanfare was to attract the audience's attention to the recitation of the declaration. This is still the residual generic meaning of the fanfare in the current ceremony. The particular fanfare played nowadays – the opening fanfare from the Finnish military march 'Marshal's Silver Trumpets' by Artturi Rope – is, once again, associated with certain 'fateful events' and 'times of war and crisis' in the Finnish past, namely the Second World War and the Thirty Years War.

The exact year of composition is not known but Rope is assumed to have written the march sometime between 1928 and 1930. In 1928, General Carl Gustaf Mannerheim, the Honorary Chief of the Finnish White Guard, presented eight silver trumpets to the Guard. Rope played in the White Guard's band at the time. The original title was 'Fanfare March' but, apparently after the promotion of Mannerheim to Field Marshal, Rope replaced it by the present title (Vuolio 2006:84). During the Second World War, Mannerheim was the commander-in-chief of the Finnish Defence Forces and, between 1944–1946, the sixth president of Finland. The entire country became familiar with the 'Marshal's Silver Trumpets' during the Second World War, as it was played as an opener in brother-in-arms gatherings broadcast live by the national broadcasting company Yleisradio. It was also used as the title tune of the war reviews shown by the Defence Forces shown in cinemas (Vuolio 2006:84; YLE 2014).

The opening fanfare of 'Marshal's Silver Trumpets' is written in the style of European sixteenth and seventeenth century cavalry calls and fanfares. They used the common-chord range of the natural trumpet and were usually centred on the 4th harmonic; they frequently used the 3rd and 5th harmonics and rose above the 5th harmonic only when there was an optional flourish up to the 8th at the end (Baines 1974:2). These kinds of cavalry calls were also in use in the Swedish army, as the so-called Delitzsch signals from the Thirty Years War show (Vuolio 2006:20–21, 88). Indeed, the opening fanfare of 'Marshal's Silver Trumpets' appears to be modelled after a couple of Delitzsch signals (Example 1).

Given that the fanfare is detached from the march and is incorporated in the ceremony between the cathedral bells and the recitation of the declaration, its residual generic function is emphasized at the cost of its intertextual connections and dense historical background. In itself, in the context of the current ceremony, it suggests a residual sense of continuity with the medieval and early modern past of Finland.

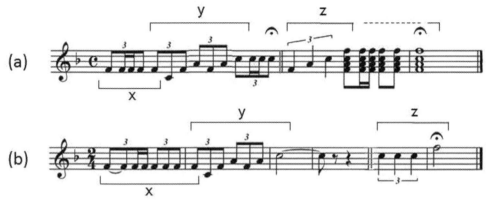

Example 1: (a) Delitzsch signals VI: 4 and VII: 3; (b) the beginning and ending of the opening fanfare of 'Marshal's Silver Trumpets' (Artturi Rope). Motives: repetition on the 4th harmonic (x), an arpeggiated flourish from the 4th to the 6th harmonic (y); a cadential flourish up to the 8th beginning with triple quarter notes (z).
Sources: Delitzsch signals (Vuolio 2006:21), 'Marshal's Silver Trumpets' (transcription by author).

Declaration

The declaration itself is the original cause of the ceremony. In Sweden and Finland, the declaration of Christmas peace had originally a legal status based on so-called *edsöre* legislation, according to which peace was protected by an oath sworn by the king (*edsöre* = sworn oath). Medieval laws were announced to the citizens by reading them publicly. King Magnus Barnlock of Sweden (r. 1275–1290) is said to have proclaimed: 'What we ordain in writing shall be frequently announced to all men that they may observe our commands and avoid what we forbid' (Orfield 2002:254).

The declaration is assumed to have been read aloud from a piece of parchment since as early as the fourteenth century (Heikkilä and Suvikumpu 2011:25). Because no such pieces of parchment have survived, the exact wordings used before the seventeenth century are not known. Heikkilä and Suvikumpu (2011:31) assume, however, that the core content of the declaration has been to remind townspeople that Christmas peace has begun, to advise them to spend the festive season like good Christians, to threaten offenders with heavy fines and to wish all a merry Christmas. Until the seventeenth century, the declaration was probably read only in Swedish and was interpreted for the Finnish-speaking people in their own language. The first reports of reading the declaration in both Swedish and Finnish come from 1711 (Heikkilä and Suvikumpu 2011:35). The currently recited text goes as follows (translation by Turku 2014b):

Tomorrow, God willing,
is the graceful celebration of the birth of our Lord and Saviour;
and thus is declared a peaceful Christmas time to all, by advising devotion and to
behave otherwise quietly and peacefully,

because he who breaks this peace and violates the peace of Christmas by any illegal or improper behaviour shall under aggravating circumstances be guilty and punished according to what the law and statutes prescribe for each and every offence separately. Finally, a joyous Christmas feast is wished to all inhabitants of the city.

The oldest surviving document of the wording in Finnish can be traced back to the 1680s (Krötzl 1988:4; Rapola 1924:105–107). Several different versions were in use during the eighteenth and early nineteenth century. In 1827, the text used at the time was destroyed in the Great Fire of Turku. In 1831, the secretary of the council wrote a new version in Swedish. This version still mentions a fine of 40 silver marks in the case of a breach but is otherwise very close to the present wording. A new Finnish wording, written in 1833, was linguistically clumsy and contained, unlike the new Swedish text, advice to spend the Christmas feast 'so that everyone avoids drunkenness, fighting and other kinds of breaking the peace' (Heikkilä and Suvikumpu 2011, translation by author). This is an obvious remnant from the times of Queen Christina and King Charles XI. The threat of fines was removed from the text during the 1770s. In 1880, A. W. Jacobson revised the wording to be practically the same as it is today. Eventually, in 1936, the phrase 'under aggravating circumstances' was added to the text (Heikkilä and Suvikumpu 2011:38, 68).

The declaration itself is, even though its wording has changed over time, the only one of the present elements that certainly has always been a part of the ceremony. It is, then, the very custom of reciting the declaration of the Christmas peace at the Old Great Square of Turku on which the claim of 'virtually unbroken tradition' and the sense of continuity with the medieval past is based.

'Our Land'

After the declaration, the national anthem of Finland follows. Being one of the most important national symbols, national anthems are at the core of nations' identities. The national anthem of Finland is based on a poem 'Vårt land' ('Maamme' in Finnish, 'Our Land' in English), written by the Swedish-speaking poet Johan Ludvig Runeberg in 1846. The poem was immediately set to music by three composers, Runeberg himself included. In early May 1848, the German-born composer Friedrich Pacius was asked to write new music to the poem. This combination of words and music was performed for the first time in Helsinki on 13 May 1848 in a student association's spring gathering organized by docent and acting professor Fredrik Cygnaeus (Klinge 1998:11; Salmenhaara 1998:43–45). The first stanza of 'Our Land' reads as follows (translation from the original Swedish poem by Clement Burbank Shaw):

Our land, our land, our fatherland,
Sound loud, O name of worth!

No mount that meets the heaven's band,
No hidden vale, no wavewashed strand,
Is loved, as is our native North,
Our own forefathers' earth.

The year 1848 is commonly known as 'the year of revolution' and the spring of 1848 as 'the Springtime of Peoples' (Rapport 2009:112) or 'the Spring of Nations' (Lucic 2010:40). At the time, however, Finnish academia was not willing to be associated with revolutionary or separatist aspirations. Choosing 'Our Land' as the poem to be set to music, the organizers ensured that the song would not express separatist revolutionary aspirations (Salmenhaara 1998:44). Instead of prompt and violent change by revolution, 'Our Land' set up an idyllic landscape, belief in fate and maturing from within (Klinge 1998:18). Journalist, poet and novelist Zacharias Topelius published a description of the gathering on 17 May in *Helsingfors Tidningar*. Later in the same year, a sheet music arrangement of the song was included in Runeberg's first volume of *The Tales of Ensign Stål*. According to Klinge (1998:24), Runeberg, Pacius, Cygnaeus and Topelius on 13 May 1848 gave expression to the kind of patriotism on which Finnishness was to be constructed.

'Our Land' gained the status of a national anthem only gradually. In the 1850s and 1860s, it became an established item in the repertoire of student choirs. During the 1870s, it was the most popular song in both the Finnish- and Swedish-speaking schools. From the 1850s to the 1880s, it was commonly performed on official festive occasions, usually paired with 'God Save the Czar!', the national anthem of the Russian Empire since 1833 (Junkkari 1998:73–80). Towards the 1890s and early 1900s, particularly during the so-called first Russification period (1898–1905), 'Our Land' became a standard number at several patriotic and religious-political meetings – together with 'A Mighty Fortress' and 'The March of the Pori Regiment' (Rantanen 2013:219–256; Goss 2009:194–196). It became the official national anthem after Finland gained independence in 1917. Today 'Our Land' is, as the national anthem, indisputably one of the most important sites of the Finnish national memory. As such, it accentuates a sense of a Finnish identity and continuity with the formative years of Finland as an independent nation.

'The March of the Pori Regiment'

Curiously enough, the Christmas peace ceremony ends with a bellicose military march. As a genre, the military march originated in the sixteenth century to accompany orderly military movements and processions. Due to the decline of the role of the infantry regiment after the First World War, the direct military function of the march ceased but the ceremonial function remained. Military marches are still used in, for example, parades, coronations, military events and festivities to accentuate the stately and ceremonial character of the event (Schwandt and Lamb 2014). This is also the function of 'The Pori March' in the Christmas peace ceremony.

The exact origin of this particular march is not known. The main part of the melody (sections A and B) is probably of French origin. In the mid-eighteenth century, it was played in Denmark and later in the same century in Sweden and Finland. Christian Kress, the German-born conductor of the Life Regiment of the Queen Dowager Lovisa Ulrika of Sweden, arranged the march for military band. During the early years of Finland as a grand duchy of the Russian Empire, it was rarely played in Finland. The currently known form of the march was provided in 1851 by another German-born musician, Konrad Greve, the conductor of the Grenadier-Sharpshooter Regiment of Turku. Greve used the march as incidental music in a play called *Ur livets strid* (From Life's Struggle). Johan Ludvig Runeberg wrote a poem to Greve's version, now titled 'The March of the Pori Regiment' (Vuolio 2004:65–66). It was published as the opening poem of the second volume of *The Tales of Ensign Stål* in 1860. The first two stanzas read as follows (translation by Henry Norman):

Sons of a race whose blood was shed,
On Narva's field; on Poland's sand; at Leipzig; Lutzen's dark hills under;
Not yet is Finland's manhood dead;
With foemen's blood a field may still be tinted red.

All Rest, all Peace, Away! begone!
The tempest loosens; lightnings flash; and o'er the field the cannon thunder
Rank upon rank, march on! march on!
The spirit of each father brave looks on as brave a son.

According to Glenda Goss, the patriotic *Tales of Ensign Stål* 'supplied Finns with the central images and strongest vision of who they aspired or saw themselves to be' (2009:27). Instead of the idyllic 'motherly face' of the fatherland portrayed in 'Our Land', 'The Pori March' is openly bellicose. The first stanza refers to the glorious past of the Finnish soldiers in the Swedish army during the seventeenth and early eighteenth centuries. 'Narva's field' is a reference to the battle of Narva (1700) where the Swedish army led by King Charles XII defeated the Russian forces. 'Poland's sand' is associated with a series of wars between Sweden and the Polish-Lithuanian Commonwealth between the sixteenth and eighteenth centuries, most notably to the Polish-Swedish War (1626–1629). The 'Lutzen's dark hills', in turn, refers to the battle of Lützen (1632) where the Swedish army defeated the forces of the Holy Roman Empire at the cost of the life of King Gustaf II Adolf of Sweden. The 'cannon thunder' mentioned in the second stanza was also incorporated in the musical arrangement of the march's trio section in the early 1860s when Filip von Schantz added rhythmically irregular drum beats to mark cannon shots (Vuolio 2004:67).

Together with 'A Mighty Fortress' and 'Our Land', 'The Pori March' was among the standard repertoire played in the patriotic and religious-political meetings in the late nineteenth and early twentieth centuries. Since 1918, it has been the official honorary and parade march of the Finnish Defence Forces. It is also one of the four symbols of the president of the Republic of Finland, the other three being the flag, the coat of arms and the decorations (President

2014). It is usually played at all official ceremonies involving the president of Finland. Like 'Our Land', it belongs to the most important sites of Finnish national memory. Like 'Our Land', it accentuates a sense of Finnish identity and continuity with the formative years of Finland as an independent nation.

Conclusion

The annual declaration of Christmas peace on Christmas Eve at noon on the Old Great Square is a highly institutionalized ritual performance with a fixed position in the cultural life of both the inhabitants of Turku and the Finnish people as a whole. With its assumed 700-year history, the ceremony maintains a residual sense of continuity with the national past from the Middle Ages to this day. Each element (number) of the ceremony contains references to or is otherwise associated with the memory of certain crucial events and epochs in the Finnish past. Put together, the symbolic meanings associated with the individual elements strengthen each other recursively, making the ceremony as a whole an extremely dense site of Finnish national memory.

Despite the sense of continuity with the past, there have been ruptures, breaks and transformations in the tradition. There have been at least two major revitalizations, both of which were referred to in the above analysis. It is probably no coincidence that both of these coincide with the 'two great phases of royal ceremonial efflorescence' in Europe (Cannadine 2000:161). The first of these took place in the sixteenth and seventeenth centuries and was centred particularly on the renaissance court of the Vasa Dynasty and the absolute sovereignty of King Charles XI. Remnants of royal Christmas peace ordinances can still be recognized in the wording of the current declaration text. Moreover, the custom of accompanying the ceremony with musical performances dates back to this period. The second major revitalization took place in the end of the nineteenth century, when the ceremony received approximately its current form. This can be seen as part of the mass production of invented traditions in Europe in 1870–1914 (Hobsbawm 2000b; Cannadine 2000:161). The revitalization of the Christmas peace tradition during this latter phase was not only connected with but also an expression of the emerging Finnish national identity.

Turku is the only city where the tradition of the Christmas peace declaration is said to have been virtually unbroken since the fourteenth century. Why is this the case? An obvious explanation would be that as the legal status of the ceremony – its original justification – weakened and the continuation of the tradition was questioned after the mid-nineteenth century, the ceremony was harnessed to serve the purposes of the growing nationalist movement. The 'medieval core' (cathedral bells, fanfare, declaration) was taken to refer to the long history of Finland as part of Sweden. The openly patriotic 'Our Land' and 'The March of the Pori Regiment' were included in the ceremony; the latter referring explicitly in its lyrics to the glorious past of Finnish soldiers in the Swedish army. 'A Mighty Fortress' had already had a special position in the Nordic countries since the sixteenth century. As the 'battle hymn of the Reformation', it now represented defence against the Russian Orthodox Church and, more generally, the 'one law, one church, one language' policy of the Russian Empire. One can conclude that without the Russification policy of the Russian Empire and the growing nationalism in Finland, the tradition of the declaration of Christmas peace could also have been waned in Turku.

Today the ceremony is predominantly residual much in the same sense as ceremonies of organized religion and monarchy are in the European contemporary dominant culture (cf. Williams1977:122). Yet a debate in the Finnish Parliament on the presidential prayer-day declarations in 2003 showed that religious-patriotic dimensions still count. While the majority of Finns probably do not themselves subscribe to all the literal wordings or the overall religious-patriotic spirit proclaimed by the ceremony, there is a considerable minority still committed to the 'core Finnish values' represented in the Christmas peace ceremony. Moreover, even the liberal majority is willing to preserve the tradition for its own sake, as a culturally meaningful tradition (Ihalainen 2005:103, 108).

The declaration of Christmas peace is a highly symbolic ritual that takes place in a highly symbolic space at a highly symbolic time. In Evangelic Lutheran countries like Finland, Christmas is the most important annual feast and holiday. Due to Turku's historical role in spreading and maintaining Christmas traditions in Finland – not least the putatively 700-year tradition of the declaration of Christmas peace – Turku City Board declared Turku in 1996 the official Christmas City of Finland (Hansen et al. 2004:20–21). Apart from its function in maintaining cultural memory, the declaration of Christmas peace, both as an actual live performance on the Old Great Square of Turku and as radio or television broadcast, acts nowadays as an annual ritual marking a difference between the routines of daily work and the peace of the Christmas holidays.

References

Anon. (1851), 'Joulu-Juhlasta', *Sanomia Turusta*, 23 December 1851, pp. 201–207.

Arnold, John H. and Caroline Goodson (2012), 'Resounding Community: The History and Meaning of Medieval Church Bells', *Viator*, 43:1, pp. 99–132.

Assmann, Jan (1995 [1988]), 'Collective Memory and Cultural Identity', Trans. John Czaplicka, *New German Critique*, 65, pp. 125–133.

Baines, Anthony (1974), 'The Evolution of Trumpet Music up to Fantini', *Proceedings of the Royal Musical Association*, 101, pp. 1–9.

Boissevain, Jeremy (2013), *Factions, Friends and Feasts: Anthropological Perspectives on the Mediterranean*, New York: Berghahn Books.

Braunfels, Wolfgang (1990 [1988]), *Urban Design in Western Europe. Regime and Architecture, 900–1900*, Trans. Kenneth J. Northcott, Chicago: University of Chicago Press.

Cannadine , David (2000 [1983]), 'The Context, Performance and Meaning of Ritual: The British Monarchy and the "Invention of Tradition", c. 1820–1977', in Eric Hobsbawm and Terence Ranger (eds), *The Invention of Tradition*, Cambridge: Cambridge University Press, pp. 101–164.

Carroll, Michael P. (1989), *Catholic Cults & Devotions: A Psychological Inquiry*, Montreal: McGill-Queen's University Press.

Dahlström, Fabian and Erkki Salmenhaara (1995), *Suomen musiikin historia 1: Ruotsin vallan ajasta romantiikkaan*, Porvoo: Werner Söderströmin Osakeyhtiö.

Dohrn-van Rossum, Gerhard (1996 [1992]), *History of the Hour: Clocks and Modern Temporal Orders*, Trans. Thomas Dunlap, Chicago and London: Chicago University Press.

Foucault, Michel (1972 [1971]), *The Archaeology of Knowledge*, Trans. Alan Sheridan, New York: Pantheon.

Goff, Jacques de (1982 [1977]), *Time, Work & Culture in the Middle Ages*, Trans. Arthur Goldhammer, Chicago and London: University of Chicago Press.

Goss, Glenda Dawn (2009), *Sibelius: A Composer's Life and the Awakening of Finland*, Chicago and London: University of Chicago Press.

Haines, John (2014), *Music in Films on the Middle Ages: Authenticity vs. Fallacy*. New York: Routledge

Hansen, Külli, Elena Di Stefano, Dragan Klain, Ugo Bachella and Elena Distefan (2004), *Festivals: Challanges* [sic] *of Growth, Distinction, Support Base and Internationalization*, Tartu: Tartu Linnavalitsus.

Hansson, Karl-Johan (2008), 'Martin Luther's Hymns in the Life of the Northern People', in Sven-Åke Selander and Karl-Johan. Hansson (eds), *Martin Luthers psalmer I de nordiska folkens liv*, Lund: Arcus, pp. 730–740.

Hebdige (2006 [1979]), '(i) From Culture to Hegemony; (ii) Subculture: The Unnatural Break', in Meenakshi Gigi Durham and Douglas M. Kellner (eds), *Media and Cultural Studies: KeyWorks*, Malden: Blackwell, pp. 144–162.

Heikkilä, Tuomas and Liisa Suvikumpu (2011), *Suomen Turku julistaa joulurauhan – Åbo kungör julfred*, Helsinki: Kirjapaja.

Helin, Mari, Kaarin Kurri, Aki Pihlman, Iina Paasikivi and Aki Männistö (2011), *The Oldest Parks in Turku: Cathedral Park – Brahe Park – Porthan Park*, Turku: Turku Administration Printing Services.

Hietala, Marjatta (1999), 'The Townbuilding and the Typology of Finnish Towns until 1720', in Julia-K. Büthe and Thomas Riis (eds), *Studien zur Geschichte Ostseeraumes III: Stadtwerdung und Städtische Typologie des Ostseegebietes bis zur Mitte des 18. Jahrhunderts*, Odense: Odense University Press, pp. 42–54.

Hobsbawm, Eric (2000a [1983]), 'Introduction: Inventing Traditions', in Eric Hobsbawm and Terence Ranger (eds), *The Invention of Tradition*, Cambridge: Cambridge University Press, pp. 1–14.

Hobsbawm, Eric (2000b [1983]), 'Mass-Producing Traditions: Europe, 1870–1914', in Eric Hobsbawm and Terence Ranger (eds), *The Invention of Tradition*, Cambridge: Cambridge University Press, pp. 263–307.

Ihalainen, Pasi (2005), 'The Lutheran National Community in 18th Century Sweden and 21st Century Finland', *Redescriptions: Yearbook of Political Thought and Conceptual History*, 9, pp. 80–112.

Jovinelly, Joann and Jason Netelkos (2007), *The Crafts and Culture of a Medieval Town*, New York: Rosen.

Junkkari, Olli (1998), 'Kuorolaulu ja Maamme-laulun leviäminen', in Laura Kolbe, Risto Valjus and Johan Wrede (eds), *Soi sana kultainen: Maamme-laulun viisitoista vuosikymmentä / Vårt land: Vår nationalsång 150 år*, Helsinki: Yliopistopaino, pp. 69–81.

Kantonen, Taito A. (1951), 'The Finnish Church and Russian Imperialism', *Church History*, 20:2, pp. 3–13.

Kirby, David (2006), *A Concise History of Finland*, Cambridge: Cambridge University Press.

Kivimäki, Ville and Tepora, Tuomas (2012), 'Meaningless Death or Regenerating Sacrifice? Violence and Social Cohesion in Wartime Finland', in Tiina Kinnunen and Ville Kivimäki, (eds), *Finland in World War II: History, Memory, Interpretations*, Leiden: Koninklijke Brill NV, pp. 234–275.

Klinge, Matti (1998), 'Euroopan kumousvuosi ja suomalaisuuden synty', in Laura Kolbe, Risto Valjus and Johan Wrede (eds), *Soi sana kultainen: Maamme-laulun viisitoista vuosikymmentä / Vårt land: Vår nationalsång 150 år*, Helsinki: Yliopistopaino, pp. 11–25.

Korsyn, Kevin (1999), 'Beyond Privileged Contexts: Intertextuality, Influence and Dialogue', in Nicholas Cook and Mark Everist (eds), *Rethinking Music*, Oxford: Oxford University Press, pp. 55–72.

Kramer, Lawrence (1990), *Music as Cultural Practice, 1800–1900*, Berkeley: University of California Press.

Krötzl, Christian (1988), 'Joulurauhasta kylpyrauhaan: Keskiajan erillisrauhat', *Rauhantutkimus*, 4:2, pp. 3–10.

Kurkela, Vesa (2011), 'Jumala ompi linnamme: Yhteiskunnallinen virsi ja sen suomalainen reseptiohistoria', *Hymnos*, pp. 83–97.

Leaver, Robin A. (1992), 'The Chorale: Transcending Time and Culture', *Concordia Theological Quarterly*, 56:2–3, pp. 123–144.

Leeuwen, Jacoba Van (2006), 'Praise the Lord for this Peace! The Contribution of Religious Institutions to the Ceremonial Peace-Proclamations in Late Medieval Flanders (1450–1550)', in Paul Trio and Marjan de Smet (eds), *The Use and Abuse of Sacred Places in Late Medieval Towns*, Leuven: Leuven University Press, pp. 47–70.

Loewe, Jost A. (2013), 'Why Do Lutherans Sing? Lutherans, Music, and the Gospel in the First Century of the Reformation', *Church History*, 82:1, pp. 69–89.

Lucic, Renéo (2010), 'The Emergence of the Nation-State in East-Central Europe and the Balkans in Historical Perspective', in Sabrina P. Ramet (ed.), *Central and Southeast European Politics since 1989*, Cambridge: Cambridge University Press, pp. 39–63.

MacClancy, Jeremy and Robert Parkin (1997), 'Revitalization or Continuity in European Ritual? The Case of San Bessu', *The Journal of the Royal Anthropological Institute*, 3:1, pp. 61–78.

Manning, Frank (1983), 'Cosmos and Chaos: Celebration in the Modern World', in Frank Manning (ed.), *The Celebration of Society: Perspectives on Contemporary Cultural Performance*, Bowling Green: Bowling Green University Popular Press.

Merriam, Alan P. (1964), *The Anthropology of Music*, Evanston: Northwestern University Press.

Nettl, Bruno (1983), *The Study of Ethnomusicology: Twenty-Nine Issues and Concepts*, Urbana and Chicago: University of Illinois Press.

Nora, Pierre (1996), 'General Introduction: Between Memory and History', in Lawrence D. Kritzman and Pierre Nora (eds), *Realms of Memory: Rethinking the French Past, Vol. I: Conflicts and Divisions*, Trans. Arthur Goldhammer, New York: Columbia University Press, pp. 1–20.

Orfield, Lester Bernhard (2002 [1953]), *The Growth of Scandinavian Law*, Union: The Lawbook Exchange.

Paarma, Jukka (2000), '"Abide in Me, and I Will Abide in You" – Sermon at the Festal Mass to Celebrate the Millennium Year 2000 and the 700th Anniversary of Turku Cathedral, on Trinity Sunday, 18 June 2000, *Evangelical Lutheran Church of Finland*, http://www.evl.fi/arkkipiispa/18600ENG.HTM. Accessed 4 February 2014.

President (2014), 'The Pori March', *The President of the Republic of Finland*, http://www.tpk.fi/public/default.aspx?nodeid=44828&contentlan=2&culture=en-US. Accessed 6 February 2014.

Pulma, Panu (2003), 'Rauhoituspolitiikan kausi', in Seppo Zetterberg (ed.), *Suomen historian pikkujättiläinen*, Helsinki: WSOY, pp. 373–392.

Rantanen, Saijaleena (2013), *Laulun mahti ja sivistynyt kansalainen: Musiikki ja kansanvalistus Etelä-Pohjanmaalla 1860-luvulta suurlakkoon*, Helsinki: Sibelius-Akatemia.

Rapola, Matti (1924), 'Suomenkielinen joulurauhan julistus 1600-luvulta', *Turun historiallinen arkisto*, 1, pp. 104–116.

Rapport, Mike (2009), 1848: *Year of Revolution*, New York: Basic Books.

Ratner, Leonard G. (1980), *Classic Music: Expression, Form, and Style*, New York: Schirmer.

Relph, Edward T. (1976), *Place and Placelessness*, London: Pion.

Rüsen, Jörn (2007), 'How to Make Sense of the Past – Salient Issues of Metahistory', *The Journal for Transdisciplinary Research in Southern Africa*, 3:1, pp. 169–221.

Salmenhaara, Erkki (1998), 'Fredrik Pacius ja Maamme-laulu', in Laura Kolbe, Risto Valjus and Johan Wrede (eds), *Soi sana kultainen. Vårt land. Maamme-laulun viisitoista vuosikymmentä. Vår nationalsång 150 år*, Helsinki: Yliopistopaino.

Schwandt, Erich and Andrew Lamb (2014), 'March', *Grove Music Online*, http://www.oxfordmusiconline.com/subscriber/article/grove/music/40080. Accessed 5 September 2014.

Schweitzer, Albert (1955), *J. S. Bach*, Vol. I, Trans. Ernest Newman, New York: Macmillan.

Seppänen, Liisa (2011), 'Lost but Found Underground: Construction, Development and Maintenance of Medieval Streets and Squares of Turku (Finland)', in Wolfgang Börner, Susanne Uhlirz and Lotte Dollhöfer (eds), *CHNT 16: International Conference on Cultural Heritage and New Technologies – Proceedings*, 14–16 November, Wien: Museen der Stadt Wien – Stadtarchäologie, pp. 476–490.

Sundman, Mikael (1991), 'Urban Planning in Finland After 1850', in Thomas Hall (ed.), *Planning and Urban Growth in the Nordic Countries*, London: Routlege, pp. 68–132.

Tucker, Spencer C. (2011), *Battles that Changed History: An Encyclopedia of World Conflict*, Santa Barbara: ABC-CLIO.

Turku (2014a), 'The Brinkkala Mansion', *City of Turku: The Old Great Square*, http://www.turku.fi/public/default.aspx?nodeid=15007&culture=fi-FI&contentlan=2. Accessed 6 September 2014.

—— (2014b), 'The Declaration of Christmas Peace', *City of Turku: Events and Leisure*, http://www.turku.fi/christmaspeace. Accessed 6 September 2014.

Vapaavuori, Hannu (2008), 'Tröst i krisis och pomp vid fest i Finland', in Sven-Åke Selander and Karl-Johan Hansson (eds), *Martin Luthers psalmer I de nordiska folkens liv*, Lund: Arcus, pp. 48–61.

Vuolio, Jukka (2004), 'Kunniamarssit – yleiseurooppalaista tunnusmusiikkia', *Musiikin suunta*, 26:1, pp. 61–70.

Vuolio, Jukka (2006), *Soi raikuen torvet ja rummut: Suomen sotilasmusiikin perinteitä sanoin, kuvin ja sävelin*, Helsinki: Kaartin jääkärirykmentin kilta ry.

Welin, Sanfrid (1936), 'Julfredens utblåsande: Ett bidrag till kännedomen om en gammal sed', in Salomon Kraft (ed.), *RIG: Tidskrift utgiven af föreningen för Svensk kulturhistoria*, Stockholm: Thule, 19, pp. 191–194.

Whitrow, Gerald James (1988), *Time in History: Views of Time from Prehistory to the Present Day*, Oxford: Oxford University Press.

Williams, Raymond (1977), *Marxism and Literature*. Oxford and New York: Oxford University Press.

Wilson, Archibald W. (1914), *The Chorales: Their Origins and Influence*, London: Faith Press.

YLE (2014), 'Asemiesillat viihdyttivät jermuja ja siviilejä', *Elävä arkisto*, http://yle.fi/elavaarkisto/artikkelit/asemiesillat_viihdyttivat_jermuja_ja_siviileja_54184.html#media=54188. Accessed 13 February 2014.

Notes

1   It is important to note that in 1150 there was no Finland, or Sweden, in the sense that the concepts are understood today. The area of present-day Finland gradually became a fully consolidated part of the Swedish kingdom as a result of a process that started in the twelfth century.

2   There are several different versions and translations of this motto. Kirby (2006:90) translates it as 'Swedes we are no longer, Russians we cannot be, therefore let us be Finns', whereas Kantonen (1951:6) gives the following translation: 'Swedes we are no longer; Russians we never can be: therefore we must be Finns'. The original Swedish form is usually stated as 'Svenskar äro vi inte längre, ryssar vilja vi inte bli, låt oss alltså bli finnar', which strictly speaking means 'Swedes we are no longer, Russians we do not want to become, therefore let us be Finns'.

3   Nils Pinello had started his café in the park already in the 1840s, but in the central square further away from the river. In 1862, this became the location of the statue of Henrik Gabriel Porthan (hence the name 'Porthan Park'), and in 1863 the Pinella building was moved to its current place above the colonnade (Helin et al. 2011:9).

4   Edelfelt's triptych was destroyed during the massive bombings of Helsinki by the Soviet Union air force in early 1944. Artist Johannes Gebhard reconstructed the triptych in 1961 on the basis of survived sketches, photographs and copies.

Chapter 3

Authenticities on Display: Reflections on a Staged Pink Floyd Concert

Lars Kaijser

In 2010, an article in *Dagens Nyheter* – a daily Swedish paper with national coverage – stated that the original Pink Floyd was to reunite for one night in Stockholm (Kronbrink 2010). A hitherto unknown taping of a Pink Floyd concert from 1967 had emerged and an audience would now for the first time be able to listen to this recording. The band was to be present at the concert as mannequins. Pink Floyd belongs to the canon of rock and popular music, and the discovery of the tape caught media attention. The stories told in the Swedish paper would reappear in both Swedish and international papers such as *The Observer* and the music magazine *Rolling Stone*. The history behind the news was that Pink Floyd in the autumn of 1967 did a tour of Europe and Scandinavia. In Stockholm, they played a Sunday afternoon concert at a venue called Gyllene Cirkeln (The Golden Circle). The audience consisted of 275 guests who had to pay a cover charge that also included a meal. One man had recording equipment placed at the venue. He had asked Pink Floyd if it was okay to tape their show. It was. Unfortunately, the sound system did not work properly during Pink Floyd's set and it was almost impossible to distinguish the vocals. The man who did the recording was disappointed with the result and the tapes were shelved. Some 40 years later, one entrepreneur in the prog-rock heritage business got to listen to the tapes and after some persuasion he was allowed to organize an event around the recorded concert. The event was to be called The Pink Floyd Happening and took place during two evenings in May 2011.[1]

The planned event asserted several claims to authenticity. The same venue as in 1967 was to be used and Pink Floyd would be present as look-alike mannequins dressed in exactly the same way as when they first played at Gyllene Cirkeln. The event was said to have a certain historical importance. For a start, Pink Floyd here debuted 'Set the Controls for the Heart of the Sun', a tune that was not released on record until a year later. This fact, according to the organizer, made the recording significant as it in some way altered the history of Pink Floyd (Dimle: 19 April 2011 interview). Of more importance was that it would be the first playback of the 1967 Stockholm recording. This recording was unique in its own way as one of the few live recordings capturing a complete Pink Floyd show with Syd Barrett still in the band. In 1967, Pink Floyd had released their first album and a couple of singles. During the first years, Syd Barrett was the driving force in the band, writing most of their songs and singing lead vocals. The band belonged to the London underground scene. They were playing improvisational psychedelic music and were recognized for their light shows. The Pink Floyd line-up at this time was Syd Barrett on guitar and vocals, Nick Mason on drums, Roger Waters on bass and vocals and Rick Wright on keyboard and vocals. This changed gradually later in 1967 as Syd Barrett, due to drug use in combination with mental-health issues, was gradually left out of the group. He was replaced by David Gilmour in early 1968.

This line-up would later be famous for spectacular stage shows and albums like *Dark Side of the Moon*, *Wish You Were Here* and *The Wall*. Syd Barrett, on the other hand, became mythologized as one of pop music's lost geniuses and died as a recluse in 2006 (Heylin 2012).

The Pink Floyd Happening will be used in this chapter as a starting point for discussing how representations, performances or enactments of the past can be interpreted in terms of authenticity, historical accuracy and notions of zeitgeist. My inspiration for approaching the concept of authenticity initially derives from studies of tourism and cultural heritage, where ideas of the authentic have been ascribed to an original and unspoiled past (Lowenthal 1985; MacCannell 1999/1976; Bendix 1997; Dicks 2003). As such it has been an important theme in ideas about an emerging modern society. The past has been understood to inhabit a more natural way of living, and authenticity has been found in past customs and practices. Pink Floyd and the 1960s psychedelic music scene could hardly be seen as part of an emerging modernity but belonging to later twentieth century and a modernity giving way to what Anthony Giddens referred to as late or radicalized modernity (1990:150). Here, Pink Floyd and their contemporaries could be seen as both pioneers and originators in a social era characterized by increased global relations and the establishment of what has been defined as 'a pop/rock cosmopolitan taste culture', that is, a de-territorialized social community constituted through knowledge of popular music (Regev 2002:656). At the Pink Floyd Happening, the musicians as well as the organizing entrepreneur and the mannequin maker were seeking to establish the impression of a reliable representation of the original concert. Authenticity could in this case be understood, in the words of Hugh Barker and Yuval Taylor, as an 'absolute, a goal that can never be fully attained, a quest' (2007:x). An endeavour for this could be detected when talking to the participant audience as well as to musicians and in the arrangements with the mannequins. This was, after all, an entrepreneurial and not an erudite setting. This aim, as I interpret the situation, was not so much an outright staging of the past, but more to find a common ground where values of the late 1960s could be played out and enjoyed.

A focus on authenticity also follows a well-trodden track in popular music research, where authenticity has been recognized as authentic musical expressions and acknowledged as individual artistry (see, e.g., Peterson 1997; Grazian 2004; Barker and Taylor 2007). This connects to the idea of an authentic origin, placing the authentic sometimes in the past (early-twentieth-century blues) or in certain ethnic or social communities (world music comes to mind). In this chapter, the concept of authenticity is significant in both an emic and an etic sense. It was used by the participants in a multitude of ways. As I will show, it was used in a more ideological way, pointing to an understanding by which the 1960s Pink Floyd was valued as more authentic than later reincarnations of the band. This mirrors a common notion that some popular music, such as rock, carries a more authentic expression that could be traced both to the artist and to the circumstances of the musical production, whereas pop is less authentic and a more fabricated cultural product (Shuker 2001/1994:8, 34–35). This articulates the well-documented division between art and commerce. The idea of an authentic artistry carries a value of authentic as a personal and recognizable expression. The myth of Syd Barrett as a childlike genius could also be an example of this.

I will primarily – but not solely – work with a twofold concept of authenticity adapted from the consumer researchers Kent Grayson and Radan Martinec (2004). Their conceptualization of authenticity stems from more quantitative studies of marketing, while my approach is rooted in qualitative studies. I found that the conceptualization also works in studies of small-scale entrepreneurs as in the case of the Pink Floyd Happening. An aspiration for authenticity was articulated in relation to both people and things that were part of the actual 1967 concert and to aesthetic similarities (like the mannequins and what Pink Floyd actually looked like in 1967). Following Grayson and Martinec, iconic authenticity is related to look-alike and an authenticity based on the physical senses and a possible experience of being there. This is analytically separated from indexical authenticity and things with a factual relation to the represented event, and an authenticity based on facts – or in other words a more semiotic authenticity built on an acknowledged relation between the representational event and the materialities participating in the event.

I will start by describing how the event evolved during the Pink Floyd Happening. Then, I will point out some important features of how the event was approached and apprehended by visitors. The second half of the chapter is devoted to a discussion of the different ways in which authenticity was realized. I took part in some of the preparations and I closely followed the work during the two days of the happening. My participation in the event is the empirical starting point for this chapter.

The event

The actual event took place at Gyllene Cirkeln on 3 and 7 May 2011. The venue had been an important scene for jazz and for an emerging Swedish underground rock in the 1960s. It had continued as a restaurant and in 2011 it was redecorated in a 1960s retro style. The venue was a long rectangular room with a restaurant at one end. For the Pink Floyd Happening, two stages were created in the room. The stage for the tribute act was placed at the opposite end of the restaurant and in the centre was the stage with the Pink Floyd mannequins dressed to look as the band did in 1967 and equipped with appropriate instruments. Added to this was a small area displaying records, DVD's and other items for sale. Compact discs were laid out on a table and stacked in plastic trays along with vinyl records in cabinets. One could find the official records by Pink Floyd, together with bootlegs, as well as other records from progressive artists. On the wall behind the tables, the organizer hung sleeves from LP records of particular importance for the evening. There were early Pink Floyd albums, bootlegs and records by artists playing in the evening's tribute act. Also on sale were enlarged black-and-white photographs of Pink Floyd taken at Gyllene Cirkeln in 1967.

A soon as the doors were opened, a crowd of people started to gather around the stage with the mannequins. The mannequins were illuminated by a liquid light projection that slowly changed the colour of the scene. Members of the audience took turns having their picture taken in front of the mannequins. Occasionally, a small line of people queued up waiting for their turn. On the days that followed some of these pictures would be found on websites on the Internet, together with comments on the event. The open stage seemed to invite the audience to interact with the mannequins. At the same time, the mannequins were on a low stage fenced off with a rope so that the audience also kept their distance. As the time for the show drew near, more and more people stood in front of the small stage, forming a crescent-shaped formation fixing the mannequins with their eyes.

The audience consisted primarily of older men born in the 1940s and 1950s but there were women and younger people there as well. I got the impression that most of the participants were from the Stockholm area but some visitors – diehard fans I am guessing – had flown in from Germany and Britain to have the opportunity to listen to the recorded concert. The Pink Floyd Happening was organized to coincide with Roger Waters bringing The Wall show to Stockholm. When walking and eavesdropping among the audience at Gyllene Cirkeln, it was possible to hear comments on Roger Waters' show as well as on Rush, who had played in Stockholm during the same week. Pink Floyd had played several times in Stockholm and I heard people sharing their experience of seeing the 1967 concert; as well as a performance in 1971. For some who were not there in 1967, the happening was an opportunity to hear what they had originally missed.

Figure 1: The Pink Floyd mannequins on stage at Gyllene Cirkeln in May 2011. Photo by the author.

The playback of the taped concert was introduced by the man – Anders Lind – who originally recorded the concert. On the first night, a journalist helped out by putting questions to Lind and somehow also coordinated questions from the audience. On the second night, Lind did the introductions by himself. He also invited onto the stage a woman who had worked at Gyllene Cirkeln in 1967 and as an eyewitness she talked about the time when Pink Floyd visited Stockholm. Anders Lind carefully described the circumstances of the recording. He recalled that in 1967, a Swedish band called Hansson & Karlsson played at Gyllene Cirkeln and he used to tape their performances. His tape recorder was heavy and he was to record more of Hansson & Karlsson so he had his recording equipment placed at the venue all through the weekend. When Pink Floyd arrived, he asked if it was all right with them if he taped their show, and it was, as long as he didn't do anything stupid with the tape. The PA system, however, was a bit out of order and the microphones did not work properly during Pink Floyd's set. He was disappointed with the recordings and stored them away. Then several years later, it occurred to him that most of the music Pink Floyd played was instrumental. He gave the tapes another try and found out that they were really good. He said that Pink Floyd played in a rough style more to be compared to grunge. During his presentation, he held up one of the two microphones that he had used during the recording, and he pointed at his tape recorder that was placed on the stage by the feet of the mannequins. He also reported that, for copyright reasons, he had omitted one song from the set that had not been published by Pink Floyd, a tune or maybe more correctly an improvisational piece called 'Before or Since'.[2] Otherwise, it was the whole concert. The audience was allowed to ask questions. One topic that I heard referred to on several occasions was the question of where the stage originally had been placed. Some stated that it had been on the opposite side from where the stage was during the Pink Floyd Happening. Anders Lind, however, was certain of his recollection: the stage was correctly placed. They had checked with pictures taken in 1967 and were sure where to put the stage.

The tape with the concert took approximately 42 minutes. Pink Floyd played 'Matilda Mothe' 'Pow R. Toc H', 'Scream Thy Last Scream', 'Set the Controls for the Heart of the Sun', 'See Emily Play' and 'Interstellar Overdrive'. The music was loud, but not too loud. The audience participated in the show following the script for a regular concert. They moved along to the music, and clapped their hands between the songs. Some of the songs were greeted more enthusiastically, and the more pop-like hit of 'See Emily Play' received both applause and whistles. Parts of the audience sang along to the chorus-like segments of the song and 'There is no other day' was heard together with the taped music. A flickering light show dramatized the scene, with colours changing in red, green, blue and yellow. Together with shadows made by the playing lights, it gave life to the mannequins. When I spoke to a man who had visited both of the shows he said that he preferred the Tuesday show. The sound was better. He thought that it depended on where he had placed himself during the concert. The sound altered when moving around in the venue. But it could also be related to the fact that he heard the recording for the first time on Tuesday, while Saturday was

Figure 2: When Pink Floyd played in 1967, approximately 275 people attended the show. The Pink Floyd Happening was attended by approximately 350 persons each night. Photo by the author.

good but more a repetition. The audience was also more rowdy on Saturday. Afterwards, the organizer said that it was just like looking at an audience following a game of tennis, when they occasionally stared at Rick, and sometimes at Syd, depending on who had a solo part. I did not see this myself, but I heard this observation retold several times.

The initial idea of the organizer had been to let the opening acts from 1967 – the local acts Bambo and Sleepstones – to open once again for Pink Floyd. This had been impossible to accomplish, however. Instead a tribute act, called Lost in Rick Wright's Wardrobe, finished the evening with a set of Pink Floyd songs from the years 1967–1969. The band consisted of six members, filling the Pink Floyd songs with sounds of flutes and vibes and two female singers taking the lead, thus giving the song a more mellow and folky sound than the raw versions that Pink Floyd themselves had delivered earlier on.

When the two acts had finished their set and the audience was leaving the club, a more relaxed relationship appeared towards the mannequins. Possibly fuelled by drinking and possibly inspired by others, some people climbed onto the stage, taking pictures of each other posing between the mannequins or with one arm on a band member's shoulder. Someone even took the opportunity to have his picture taken while he produced a recorder and did an impromptu interview with Syd Barrett.

The event was very well received. One of the most influential daily papers in Sweden described it as a nerd record, but also as a great success (Backman 2011). Pink Floyd was acknowledged for the raw power of their music and for their innovative improvisation. The tribute band was recognized for their youth, their charm and praised for their reinterpretation of Pink Floyd.

The ambiguous past

In his book *Retromania* (2011), Simon Reynolds argues that the popular music scene has been preoccupied by its own past during the last decade or so. This could be described as an overall zeitgeist characterizing the turn of the twenty-first century (Dicks 2003). The staging of shows and concerts portraying musical pasts follows this well-established route. There is a succession of tribute acts portraying most of the famous pop idols from the 1950s onwards (Homan 2006). Elvis, the Beatles, ABBA and Pink Floyd all have their tribute acts touring and re-enacting their concerts. These shows can probably be seen, in the light of Barbara Kirshenblatt-Gimblett's findings, as places for visiting imagined and virtual worlds (1998); in this case, the imagined origin of a Swedish psychedelic scene. The tribute acts make it possible to experience or re-experience musical pasts. This could also be said of the Pink Floyd Happening. It was organized by Stefan Dimle, a well-known character on the Stockholm music scene, who through his record company, called Mellotronen, reissued and distributed progressive music from the 1960s and the 1970s. He had also ran record stores and organized reunion shows where artists from the Swedish 1970s progressive music scene had reunited and played. When talking about the Pink Floyd Happening, he expressed a desire for authenticity and said that his intention was to reconstruct the actual evening (Dimle: 19 May 2011 interview). He had a weak spot for non-official recordings, bootlegs that made it possible to hear how the music actually sounded when played live. Here, the Pink Floyd Happening was one of his ways to incorporate his interest in the non-official or alternative histories into his entrepreneurial activities.

During the two nights of the Pink Floyd Happening, documentary film-maker Mikael Katzeff was present on the premises conducting unplanned on-the-spot interviews with different people working with or attending the event. Later, when allowed to watch the recordings, I was able to follow how Katzeff talked to the organizers, to the audience and to the musicians. One of his recurring questions, asked with sincere astonishment, was 'Why should we listen to a 44-year-old recording?' The common short answer was that it offered the opportunity to listen to the music and the exclusive opportunity to listen to something that had not been released before. Many of the participants referred to other known recordings of Pink Floyd in 1967, one made in Copenhagen and the other one in Rotterdam, though they dismissed them both as lacking in sound quality. The recording at Gyllene Cirkeln was found to be superior in sound, capturing Syd Barrett's guitar playing in splendid form.

Mikael Katzeff has a long history as part of the Swedish alternative music scene from the early seventies on. Several of the people whom he engaged in interviews were old acquaintances. Those interviews did not dwell on the importance of the music; instead, they moved towards reflections on the late 1960s when Pink Floyd and psychedelia entered Stockholm. Pink Floyd was not the target of their discussion, but more a vehicle for reaching the 1960s. The emphasis was on ambivalence towards the changing times. The late 1960s were interpreted through a cultural-historic filter melded together with their own memories and nostalgia of their youth. The interviews constituted – through reference to and acknowledgement of important events, artists, people and places – what could be called an *affective alliance* (Grossberg 1997; see Hyltén-Cavallius and Kaijser 2012:68–69). Affective alliance refers to a shared inclination towards similar cultural expressions. The alliance is built on both identification and recognition, uniting certain people in their way of relating to others and in their way of relating to the past. This means sharing both memory and forgetfulness. During the evening, I could hear how the audience, trying to find a consensus on the interiors of Gyllene Cirkeln in the late 1960s, discussed where the stage was located and where there had been stairs leading to the entrance floor, at the same time as they tried to figure out which concerts they had been to – why or why not, and with whom.

September of 1967 was seen as an important time for psychedelic music in Sweden. When interviewed, Stefan Dimle talked about the week when psychedelia was born in Sweden, referring to events occurring at the same time. Pink Floyd was in Stockholm, Jimi Hendrix played at Konserthuset around the same time, Mecki Mark Men recorded their first LP and Filips – an underground club – opened (Dimle: 19 April 2011 interview). The claim about the birth of psychedelia in Sweden should not be taken literally. I find it more of a marketing strategy defining the importance of the Pink Floyd Happening on the market of competing activities relating to the popular music heritage. It is at the same time possible to see that the venues mentioned were culturally important. Motti Regev has written on the subject of pop-rock cosmopolitanism (2013). In his characterization of an aesthetic cosmopolitanism, he emphasizes one feature: the quest for recognition in what 'individual actors around the world believe to be the innovative frontiers of creativity and artistic expression' (Regev 2013:6). The psychedelic music of the late 1960s was part of an emerging cosmopolitan music scene originating in the United States and England. Within this pop-rock cosmopolitanism, it is possible to detect both centres and peripheries. The places mentioned in his article, Gyllene Cirkeln, Konserthuset and Klubb Filip, were all crucial in paving the way for the inclusion of Sweden in the cosmopolitan scene. This moves the Swedish music scene from the periphery towards a psychedelic centre in London or maybe San Francisco. It is at the same time possible to identify a Swedish psychedelic scene incubating at the clubs and concert venues. International artists played the venues but they were also important for the pioneering Swedish artists who would influence the late 1960s and early 1970s Swedish music scene and who only partially – and in some cases not until decades later – would touch a more international scene (Hyltén-Cavallius and Kaijser 2012).

Both Gyllene Cirkeln and the club Filips were often referred to in the aforementioned interviews by documentary film maker Katzeff. During the interviews, he and the interviewees shared and exchanged personal recollections of concerts that they had experienced. Cream, Jimi Hendrix, The Mothers of Invention with Frank Zappa, The Doors and Jefferson Airplane (all part of canonical psychedelic music history) played in Stockholm during the autumn of 1967 and the spring of 1968. Jimi Hendrix had visited both Gyllene Cirkeln and Filips and his jams together with Hansson & Karlsson were mentioned on several occasions during the event. There was also agreement among the interviewees that they did not understand, at that time, the importance of what they were part of. This related to visiting the concerts as well as how they treated the paraphernalia of the time. One man told the story of how he had bought posters, ordered from London, and how he had them on the wall as a teenager. Later he ripped them down and threw them away. He shook his head and said that he should have kept them. For the people interviewed this was part of their adolescence. The time was innocent on a personal level, but also on a social level, and they laughed at the need to include a meal in the ticket for the Pink Floyd concert in 1967. But the conversations also turned towards more serious subjects. The past was not all rosier. The regulations were liberal towards narcotics, which were an important part of psychedelia. They all had friends whom they had lost to drug abuse. As one man put it, 'We were the generation who took the blow from a liberal drug policy'.

This way of addressing the 1960s also set an interpretative frame for the Pink Floyd biography. When the film maker in his interviews with the audience at the happening expressed his opinion of the show, he said that it exposed how Pink Floyd changed from a small rock band touring in a Ford Transit to a global brand travelling the world with 58 trucks. The last was a nod to Roger Waters and his staging of The Wall. Thereby, the 1967 edition of Pink Floyd was also categorized as more authentic than the later Pink Floyd. By this logic, the early Pink Floyd were regarded as more genuine, because of their participation in the pioneering London underground music scene. Following an established pattern where authenticity is viewed in contrast to the commercial, the commercial success and the stadium band that Pink Floyd later would develop into were seen as opposed to artistic originality and integrity. The idea is that alternative music or an underground scene is linked to counter-culture and a more authentic way of creating music. This was expressed in different ways both as a question of size – travelling in a small bus/the limited use of instruments on stage – and as a rawer, less finely tuned sound.

The story of Syd Barrett in itself neatly encapsulates the changes and consequences of the late 1960s. To a certain extent, the event was built upon the anticipation of hearing the recording of Pink Floyd and how they actually sounded live in 1967. This was to be one of the last occasions when Syd Barrett was able to take part in a Pink Floyd show in spirit and body. His confused behaviour during some of the gigs in the autumn of 1967 is an important part of the myth of Syd (Heylin 2012:2–3). From a narrative point of view, it is possible to identify Syd Barrett, with his child-like lyrics, his genius and his estrangement from Pink Floyd as well as from public life, as a trickster, an instigator of the ethos of 1967 (see Hyde

Figure 3: The Syd Barrett mannequin is trying to hide his eyes in the afternoon before the show at Gyllene Cirkeln in 2011. Photo by the author.

1998:6–8). He could be perceived as an authentic character, in the sense of being original and honest and thus making Pink Floyd and psychedelia happen, but not being part of things to come.

It was the afternoon before the first show. I followed the work of installing the mannequins on the stage. Two women were trying to improve the Syd Barrett mannequin. One of them said that Syd's eyes looked a bit peculiar. The other one said that it had to be drugs. She then turned to me and said 'Do you think he's taken something?' Syd Barrett's eyes exemplified one of many ways in which I met and noticed how the myth of Syd Barrett was articulated throughout the Pink Floyd Happening.

At the same time that little dialogue shows one important feature of how the event was anticipated and perceived. A playful frame surrounded the event and it was – to a certain degree – performed tongue-in-cheek. This was manifested in various ways. The restaurant served dishes with names alluding to different Pink Floyd songs like Corporal Egg (Corporal Clegg), A Sausage Full of Secrets (A Saucer full of Secrets) and Candy and a Currant Bun. There were also drinks served in the same manner with names like Crazy Diamond and Apples & Oranges. Likewise, the playful mode was evident when the audience approached the mannequins, laughing and having their pictures taken. When addressed, most participants emphasized the fun of the event, describing it as funny, corny or weird. I could however sense ambivalence about taking part in the event. I had a feeling that some of the participants became self-conscious and felt they were crossing the fine line between a healthy interest in popular music and a more uncomfortable participation in a slightly unsettling scenario, inhabited by fanatics or caricatures of pop nerds. Someone described it as ghostlike. At the same time, the audience accepted the play matrix and, as I have described, participated in the concert.

Materializing the music

The taped concert was the obvious centre for the staged concert. At the same time, the mannequins were the visual focal point during the event. As described above, the audience gathered around them during and before the playback of the tape. They were also the equally obvious image in reviews of the event and a backdrop for people wanting to remember the occasion. The work of producing the mannequins displayed an array of different examples of authenticity.

The mannequins could be seen as an example of an iconic authenticity. They looked like the 1960s, or at least like the idea of the 1960s, and they looked like Pink Floyd in 1967. They made it possible for the audience listening to the tapes, at least if they gazed with their eyes half open, to get the sense of seeing Pink Floyd. The iconic authenticity works with the senses, giving the audience the possible experience of being at the original concert. This was also the most important guideline when the mannequins were produced, a work that evoked the difference between an iconic and an indexical authenticity. That is an authenticity in a more semiotic way or look-alike, and an authenticity based on a more factual relation between a historical incident and the representation of the same incident.

Sitting on the floor at the home of one of the singers in Lost in Rick Wright's Wardrobe, I followed the work on the Pink Floyd mannequins, a work involving sculpturing and painting, as well as dressing and arranging them in fitting postures. Meanwhile, I listened to discussions and talk of details, as the makers tested out the best ways of making the mannequins appear as Pink Floyd. The mannequins were to 'perform' Pink Floyd, and as such they had to have ethnicity, gender and character. At first this was a question of a visual authenticity, that is, they had to have the proper look. As I followed the work with one of the mannequins, Nick Mason, I was told that his face had become too reddish. The mannequin maker said she needed to repaint the face to get the pale English skin, expressing an idea of Englishness. She said that he had changed from looking like a southern-state officer to becoming an Italian con artist (she used the Swedish expression 'sol-och-vårare'). Our conversations went from using the right colour for the face and arranging the mannequins so that they could hold their musical instruments in the proper way, and further onto the relations within the band. I was told that it was a challenge to find mannequins that could handle the musical instruments. Six or seven mannequins were bought, dismembered and put together again. Arms that could play a guitar were taken from one mannequin and put

Figures 4–5: Nick Mason, from a head to a full-fit drummer. Photo by the author.

on another one, whose legs and torso better matched the posture of someone playing music. Three of the mannequins used were female as there were more female mannequins on the market. This was not portrayed as a problem, as both Rick Wright and Syd Barrett were said to be somewhat androgynous. Throughout the modelling of the mannequins, gender was treated as something that it was possible to both blur and transgress. Roger Waters was seen as a larger man, and more broad-shouldered. For him they used a male mannequin. The hairdo was made to look as the band did in pictures. One of the mannequins, Roger Waters, was able to use a female wig from one of the mannequins. For the others, wigs were bought at a store selling costumes, joke items and other amusements. Rick Wright and Syd Barrett wore Ringo Starr wigs.

The mannequins were dressed to look as Pink Floyd did in pictures from 1967. The clothes, however, were mainly clothes from the 1980s bought in second-hand shops around Stockholm. The mannequin maker said that she had visited a lot of shops, but that there also were many friends who had helped her in the search for garments that could perform and effectively convey a sense of the late 1960s. Elisabeth Guffey (2006) has stated that retro styles can be characterized by an eclectic and anachronistic bricolage where irony and playfulness can be more important than memory or context. This was true also for the ways in which the mannequins were dressed. One of Guffey's examples was the London psychedelic boutique Granny Takes a Trip, a shop dedicated to vintage clothes and catering for the young swinging London with Pink Floyd as one of the customers. It would be possible to argue that the way the clothes were chosen for the mannequins echoed the 1960s approach to past clothing not by recapitulating new styles but by creating new hybrid forms (Guffey 2006:57). Sometimes, female clothes were bought and remade to fit the mannequins. The mixture of colours in the way that Pink Floyd was dressed was important, but tricky to apply. The pictures of Pink Floyd playing at Gyllene Cirkeln were in black and white. The clothes used in the pictures from the concert were therefore compared with clothes worn by Pink Floyd in pictures taken in colour. The woman who made them told me that she had a green coat for Rick Wright, because this was how she had imagined it. Later she found a picture in colour and she realized that it was in red so she had to buy a new one. The same went for the shirt; she had one that looked correct in the black-and-white photo, but it lacked the mixture of red, black and silver of the original shirt in a coloured picture.

The woman who made the mannequins told me that at first she studied pictures of the band. But then she started to watch old film clips on Youtube. When doing so she gained a better view of their attitude and their character, and a way of grasping their features and peculiarities. There was a laptop on a chair by the dismembered mannequins and I was shown a clip from a 1967 interview with Roger Waters and Syd Barrett (The clip featured the interview as well as Pink Floyd playing 'Astronomy Domine', making it possible to get a sense both of their music and their light show[3]). The musician tries in a polite way to answer the rather hostile questions from the reporter – or more correctly, the critic – Hans Keller about their loud music. Keller finishes the interview with a judgement: 'My verdict is that it is a little bit of a regression to childhood, but after all, why not?' After showing me the clip she laughed, repeated the critic's last words and commented that Syd had a very thin face on that clip. The moving images made it possible to catch facial expressions as well as getting a sense of the ethos of the time.

The work with the mannequins also encapsulated stories of the band members and the relations within the band. Pink Floyd's biography has often been told and has been the subject of many books and magazines (Liljegren 2010; Mason 2005). One important feature is the estrangement between Roger Waters and Rick Wright. At the time when Pink Floyd visited Gyllene Cirkeln, Syd Barrett was the dominant creative force in the band. Later, when he left, Roger Waters slowly took on that role. In the early days, Rick Wright wrote and sang several of their classic songs. By the time – in the late 1970s – when they recorded *The Wall*, Roger Waters was the sole leader of the band and he forced Rick Wright to leave. Wright took part in the production of *The Wall* but only as a salaried session musician. Fragments of this story echoed when the mannequins were made. I was told that Roger was a bit of a bully and Rick had to put up with this. The woman who made the mannequins said that she had affection for Rick and he became her favourite. She continued by saying that even though he was in the background, his influence was fundamental for the musical atmosphere. He

Figure 6: A computer was placed on a chair in the room where the mannequins were made. Here is a picture of Syd Barrett when interviewed by Hans Keller (from the Youtube clip *PINK FLOYD BBC 1 1967 Astronomy Domine Unedited*). Photo by the author.

wrote the best songs, but due to Roger's bullying he slowly faded away. Standing in front of the Roger mannequin it was possible to apprehend him as intimidating, broad-shouldered and leaning over you. Rick, on the other hand, looked a bit uncomfortable and more timid. In this way, the arranged mannequins staged an anachronistic narrative. They depicted not so much the relations within the band at the time as the relations that would evolve over the years to come.

There were several other actors in the mannequins' performance. The instruments and devices that were part of the staging brought their iconic authenticity to the show. Some of the visitors attending Gyllene Cirkeln, who had also been present at the 1967 show, stated that in 1967 it was not just the band that was important. Sometimes, they went for the light show. Pink Floyd was one of the bands that were famous not just for the music but also for their light shows. So – for those visitors at least – the light show did not just bring life to the mannequins, but also helped to authenticate the event.

The instruments used had been borrowed from friends and musicians. The instruments were iconic in that they looked like the instruments used by Pink Floyd. At the same time, their iconicity was constrained by some important conditions. If the clothes looked correct, their origin was of no importance. The same did not go for the instruments, where brand and to a certain degree also type and model were prominent features for those in the know. Musical instruments, amplifiers and other devices are often important cues when identifying a popular music artist with their sound and style. One prime example of this is how the Beatles on occasion can be reduced to a Hofner bass (Paul McCartney), a Rickenbacker guitar (John Lennon), a Gretsch guitar (George Harrison) and a Ludwig drum kit (Ringo Starr). When it comes to musical instruments, the indexical and iconic authenticity sometimes seems to interlock. They need to look like the original instruments, but at the same there is also an authenticity in the brand as an index of the instruments originally used. At the Pink Floyd Happening, Syd Barrett and Roger Waters were equipped with guitar and bass similar to those that Pink Floyd used in 1967 – if not the same model, at least the same brand. Syd played what looks like a black-and-white Danelectro and Roger a Rickenbacker bass. The keyboard used on stage by Wright in 1967 was a Farfisa Compact Duo with double manual. At the Pink Floyd Happening a simpler Farfisa Compact Deluxe with one manual was used instead. The difference was said not to matter as long as it looked old. Also on stage was an echo unit, a Binson Echorec 2, favoured by Rick and Syd. The echo did not work, but as someone said, that didn't really matter. What it did was to contribute to an aesthetic representation and a materialization of the recorded concert, showing one of the important devices in making the original Floyd sound.

The use of technical devices when setting the stage for the mannequins also provided space for a more indexical authenticity. The man who originally taped the concert was important for this. He brought the two microphones used in 1967, and he was said to have placed the original Revox tape recorder on the stage, playing the original tape. This was not completely true. The tape recorder on stage was identical to the one used in 1967, but it was not the actual one that was used. Lind had still the tape recorder used in his possession but it was located in his home in another part of Sweden. But it weighed 30 kilos and was too cumbersome to carry with him to Stockholm. The audience did not know this and members of the audience took a great interest in the tape recorder. To them it was the device that had taped Pink Floyd and other artists such as Jimi Hendrix and Hansson & Karlsson. Just like the mannequins, it was a subject for photographers, and I saw several persons with cameras or their telephones leaning over the recorder, studying it in detail. Thus, the tape recorder on the stage blurred the line between iconic and indexical. It was possible to view it as indexical, as this was what said during the introduction before the playback, but at the same time there was no factual relation between the recorder and the event. But it looked the same and in that way it fulfilled a role as an iconic item in the same way as the echo-unit.

Figure 7: The Binson Echorec 2 on stage at Gyllene Cirkeln. The device is mentioned in several articles on Pink Floyd. It was used both by Rick Wright and Syd Barrett, and later by David Gilmour who used it during most of the live shows in the 1970s (Riis: 'Binson Echorec'). Photo by the author.

The most important authentication, as I understand it, was not the devices but Anders Lind himself being present at the event, linking the staged event to the actual concert. Even though several of the concert goers in 1967 were present at the staged event, Lind was the only one among the organizers of the Pink Floyd Happening who had been there. With this in mind, there were several ways of establishing a relation to the 1960s psychedelic scene. The people who took part brought different authenticities to the show. This I will show in the next section.

Embodying a time and a soundscape

In a previous section, I argued that members of the audience who had been around in the late 1960s constituted an affective alliance. In a way these visitors brought an indexical authenticity to the show. They might not have looked like they did in 1967. On the contrary, they were older and presumably moved differently and weighed more than they did the first time they saw Pink Floyd. So they did not bring an iconic authenticity to the Pink Floyd

Happening, but they had been at the original concert and thereby they could be linked to the murmur heard on the recorded tape. There was also another affective alliance that could be detected during the Pink Floyd Happening, an alliance that could be discussed in terms of iconic authenticity. This consisted of the tribute band, Lost in Rick Wright's Wardrobe and the friends they brought to the show. The organizer of the event had chosen the band because they did something else with Pink Floyd's tunes. Shaping the songs in new arrangements made Pink Floyd's music more distinctive, giving them a unique value and a prominence of their own.

Lost in Rick Wright's Wardrobe was originally called Lost in Rick's Wardrobe, derived from the progressive musician Rick Wakeman, but for the Pink Floyd Happening, they changed their name to reference Pink Floyd's keyboard player. The band had got together one year before the Pink Floyd Happening. The band has now broken up, but the members work together in new forms and in other collaborations. They had not intended to play Pink Floyd. They liked Pink Floyd; several of the members said that they had grown up with them as their parents listened to them. But there were too many tribute bands playing Pink Floyd and they wanted to do something else. On their Facebook page, they presented themselves as: 'We will carry you away back to the late sixties/early seventies, to England, to obscure clubs and arenas [...] and give you only the best songs from the best (mainly British) PROG ROCK BANDS: King Crimson, Gentle Giant, Curved Air, Mellow Candle, Pink Floyd, Genesis, van der Graaf Generator, Camel, Pentangle, Soft Machine, Focus and more [...]' (Lost in Rick Wright's Wardrobe's Facebook page). Thus, they aimed for a progressive music scene consisting of both the most canonical and the alternative artists of that time.

The band did not try to recreate Pink Floyd by playing note-for-note versions of their tunes. Instead, they said, they tried to work in the spirit of the young Pink Floyd, improvising as Pink Floyd did when playing live in the 1960s. But whereas Pink Floyd were four people using guitar, bass, keyboard and drums live, Lost in Rick's Wardrobe's six members brought guitars, bass, drums, keyboard, mellotron, vibes, flute, gong-gong and female voices. They were representing a modus – that is, a more affective rendering of the improvising Pink Floyd – and not an accurate musical adaptation of the original Floyd. In that way they articulated themselves not so much as a cover band or a tribute act but as artists on their own striving for an authentic originality.

The bass player of Lost in Rick Wright's Wardrobe David Svedmyr said that he was inspired by the first four records made by Pink Floyd, the ones made between 1967 and 1969 (Isaksson and Svedmyr: 16 May 2011 interview). The music they played during the Pink Floyd Happening was entirely from this period. He said he found music from this period more open, not so pre-planned. More generally, he favoured music made between 1967 and 1971. Contemporary music he considered more controlled and ready-made, or in other words less authentic. Thus, he made a similar distinction as the person mentioned before, who contrasted the early Pink Floyd and Roger Waters touring *The Wall*. When I asked him if there was any music from today that interested him, he said that he liked music made with the same starting point and the same direction as himself, like the Swedish Dungen, and

Figure 8: Lisa Isaksson and Mikael Lennholm of Lost in Rick Wright's Wardrobe. Photo by the author.

Den stora vilan or the US contemporaries Devendra Banhart and Joanna Newsom. Another member of Lost in Rick Wright's Wardrobe described such music in generic terms as folk, psych or acid-folk and discussed her own musicianship in these categories. The show that was taped in 1967 captured a Pink Floyd playing what could be described as heavier rock; the man who taped the concert even described it as grunge. Lost in Rick Wright's Wardrobe did not play heavy rock, instead they framed the tunes with a more folkish impression, putting Pink Floyd in a more pastoral setting and in this way presented an updated authentic psychedelia.

So Lost in Rick Wright's Wardrobe brought another sound to the event. This also evoked another affective alliance. The members of Lost in Rick Wright's Wardrobe were part of a contemporary neo-psychedelic scene, where the music of the late 1960s and early 1970s was highlighted in different ways. They arranged concerts with Swedish progressive artists; they organized clubs and played in different constellations drawing influences from the scene of which the early Pink Floyd was part. In a way it is possible to say that they brought authentic psychedelia to the show. Tickets for the Pink Floyd Happening were fairly expensive. At the same time, there was a lot of work at Gyllene Cirkeln in the two days before the show. The organizer of the event made a call for helping hands, in exchange for tickets to the show.

Figure 9: David and Johan Svedmyr of Lost in Rick Wright's Wardrobe. Photo by the author.

A lot of friends from the social network of Lost in Rich Wright's Wardrobe responded to the call; they helped to build the two stages, carrying sound equipment and installing the mannequins. Later they took part in the live shows. They were, on average, younger than the rest of the audience. And they vitalized the audience, moving and dancing in a different way. While the older audience tended to move more slowly as they moved their heads forward and back and stamped their feet, the younger helpers swayed sideways in a more animated style. In doing so, they also contributed to the authenticity of the live show, embodying a more alternative, hippieish ethos.

If the audience that took part in the late 1960s made up an affective alliance based on having been part of that period, nostalgia and a sense of change, the members of Lost in Rick Wright's Wardrobe and their friends projected a different relationship to the late 1960s. The most obvious reason was the differences in age. The members of Lost in Rick Wright's Wardrobe were born in the 1980s. For them, the music and the 1960s were more of an aesthetic treasury where they could find inspiration for present creativity. Also important was an idea of the 1960s as a time of alternative and more ideal ways of living. For the people born in the 1980s, the 1960s was not nostalgia born out of experience, but more about a possible choice of future, more of a retrospective utopia than nostalgia.

Final words

In the first interview, Stefan Dimle, the man who organized the Pink Floyd Happening, said that the playback in some way would change history. These are bold words. But they have some relevance insofar as the recording shed some new light on how Pink Floyd sounded live with the Syd Barrett line-up. At the same time, these new insights appear to have had a very limited impact. It seems more likely that the event will stay in memory as an amusing and diverting incident.

The Pink Floyd Happening worked as a meeting place for different and various ways of apprehending the past. The event was characterized by eclecticism and an anachronistic bricolage, where irony and play sometimes were more important than memory and context. The recording, once thought of as a failure, was interpreted as a lost treasure, a sound fragment, representing another time and to some of the younger visitors another future. It was an arena for fun, but also a stepping stone towards recollections of the past. In this, it evoked a historical consciousness. The happening addressed a certain time-space in music history and its representation held various authenticities. It was to be identified and recognized through iconic images of clothes, instruments and bodies, but also in sounds and artistry. Layers of authenticity worked together at the event – not competing, but complementing each other.

The Pink Floyd Happening was a staging of a historical music event in an entrepreneurial setting. This had consequences for the demands of the accuracy valid at the event. The Pink Floyd Happening can be related to the tourist economy and entertainment (Kaijser 2012). The ideals were not academic rigour or accurate use of historical sources, but to amuse and at the same time give the participants a sense of the Pink Floyd concert. This does not mean that it merely entertained, but the representations, as we have seen, were made with a sense of humour. This carried an authenticity more related to senses and recognition through indexicality and iconicity than to source criticism. One of the features of the event was the importance of the play frame. It invited the participants to take part in the concert as an audience, a role that they performed according to a standard. In a way I find this to be the most authorizing feature of the Pink Floyd Happening.

References

Backman, Dan (2011), 'Svulstigare än någonsin', Svenska Dagbladet, 5 May.

Barker, Hugh and Yuval Taylor (2007), Faking It: The Quest for Authenticity in Popular Music, London and New York: W.W. Norton.

Bendix, Regina (1997), In Search of Authenticity: The Formation of Folklore Studies, Madison: University of Wisconsin Press.

Dicks, Bella (2003), Culture on Display: The Production of Contemporary Visitability, Maidenhead and Berkshire: Open University Press.

Dimle, Stefan (2011), (organizer of the Pink Floyd Happening), personal interview, 19 April and 21 August.

Fagoting, Alex (2011), 'EMI Blackmails Pink Floyd Fans!' *The Holy Church of Iggy the Inuit*, http://atagong.com/iggy/archives/2011/05/emi-blackmails-pink-floyd-fans. Accessed 16 June 2014.

Giddens, Anthony (1990), *The Consequences of Modernity*, Cambridge: Polity Press.

Grayson, Kent and Radan Martinec (2004), 'Consumer Perception of Iconicity and Indexicality and Their Influence on Assessments of Authentic Markets Offerings', *Journal of Consumer Research*, 31, pp. 296–312.

Grazian, David (2004), 'The Symbolic Economy of Authenticity in the Chicago Blues Scene', in Bennett, Andy and Richard A Peterson (eds), *Music Scenes, Local, Trancelocal, and Virtual*, Nashville: Vanderbilt University Press.

Grossberg, Lawrence (1997), *Dancing in Spite of Myself, Essays on Popular Culture*, Durham: Duke University Press.

Guffey, Elisabeth C. (2006), *Retro, the Culture of Revival*, London: Reaktion.

Heylin, Clinton (2012), *All the Madmen: Barrett, Bowie, Drake, Pink Floyd, The Kinks, The Who and a Journey to the Dark Side of British Rock*, London: Constable.

Homan, Shane (2006), *Access All Eras: Tribute Bands and Global Pop Culture*, Maidenhead and Berkshire: Open University Press.

Hyde, Lewis (1998), *Trickster Makes This World*, New York: North Point Press.

Hyltén-Cavallius, Sverker and Lars Kaijser (2012), 'Affective Ordering: On the Organization of Retrologies in Music Networks', *Ethnologia Scandinavica*, 42, pp. 64–85.

Isaksson, Lisa and David Svedmyr (2011), (members of Lost in Rick Wright's Wardrobe), personal interview, 16 May.

Kaijser, Lars (2012), 'Fragments in Motion: Reflections on a Guided Tour, the Beatles and the Organizing of History', Conference Proceedings, *Soundtracks: Music, Tourism and Travel Conference*, International Centre for Research in Events, Tourism and Hospitality (ICRETH), 6–9 July, Liverpool, United Kingdom.

Kirshenblatt-Gimblett, Barbara (1998), *Destination Culture: Tourism, Museums and Heritage*, Berkeley, Los Angeles and London: University of California Press.

Kronbrink, Hans (2010), 'Svensk bakom unik Pink Floyd-konsert', *Dagens Nyheter*, 4 December, http://www.dn.se/kultur-noje/nyheter/svensk-bakom-unik-pink-floyd-konsert/. Accessed 3 June 2014.

Liljegren, Bengt (2010), *Pink Floyd, Musiken, människorna, myterna*, Lund: Historiska Media.

Lost in Rick Wright's Wardrobe's Facebook page, https://www.facebook.com/groups/138780816 136350/?fref=ts. Accessed 5 January 2014.

Lowenthal, David (1985), *The Past is a Foreign Country*, Cambridge: Cambridge University Press.

MacCannell, Dean (1999/1976), *The Tourist: A New Theory of the Leisure Class*, Berkeley, Los Angeles and London: University of California Press.

Mason, Nick (2005), *Inside Out: A Personal History of Pink Floyd*, London: Phoenix.

Peterson, Richard A. (1997), *Creating Country Music, Fabricating Authenticity*, Chicago and London: Chicago University Press.

PINK FLOYD BBC 1 1967 Astronomy Domine, Daily Motion, http://www.dailymotion.com/video/xwljyx_pink-floyd-astronomy-domine-bbc-1-1967_music. Accessed 9 December 2015.

Regev, Motti (2002), 'Critics, Aficionados, Cognoscenti: Pop/Rock Expertise and Cosmopolitanism', in Kimi Kärki, Rebecca Leydon and Henri Terho (eds), Conference

Proceedings, *Looking Back, Looking Ahead: Popular Music Studies 20 Years Later,* Conference Proceedings, Turku: IASPM-Norden.

Regev, Motti (2013), *Pop-Rock Music: Aesthetic Cosmopolitanism in Late Modernity*, Cambridge and Malden: Polity Press.

Reynolds, Simon (2011), *Retromania: Pop Culture's Addiction to Its Own Past*, London: Faber and Faber Ltd.

Riis, Bjørn, 'Binson Echorec', http://www.gilmourish.com/?page_id=74. Accessed 2 June 2014.

Shuker, Roy (2001/1994), *Understanding Popular Music*, 2nd edition, London and New York: Routledge.

Fieldwork material

The material for this chapter is based on fieldwork at the home of Lisa Isaksson who made the mannequins (27 April 2011) and during the two days when the Pink Floyd Happening was held (3 May 2011 and 7 May 2011). Field notes, photographs and the recorded interviews are archived by the author. I have also gained access to some of the interviews made by the documentary film maker Mikael Katzeff during the events in 2011 and to a raw version of a documentary of the Pink Floyd Happening. Copies of this material are archived by the author.

Notes

1 I am grateful to the Bank of Sweden Tercentenary Foundation for funding this study as part of project *Echo Affects*. I thank Mikael Katzeff who let me view some of the film clips recorded at the event.

2 Lind took the name of the tune from Roger Waters' presentation of the song during the concert where Waters said 'nobody is ever gonna hear that one again, before or since' (Fagoting 2011).

3 This clip has later been removed from YouTube for copyright reasons The clip is available at: http://www.dailymotion.com/video/xwljyx_pink-floyd-astronomy-domine-bbc-1-1967_ music

Chapter 4

On the Remembered Relationship between Listeners
and C-Cassette Technology

Kaarina Kilpiö

In the 1970s and 1980s, the range and means of shaping public and private soundscapes multiplied. Cassettes and cassette players widened the scope of mobile music-related practices initiated by portable gramophone players, transistor radios and car radios. With home-taped cassettes, music could not only be detached from the domestic listening space, but also compiled into sequences in ways the cassette user desired. The compact cassette further strengthened music's role as an everyday companion. An audible change also occurred in background music practices: commercial background music products faced challenges from affordable systems based on C-cassette technology.

However, none of the changes described above was actually accomplished by 'technology' or 'cassettes'. It was the listeners who used sound technologies and who acted in ways that resulted in irrevocable changes in music listening. Although user-centred academic studies exist on current use of music and technology (see, e.g. DeNora 2000), research on the past use of music technologies has not been as frequent in western European countries and the United States. If we are to avoid casting 'technologies themselves as primary agents of historical change' (Sterne 2003:7), listening to users is essential. To fully understand the meaning of recorded music for users in everyday situations, we need to widen the scope of study and also consider technologies that are extinct or marginalized – especially those with a history of wide popularity.

A thousand stories of cassettes

Approximately one thousand Finnish cassette users wrote about their memories in 2010 in an Internet/letter questionnaire conducted by the *Musiquitous* research project.[1] In these Cassette Memories stories, C-cassette technology is remembered as a mundane part of Finnish (mostly teenage) life during the heyday of the format. Listening, recording and sharing practices are firmly intertwined with the respondents' own growing-up process, opening up a view on music's role in cultural and social memory. The respondents wrote in Finnish and Swedish. All translations of their texts into English are by the writer.

Biographical writing often employs discourses of scarcity in bygone times and strategies of survival and cleverness to overcome circumstances. These are interestingly present also in the memories of C-cassette users. The memories are by no means equivalent, for example, to depression era memories of financial struggle. Nonetheless, recurrent basic elements in describing the everyday world of the teenager include musical scarcity resulting from meagre popular music programming in Finnish public radio, low quality of sound reproduction due to the inexpensive equipment, as well as the constant lack of spending money. These accounts of reduced circumstances find their counterparts in the recollections of cunning recording strategies, of DIY skills in repairing and modifying the fallible technology, and social networking to join forces in raising the level of (music) consumption.

Questions in Cassette Memories were grouped in four sections. We started with general questions on C-cassette use: how it started and ended; how large the respondent's collection of cassettes had been; practices of buying, recording and listening to cassettes. The second section focused on the mobility of cassette technology. Respondents were asked where, when and how they listen(ed) to cassettes outside their own home. Thirdly, social aspects of cassette use were targeted – including whether the users made tapes for or received tapes from others (either with or without remuneration). This section also contained questions on the use of cassettes in rehearsing and making music together with others. The fourth and last section was an open invitation for any recollections that the respondent considered relevant.

The first and last free-form fields drew the most interesting recollections. These questions were phrased 'How did your cassette use start – and how did it end?' and 'What did we not know to ask? Other memories of the C-cassette'. In these fields, the respondents most often tell the longest stories, in which they reflect on the significance of the format, both making general arguments about music listening during the cassette era and delving into their personal history. In other words, stories about the core of cassette use seem to be written within the first and last questions. These include the influence of economic circumstances on music listening, negative reactions towards the technology and the meanings cassettes had in social intercourse.

The good years

Many respondents remember the 'cassette era' as a good time in their personal lives. Most of them were children or teenagers during the 1970s and 1980s, the heyday of the format. This was also an important period of change in Finnish popular music culture. Recorded popular music was in the process of becoming considerably more important and ubiquitous in the everyday lives of Finnish people of all ages, and especially the young population. Music was listened to in cars and as background in production and consumption spaces. Slow but steady changes also happened in the programming of the public broadcasting company Yleisradio. More music content was included in the broadcasts, and the general attitude within the broadcasting company started to move away from the policy activated by educational objectives typical of Finnish public radio in the earlier decades (e.g. Kemppainen 2011:123, 219–221).

Economically, Finland developed swiftly during the 1960s and 1970s. Young Finns were faced with a feature in their lives unknown to previous generations: the possibility of creating and modifying their identity via consumption in this new, more affluent time. This meant a distinct change in the way youth was experienced. One way of expressing personal taste via consumption was naturally through sound recordings: taping, listening, sharing and discussing popular music.

> Before, we had written down pop song lyrics from song books and lent each other our *iskelmävihkot* [pop song notebooks]. Now there was fresh energy on the music front, with the chat about who got what on their *mankka*.[2]
>
> (KM 2010: female, Kemi, b. 1953)

Although the economic standing of the average young person was higher than before, few of them still had enough resources for acquiring hi-fi equipment for their personal use. Cassette players purchased in the first wave of popularity (in the early 1970s) became home electronic devices for the whole family, and they were placed in living rooms. Although perhaps not as characteristically a social event as in the earlier days of home sound reproduction, listening and the related practices were at least audible to other family members.

With the rise in living standards during the late 1970s and 1980s, the amount of appliances skyrocketed. By 1983, there was more than one cassette player in each Finnish household (Muikku 1989:28). The older devices ended up in the bedrooms of younger household members, or they were given their own – by the 1980s increasingly mobile – gadgets. In Cassette Memories texts, bedrooms and living rooms are the spaces most frequently associated with descriptions of taping and listening practices. Mobility is also often mentioned and described, but according to Cassette Memories texts, the 'technological relationship' with C-cassettes is based on activities that took place at home, using appliances that were seldom moved around.

'I grew up in a world where cassettes were commonplace'[3]

Younger respondents (born in the late 1970s and 1980s) often mention they had access to a cassette player as early as at the age of three. They were also allowed to experiment quite freely with this durable equipment. The individual and socially innovative applications, such as mix-tapes, audio letters or 'radio plays', indicate that the technology was domesticated in quite a relaxed way, as a part of work and leisure time. They developed a different 'music technology identity' from previous generations, and recorded music on tape had a significant role in building this identity and the musical worldview of their generation.

Sherry Turkle, having studied relationships we have with technology, claims that the evocative nature of an object – its ability to give rise to associations not inherent in the object itself – is not dependent upon its instrumental power or technical superiority. It depends upon the object 'as a companion in life experience' (Turkle 2007:5). With regard to C-cassettes, this indeed seems to be true. The format is clearly a so-called 'container technology' (Sofia 2000:188–190), not inclined to evoke respect or affection as an object.

This is evident when reading the Cassette Memories respondents' texts. The theme of companionship still raises the significance of the mundane recording platform:

> I have compiled them with pieces I like, designed their covers, and they have travelled with me through the turbulences of my life. Is it any wonder that a relationship forms with this sort of objects that is much more intimate than with any purchased record?
>
> (KM 2010, male, Helsinki, b. 1980)

Controlling one's own emotions and managing self-esteem issues was a frequent theme in the recollections. 'Cassettes to me meant music and music meant a major source of strength for a child who was bullied at school as I was. I listened to music always after school' (KM 2010: female, Uurainen, b. 1983).

Affordable and malleable companions

From the point of view of young music listeners, one of the strongest benefits of empty C-cassettes was their low price. Recorded cassettes were no more affordable than vinyl records – at times the price difference actually favoured vinyl. But empty cassettes were accessible to almost all young listeners. They also carried another benefit young people appreciated, namely freedom of choice in sound contents.

As consumers, young people have been less characterized by accumulation of material possessions in the vein of 'traditional' western consumer societies; their consumption is more often connected with hedonism, making themselves noticed and open-minded (Wilska 2003:441). Those respondents whose relationship with C-cassette technology dates from their childhood or youth do in fact write differently from 'adult users', namely those with experience of one or more of the earlier formats. There are some cassette enthusiasts among the latter also, but it is clear that a tendency to perceive C-cassettes as relevant to one's own personal history is more prevalent among those users who started young. For older respondents, the format often appears as one development in a chain of listening formats. Tales of the older generations concerning their initial encounters with C-cassette equipment are demure when compared with accounts of sensory recollections from an early age.

Cassettes and the related equipment are remembered mostly with pragmatic notions of the consequences of wearing out and poor quality. The integration of music into everyday activities – its development towards a ubiquitous feature – was already heard and seen in the 1970s. This was vital also when it came to the willingness of the listeners to make compromises on sound quality. Incomplete sound information does not detract too much from the listening experience, when the sound is a part of other activities and experiences (Sterne 2006:835). A perfect musical experience is secondary to the music's compatibility with and applicability to everyday situations.

Some recollections have a positive approach to managing the weaknesses and quirks of the simple technology. In those texts, cassettes are presented as 'personalities' among music recording formats. They were 'not too easy' and there was genuine pleasure for the user in successfully repairing or manipulating the technology.

> Not even a badly ruined C-cassette was lost. Tapes run over by cars or in casings otherwise destroyed could be moved to new casings and broken tapes sellotaped anew.
>
> (KM 2010: male, Rovaniemi, b. 1973)

The respondents see this as specific to C-cassette technology and no other music-listening format. The strength of the relationship between user and technology partly results from the active role of the user in maintenance as well as a maker of recordings or listener. With their own inventiveness, efforts and dedication, they emerged as winners from situations of imminent technological disaster. This implies a certain moral order, where the user's dedication and active approach in a 'difficult' technology relationship satisfy them. It may also gain the user respect within a community, something that has been observed among TRS-80 computer enthusiasts engaging in maintaining the old computers and pushing their limits to operate alongside present-day information technology (Lindsay 2003).

Archive copies of personal history

It is not a far-fetched idea to consider this discourse of technological companions as 'personalities' from the point of view of personification in other ways as well. Auditive memories of C-cassette technology are often flavoured in the Cassette Memories texts with organic-sounding words such as warm, soft or hearty. These notions recurrently set analogue technology apart from later formats – CDs and mp3s, for instance. There is a wide spectrum of attitudes towards the 'cleanliness' of reproduced sound, and as Cassette Memories material reveals, even C-cassette sound can be ideal to many human ears. As Marc Perlman has found, the listening experience continues to be an important criterion in certain audiophile circles where 'subjectivity is a point of pride' (Perlman 2004:792).

With home-taped C-cassettes, the sonic material may also contain traces of personal history, as well as the spaces and frames of mind the recordings were made in.

> Even today, while listening to some old favourites, I get the feeling: 'hey, the piece was supposed to end here and then there would be the click [...]'
>
> (KM 2010: female, Kokkola, b. 1988)

> Funny memories are for instance those where I taped from player to player or from radio to player with no wire to connect them, wishing mom would not call for a meal or my brother come and make a racket all of a sudden. But it wasn't unusual that noises ended

up on my recordings. Once I meant to tape the end of a tape blank. I assumed, incorrectly, that outside sounds would not get recorded. While recording 'blank' I ate an apple in front of the player. Quite a crunch was stored on the tape.

(KM 2010: female, Valkeakoski, b. 1971)

Making comparisons with the 'original' clean sound and hearing mistakes on the recording is not meaningful. A significant listening experience comes to include all the material that has ended up on the tape. In their recollections of 'ruined' home tapings, many respondents note their approach to the sounds of their own bygone everyday life is very different now:

It was so great to discover tapes of my own making from the summer house a few months ago. One recording, ruined at the time by sounds of my mother's kitchen chores and my own conversation with my sister, was so cosy now. Familiar radio voices between the taped [music pieces] were also somehow touching.

(KM 2010: female, Joensuu, b. 1977)

It is often particularly in comparison to digital sound reproduction systems that some users emphasize the nature of C-cassettes as human and warm. These listeners claim they do not experience the same contact when using digital recordings as they did with previous technologies (including or meaning C-cassettes). The lack of a tangible or at least visible surface – the physical site of the recording itself – is disturbing to many when dealing with digital formats.

Of course, some music listeners never did embrace the C-cassette, which is evident also in the Cassette Memories. The most common reasons for this were complaints about the weaker sound quality, the cassette being no match for vinyl records or reel-to-reel tapes. If the users considered sound quality to be crucial for their use of music, the conclusion was that cassettes were either used in restricted circumstances, for instance in car stereos, or not at all. This presents a small but important aside that deserves to be mentioned here: non-users exist, even when it comes to cases of very 'domesticated' technologies such as C-cassettes. When making users visible in studies of technology history to counterbalance the emphasis on producers, it is wise to remember that those who prefer either using preceding technologies or choosing non-use completely can also offer interesting views on technological change (see Wyatt 2005).

Sound images of self and the nearest

With a C-cassette recorder, it was possible to 'mirror' one's own immediate sonic surroundings and also, importantly, one's own voice and manner of producing sound. The latter especially has meant a considerable change in how sound technology affected intimate auditive self-images. The recording feature was of decisive importance in 'domesticating' the C-cassette technology and making it a 'natural' part of Finnish everyday life. Several respondents report experiments with spoken and sung vocal expression as the very first activities after a cassette player was purchased and brought home. The results were listened to 'ardently', 'blushing' or 'marvelling', and form a vivid memory of many Finns.

Using cassettes as sonic family albums is repeatedly mentioned in the Cassette Memories material. Recording family members, at least small children and seniors, seems to have been a fairly common practice. Some respondents also use the concept of 'time travel' when describing their moments of reminiscing with their old cassettes. Taping for future memories means transferring the sonically communicated experience in time – an almost totally unattainable aspiration until sound recording. Early sound recording technologies inspired salesmen and visionaries to pronounce the barrier between life and death was about to be broken: 'Death has lost some of its sting since we are able to forever retain the voices of the dead' (Sterne 2003:294, 308). In the 1960s, the (reel-to-reel) tape recorder was marketed in Europe as a means for saving and archiving the memorable moments of family life and for putting together audio letters, radio plays, etc. (Bijsterveld and Jacobs 2009:29–30, 40). With C-cassettes, the recording platform was finally attainable, easy and flexible enough to be widely used for these purposes.

Death, inevitably a part of anyone's life history, is present in the Cassette Memories material as well. Several respondents report shifts in the value of mundane recordings of casual chat after the passing away of someone on that recording.

I have since lost my parents in a car accident 2006, and I have several cassettes with my mother's speech recordings. I have been unable to listen to these since, but perhaps the day will come. So I hold on to the C-cassette deck for a good reason.

(KM 2010, male, Helsinki, b. 1975)

One of the most memorable C-cassette recordings dates from February 1974, when my uncle taped my grandmother's phone call with my aunt. Grannie lived in Ilomantsi and my aunt in Helsinki, and they both missed each other very much. Only 2 months after, my grandmother died. Copies of that recording were then made for all my mother's siblings and their children.

(KM 2010: female, Joensuu, b. 1961)

What I like, whenever I like

Many respondents whose childhood or youth coincided with the heyday of C-cassette use wrote about expressions of independence and defiance that had to do with cassettes. Two types of recollections were the most recurrent: acknowledging one's own proficiency in using and manipulating the technology and the sonic environment, and taking command of space at home or elsewhere with the help of sound recordings. There is a distinct impression of empowerment in the way many respondents describe their competence:

> Dad's LPs were out of bounds, but my parents were not so meticulous with cassettes. The greatest thing about cassettes was surely that one could use them freely as one wished, rewind and fast forward.
>
> (KM 2010: female, Kotka, b. 1984)

One of the most significant changes related to C-cassettes is very much connected with empowerment felt by the users. The relationship of music and listeners was taking a new turn. I am of course referring to the increased agency and active role of the listener in manipulating sound contents. This happened with home taping and the pursuit of compiling mix-tapes.

> I never just listened to the radio. I carefully chose the programs I recorded music or radio plays from, and with cassettes I could listen to music I liked, when I liked.
>
> (KM 2010: male, Mäntsälä, b. 1970)

Almost every respondent in the Cassette Memories material was a more or less active home tapist; of nearly one thousand participants, only one claimed never to have taped on C-cassettes herself but merely bought recorded cassettes. An overwhelming majority thus taped, and seemingly felt happy and triumphant when doing so. One respondent specifically writes about the memories of a new feeling of authority:

> Memories about the first cassette players and cassettes are extremely detailed. They were of such enormous importance to us 12- to 18-year olds. Record players were uncommon at least in the countryside and we were mainly dependent on the offerings of the radio. When the recording option became a reality, it was the first time when we could decide on what we wanted to listen to at our chosen time.
>
> (KM 2010: male, Varkaus, b. 1960)

Defiant practices making use of music content seem to have varied substantially in how open they were and what kind of role music was given. Certain genres could be acceptable and others unacceptable or embarrassing in the respondent's family or circle of friends. Lyrics of songs could be seen as objectionable and listening to these songs was thus a declaration of independence from disapproving authorities, usually parents or teachers. A tangible way of taking control was to seize either technology – 'we confiscated Dad's cassettes for our own use and taped over his recordings from the radio' – or domestic space. The space of the respondent's personal room has been extremely important for recording and listening purposes. Since music, and sound in general, was important in managing emotions, many reported a need to be alone while interacting with the sound material.

> I was competent in using the record player myself quite early, but the cassette player was easy to monopolize for myself and retire to privacy, unlike the record player sitting in the middle of the living room shelving.
>
> (KM 2010: female, Askola, b. 1976)

The situatedness of listening to recorded music started to disintegrate quite early on with portable gramophones, and the launch of music appliances for cars and battery-operated recorders settled the issue. However, for the duration of the 1970s, home seems to have remained the most important space for listening as far as Finnish young people were concerned. It was only the Walkman era that truly undid the connection between music and stationary appliances. Music sidled up closer to the centre of the everyday life of Finnish youth, with phases defined in each case by home electronics purchases and independence of movement.

> To begin with: in the shared spaces of the home, then in my own room/home/summer house/friends' homes and when portable cassette players were invented, listening also proceeded to happen on trips, in the bus, train and on interrail. After I became a car owner, listening to cassettes happened mostly on drives.
>
> (KM 2010: female, Luvia, b. 1964)

Social interaction and C-cassettes

In the Cassette Memories texts, friends and pen pals are perhaps the foremost social contacts we were expecting to read about. We did find them, in fairly foreseeable and sometimes still valid forms: sharing music with peers, recommending new artists and styles, forming circles for reciprocal record copying, making compilations to serve as love letters. But according to the respondents in our material, the elementary social setting for learning music-listening habits and preferences has been family and relatives. This is partly explained by the spatial situatedness of listening described above. With large sedentary one-per-household appliances, listening was at first an activity that took place predominantly at home. Later, in the era of portable listening devices, the personal nature of the smaller devices attached new social meanings that have become an important feature in the range of normative ways of listening.

In the respondents' lives, the most important people in the surrounding environment using music technology and listening to music have been their parents and older siblings. They made the home electronics purchases (fathers, in most texts) and taught the use of the appliances. How personal taste in music started to develop is remembered very differently. Some features are present in several texts and thus can be interpreted to more or less typify C-cassette music listening in Finnish homes. Stay-at-home mothers and radio music programming are a recurrent combination in many respondents' descriptions of their growing up to radio listening. An active music listener in the family was likely to have an impact on initiating the respondent into listening and recording: either they would be seen and heard (and later mimicked) devoting their time and energy to music listening, or they could also simply recommend the young respondent something from their own broader acquaintance.

What came later would most likely be influenced by a wider set of people: friends as well as immediate and extended family. Finnish people born in the 1970s and 1980s have, while widening their milieus further and further from their homes, also acted to extend their musical social life. Apart from love and seduction 'letters', mix-tapes have also been used as testing tools and baits for musical fit when anticipating an incipient friendship.

Networks or individual contacts could also be instigated relying on music alone. Introduction would then be possible with the help of mix-tapes. You could either ask someone to record such a compilation for yourself, or simply make one yourself and hand it to the person you wished to connect with.

> I took an empty cassette to one interesting-looking character to have it filled with punk style music. We'd stalked the bod for a while so we knew where [s]he[4] lived.
>
> (KM 2010: female, Varkaus, b. 1979)

With personal music-listening appliances, listening together with others became optional for more and more young Finns. The nature of those social situations shifted slightly. They were perhaps less concentrated and intense than before the time of 'play' and 'rewind'. Focused listening took place more often in solitude, with personal devices and headphones. Social situations, on the other hand, could now serve the listeners' needs for a hobby or 'getting into' something together – forming an understanding and exchanging ideas about new records or musical phenomena.

> The cassettes were circulated among friends, and every now and then we would listen to some records together, have 'jukebox juries', etc.
>
> (KM 2010: female, Jyväskylä, b. 1976)

Sometimes, the basis of networking was financial manoeuvring, as in organizing recording circles. But in others, cassettes were more explicitly a means to an end, which could be specifically to build a sense of community for a small circle of music listeners.

> All of us had identical 'Best of' tapes in our Walkmans (the compiler replicated for others), on which we pushed play simultaneously so we could sing all together.
>
> (KM 2010: female, Helsinki and Kerava, b. 1979)

Now and then one wanted to tape and give one's favourite music to someone special. It was hoped that this would cement mutual emotional experiences. As a matter of fact, those emotions still come to life when listening to that music. ('This is what [s]he wanted to tape just for me [...]')

(KM 2010: female, Kajaani, b. 1964)

Many Cassette Memories texts also consider the relevance of cassettes in building credibility – we might also say cultural capital – within circles of friends and music listeners. Balancing one's act skilfully and finding cool new acquaintances could bring the status of connoisseur to someone with very limited financial means.

Sonic presents and letters have been quite a standard practice among Finnish C-cassette users. This is not something that only young users did. For adults, sending C-cassette greetings also served as a way of coping with the changes in everyday life brought on by internal migration and emigration to Sweden, both especially strong in the 1960s and 1970s. Family members used to having long conversations longed for each other and for interaction. Lengthy long-distance or international calls could prove too big a strain on the household budget, and letters did not convey the desired presence and intimacy. Mailing a C-cassette with familiar voices and sounds of everyday life was one solution.

A generation of active listeners

Cassette Memories texts helped us in finding answers to the main questions of our *Musiquitous* research project involving the users' views on music technology appropriation and music listening practices. Especially, the discrepancies found in users' answers validate their use in research of technology history and new uses of music. They shed light on issues that would otherwise stay unnoticed.

In the discussion initiated by Michel de Certeau (1984) and John Fiske (1989), 'poaching' and clever tactics are studied as revealing ways of evading obstacles set by subjugation. It is thus important to understand the workings of the relationship between users and the scene-changing listening format, C-cassettes. Some signs of tactics and poaching (acts that consumers feel are within their rights regardless of their illegality or at least off limits nature) are visible in the data we gathered for Cassette Memories. In this case, the most obvious strategies of the controlling and disciplinary forces would, from the young consumers' viewpoint, be the following. The record industry was selling music recordings in inelastic, uneditable packages, for prices beyond the means of many Finnish young people. Public radio and television were broadcasting meagre amounts of popular music, with a policy still emphasizing edification over entertainment more than the young listeners would have wished. At home, parents and older siblings tried to control the space, physical and sonic, and to define musical preferences suitable for children and teenagers.

The respondents report numerous significant possibilities of the format, most of which are related to modifying the contents (sonic and graphic), not developing new technical applications. I have analysed the most salient and recurring results above. The users clearly welcomed the chance to control and study time and space via sound reproduction; assessments of the experimenting and mix-tape-making practices prove this. Users made decisions concerning their own musical worldview, but also made its changes and developments comprehensible to themselves by returning to their own 'work' in their cassette collection, considering how their musical personal history had unfolded.

Jörgen Skågeby (2011) refers to cassettes and digital playlists as music media objects: discrete objects transferable and usable as communicative tools between people for music exchange and social bonding that thus become 'cultural containers' of surrounding values and practices. The memories of C-cassette users confirm that personalizing cassettes via, for example, self-made covers is a crucial practice and essential when studying this feature of the technology. A connotation made by the user, or with him/her in mind, could refer to almost any feature in music culture, in the rest of popular culture or in the social tie between, for instance, the giver and receiver of the cassette gift, for example, 'songs for smooching purposes', as one respondent nicely put it (KM 2010, female, b. 1971).

Finnish respondents repeatedly identify the most valuable pieces in their cassette collections as the ones they themselves had recorded, edited and designed sleeve artwork for. Unlike with vinyl records, the rarity of an object is not an issue when it comes to cassette use. Rather, it is the active pursuit of the user's own musical identity and the expansion in soundscape control that is most important.

Very important to some users was the sense of belonging to a larger phenomenon – a change in cultural and economic circumstances, a shift in power relations. 'C-cassettes were the best innovation of my time, it widened the scope of my life from a remote village to the whole world' (KM 2010, female, Rantsila, b. 1962). Perhaps surprisingly, cassette use was not seen as a *generational* demarcating practice in itself. But to some respondents, a turn had happened in the way music touched social relations and choices in lives.

> In my opinion, it was a truly big thing in Finland. By way of [the use of cassettes] the whole sociological map expanded and the young in my youth built their specific own identities, growing up in the process, each in their own way.
>
> (KM 2010: male, Vantaa, b. 1967)

This sense of belonging has later come to mean a generational experience for some of the respondents.

References

Bijsterveld, Karin and Annelies Jacobs (2009), 'Storing Sound Souvenirs: The Multi-Sited Domestication of the Tape Recorder', in Karin Bijsterveld and Jose van Dijck (eds), *Sound Souvenirs: Audio Technologies, Memory and Cultural Practices*, Amsterdam: Amsterdam University Press, pp. 25–42.

Certeau, Michel de (1984), *The Practice of Everyday Life*, Berkeley: University of California Press.

DeNora, Tia (2000), *Music and Everyday Life*, Cambridge: Cambridge University Press.

Fiske, John (1989), *Understanding Popular Culture*, New York and London: Routledge.

Kemppainen, Pentti (2011), *Aina soi sävelradio: Radiomusiikista musiikkiradioon/Tunes Always Play on the Radio: From Radio Music to Music Radio*, Helsinki: Avain.

KM 2010. *Kasettimuistot* [Cassette Memories], A memory data collection carried out in April–September 2010 by the research project Musiquitous and the Finnish Literature Society, Material available at the Folklife Archives, University of Tampere, Finland.

Lindsay, Christina (2003), 'From the Shadows: Users as Designers, Producers, Marketers, Distributors, and Technical Support', in Nelly Oudshoorn and Trevor Pinch (eds), *How Users Matter: The Co-Construction of Users and Technology*, Cambridge: MIT Press, pp. 29–50.

Muikku, Jari (1989), *Laulujen lunnaat: Raportti suomalaisesta äänitetuotantopolitiikasta/ The Ransoms of Songs. Report on Finnish Recording Production Policy*, Helsinki: Valtion painatuskeskus, Taiteen keskustoimikunta.

Perlman, Marc (2004), 'Golden Ears and Meter Readers: The Contest for Epistemic Authority in Audiophilia', *Social Studies of Science*, 34:5, pp. 783–807.

Skågeby, Jörgen (2011), 'Slow and Fast Music Media: Comparing Values of Cassettes and Playlists', *Transformations Journal*, 20: 'Slow Media', http://www.transformationsjournal.org/journal/issue_20/article_04.shtml. Accessed 3 July 2014.

Sofia, Zoë (2000), 'Container Technologies', *Hypatia: A Journal of Feminist Philosophy*, 15:2, pp. 181–201.

Sterne, Jonathan (2003), *The Audible Past: Cultural Origins of Sound Reproduction*, Durham: Duke University Press.

—— (2006), 'The MP3 as Cultural Artifact', *New Media and Society*, 8:5, pp. 825–842.

Turkle, Sherry (ed.) (2007), *Evocative Objects: Things We Think with*, Cambridge: MIT Press.

Wilska, Terhi-Anne (2003), 'Mobile Phone Use as Part of Young People's Consumption Styles', *Journal of Consumer Policy*, 26, pp. 441–463.

Wyatt, Sally (2005), 'Non-Users Also Matter: The Construction of Users and Non-Users of the Internet', in Nelly Oudshoorn and Trevor Pinch (eds), *How Users Matter: The Co-Construction of Users and Technology*, Cambridge: MIT Press, pp. 67–79.

Notes

1 The research project was funded by the Academy of Finland and a part of the programme MOTIVE studying ubiquitous technology.

2 From the German word *Magnetophon*.

3 KM 2010: male, Turku, b. 1983.

4 There is only one genderless pronoun 'hän' for expressing the third person in the Finnish language.

Chapter 5

Affective Memories of Music in Online Heritage Practice

Paul Long and Jez Collins

The contemporary 'memory boom' described by Andreas Huyssen (2003) comes into view across the field of popular music culture. The music industries have long repackaged and repromoted the music of the past, an enterprise supported in the United Kingdom by a wealth of publications such as *Record Collector, Classic Rock, Uncut* or *Mojo*. Likewise, television produces a prodigious amount of nostalgic music retrospectives as well as specialized 'quality' programming offering assessments of individual artists, genres and moments (see Long and Wall 2010). To this list, we should add dedicated channels such as VH1 and Vintage TV: 'a vital, unique offering for those who grew up with the many vintage artists still touring and recording as well as for a younger demographic beginning to appreciate Vintage TV's "soundtrack to the 20th century"' (Vintage TV). In addition, popular music has its own sites of special historical interest, from Memphis' Beale Street to Liverpool's Strawberry Field, each a destination for a dedicated and expanding tourist industry with music heritage recognized as an increasingly valuable part of the experience economy (Connell and Gibson 2003).

Echoing the idea of heritage as a symptom of a contemporary cultural malaise (Hewison 1987), the critic Simon Reynolds has described this range of activity as a form of 'retromania', lamenting 'pop culture's addiction to its own past' (2011). To others, this historical purview represents the democratization of the past and the terrain upon which communities might make and take meaning from it. Certainly, the reissue industry has been posited by Paul Martin as a form of public history (Martin 2000; see also Ashton and Kean 2009), while Andy Bennett identifies a form of 'DIY preservationism' (2009:475) in which music enthusiasts set up small labels or Internet sites dedicated to salvaging and preserving music outside of familiar canons. Bennett's description captures also a variety of forms of community archival projects mapped by Sarah Baker and Alison Huber (2013), activity echoed in a wealth of organized online practices devoted to music and memory (Collins and Long 2014). Across this range, practices and meanings of history, heritage, collective memory and archival formation converge, sometimes challenging the traditional parameters of culture and its preservation. Such are the cultural politics of this variety, of who determines what counts, of what is at stake, that Les Roberts and Sara Cohen have formulated a typology of discourses of popular music heritage: officially authorized, self-authorized and unauthorized. For them, popular music heritage can be understood via these categories to be a relational practice that reveals definitions of the past to be a contested and negotiated space 'ascribed with value, legitimacy and social and cultural capital' (Roberts and Cohen 2013:243).

In this chapter, we are concerned with the flourishing online world of sites devoted to popular music of the past, to its emergence and status as communal heritage and as prompt for memory. Practices in these sites can be understood in terms of Roberts and Cohen's self-authorized and, more often, unauthorized categories as communities add to, and make what they will of the available material of that which Wolfgang Ernst terms the online *an*archive (2013). The extent of the activity only hinted at in this chapter affirms that music matters in the memory of a broad range of people. Thus, we ask: *how* and *why* does music matter for so many?

In the first part of this chapter, we examine the manner in which online communities construct memories around music in the *non*-spaces of the digital world. We develop our focus in particular around memory practices that are anchored to geographically and temporally specific sites of popular music culture. These sites comprise the concert venues, clubs and record stores of specific towns and cities that are associated with particular genres and scenes. In the second part of this chapter, we build upon this evidence and discussion in order to consider how we might make sense of music that motivates memory in terms of ideas of affect. We suggest that a useful way of thinking of online memory work is in terms of the evocation of the soundscapes of the past. Participants explore feelings associated with physical spaces, of the records and bands that were encountered in them and indeed, the nature of the communities of practice that were there formed and that 'reconvene' to remember.

Constructing memories of music online

Wendy Chun suggests that 'A major – if not the major category of new media is memory' (Chun 2011:97). For her, memory is metaphor become essence in the technology of the computer, of how the digital is imagined. In addition, the content of the Internet, whether memorable or not, 'is similarly shot through with memory' (Chun 2011:97). As she notes, so much online practice is devoted to preservation: 'Memory hardens information – turning it from a measure of possibility into a "thing", while also erasing the difference between instruction and data (computer memory treats them indistinguishably)' (Chun 2011:97). Digital media, on and offline, has become an ever expanding archive that gives the appearance at least that nothing is lost.

The characteristics of the digital world described by Chun have created an apposite context for projects devoted to the commemoration of music past. As Jose Van Dijk (2006) has suggested, practices and associations of popular music cultures present frameworks for recollection. For instance, in spite of the ephemeral associations of pop, its cultural practices are characterized by forms of preservation and curation. These practices are manifest most obviously in the notion of the record collection, whether maintained in vinyl, cassette or digital files form. Here, we can see how such practices translate to online projects in which communities of interest exploit the opportunities of digital 'technologies of memory' (Smelik 2009; Van House and Churchill 2008). Online practices of 'crowd sourcing' and user-generated content creation aid the compilation of music archives and the generation of personal and communal histories.

To illustrate this online practice, the Discogs marketplace enlists user input in order to compile a database of the entirety of recorded music. A self-conscious sense of curation is invoked in the site's title and its deployment of a definition of discography as: '[t]he study and cataloguing of phonograph records. A comprehensive list of the recordings made by a particular performer or of a particular composer's works' (Discogs). Other projects concern themselves with the exploration and curation of specific stories about music and its totemic, and sometimes obscured reference points. An online version of an 'authorized' project to memorialize the Woodstock Festival of 1969 involves an attempt to register the names and memories of half a million original attendees in an 'Official Woodstock Registry'. Elsewhere, an 'unauthorized' Facebook group is dedicated to enlisting members to build a site devoted to *Altamont Festival: An Oral and Visual History*. Some of this practice connects with more commercial objectives illustrated by applications such as Songkick or Giglocker. Alongside its primary objective of selling tickets, Songkick is an enterprise that aims also to record the live music experience and, having documented over 1 million events since the 1960s, which will 'put every single concert or festival that's ever happened online' (Songkick).

For Ernst, the storage capabilities of the Internet where material awaits (re-)circulation are an expression of the logic of late capitalism, 'a part of a memory economy' (Ernst 2013:11). And the examples from this economy discussed here depend on the good will and voluntarism of contributors. We should note then that the freely given labour of contributors underwrites the value of enterprises like Songkick and indeed the various platforms that provide the frameworks for 'unauthorized' sites for memories of music. Communities are built and their interactions enabled by the technologies of memory that incorporate bespoke websites, adaptations of web log templates such as Blogger or WordPress and, most fertile of all, social media platforms such as Facebook, Tumblr, Pinterest, MySpace and the 'micro' blogging site Twitter. In each case, written expression uses typographical conventions formed in digital cultures that use emoticon shorthand and that are often ungrammatical. In examples that follow, we present any quotations verbatim.

In these online sites, a plethora of historical materials, explorations, explications and wider memory practices sits in a continuum with the presence and presentness of current music and commentary. This continuum presents a conceptual question about where the past ends and the present begins in the digital realm and how one thinks about the role and perspective of memory in relation to time, its passing and the distance of and from what is recalled. There are sites dedicated to specific artists and genres whose period of activity is long past. Across Facebook for instance, individuals who followed defunct bands in their heyday are joined in the sites they create by more recent converts of all ages, many of whom cannot claim the same experience yet for whom shared music is an important aspect of their memory. There are sites too that are dedicated to artists who have maintained lengthy careers and who continue to create new material where their catalogue of work is supported and promoted by a corporate presence alongside (and sometimes in tension with) those created by fans. For instance, on Facebook alone, the British rock musician Paul Weller has an official page for his first band The Jam and one for continuing work with the Style

Council and then as a solo artist. These sit alongside 'unauthorized' fan sites that celebrate Weller's musical incarnations, building communities of interest that can be several thousand strong. In each case, members post links to YouTube videos, SoundCloud files, Spotify playlists, between them including 'official' and 'unofficial' recordings. Unsurprisingly, such activities position such sites at the borders of legality and, where they make use of file-sharing sites such as RapidShare or MediaFire, they incur the wrath of the owners of the intellectual property that they share. Fans also upload digital scans of signed record sleeves, concert tickets, personal photographs as well as varieties of 'official' images from record company publicity or from the music press and other sources. Reciprocity is a structuring feature of community interactions here as many individuals respond to the question 'Do you remember?' and other posted invitations and comments, links or scanned artefacts with *further* links, materials and questions: 'Do *you* remember?' Above all, communities are built on the sharing of individual recollections and demonstrations of encounters with specific pieces of music, performances, videos and the place of such things in relation to their own lives, linked to both private and public events.

Commemorating the places and spaces of music online

Alongside sites dedicated to individual artists are groups devoted to particular time periods in music history. Facebook's expansive *Music of the 70s 80s 90s* promises community members that 'Through this music fan page, we can trip back to memory lane' (*Music of the 70s 80s 90s*), the aim to 'relive' the music of the past. The broad focus of this and many other sites reminds us of the normative ideas about periodization and music cultures and promotion manifest in terms such as 'swinging sixties', which in turn merge with generic categorizations such as 'the Britpop era' or 'the punk years'. In turn, such genres are also often anchored to specific geographical places and spaces: the Liverpool of Merseybeat, or the CBGB of New York punk. The memory of specific physical spaces or specialized 'nights' and events galvanizes many virtual communities. Blogs, forums, groups and pages with members and views numbering several thousand sit alongside those that have a handful of subscribers, perhaps proportionately representing micro-scenes of the past.

San Pedro 4th Street Punkhouse Resurrectors is for those 'who miss the glory days of 4th street punk-block' (*San Pedro 4th Street Punkhouse Resurrectors*); *Mabuhay Gardens – The Fab Mab* celebrates 'San Francisco's punk rock club house' (*Mabuhay Gardens – The Fab Mab*); there is a group for *Paradise Garage* New York; *The Goldmine Nightclub Canvey Island* asks of soul and funk fans 'Anybody out there remember the most famous nightclub in Essex the gold mine back in the good old days?' (*The Goldmine Nightclub Canvey Island*).

Members who build these sites speak to the *intangibility* of club nights, tacitly agreeing that there *was* such a scene, or confirm the significance of a space or genre at a particular time and place, seeking to reconvene the imagined community that made each scene. The communities can be thought of as 'imagined' since even sites servicing the memory of the smallest of venues can never attract all of its original attendees who could not in any case have known every other attendee personally or participated equally in every aspect of its character. Communities are imagined too in the virtual space of memory-making where the claims of online members to have 'been there' cannot be reliably established, nor are such credentials always necessarily sought. These issues are evinced at a Facebook group dedicated to the 1980s acid house night *Shoom 88*, which was initiated by its founder, the DJ Danny Rampling. The group's 'About' tag suggests that it is: 'For anyone who was there, says they were there or can't remember if they were there or not' (*Shoom 88*).

The reach of online groups realizes a spatial-temporal ambition not limited to venue and built environments and extending to the imagined community of the nation as defined by Benedict Anderson (1983). For instance, memories of Uganda's Hip Hop community are collated in the Facebook page *The UG – Hiphop – Archivist/Celebrate your History*, where reflections on the international origins of the genre connect with home-grown music and history. *Proyecto Memorabilia Caracas* seeks to tell the 'untold story' of pop in the Venezuelan capital (Historia jamás contada del la Música Pop en Caracas), particularly by enlisting contributions from those who participated in that story (y más importante aún quiénes participaron de estos eventos) (*Proyecto Memorabilia Caracas*).

Theorizing the project of music memory: the music itself

The many communities surveyed for this chapter exhibit a surprising degree of commonality in their approach. Typical is the sense of mission underwriting *Sydney Rave History* that aims to 'capture the rave years from 1990–1996', presenting 'a way to record the history before we all forget'. It summons members of those who constituted the community that experienced and made the 'rave years' to reconvene and make them tangible in the process of commemoration. Built from a WordPress template, posters are invited to share personal photographs and flyers, to add to a list of dates, venues, DJs, etc. There are reproductions of contemporaneous accounts of events as well as recent interviews with rave participants and uploads of around 8000 'mix-tapes', many digitized and shared by those who were part of the 'scene'. As the administrator notes: 'This is a non for profit site and we have invested time and effort in bringing it to you. We are not out to make any money, we just want to make a few people smile remembering the good old days' (*Sydney Rave History*, WordPress). The website links in turn to a Facebook group that reaffirms the communal nature of the enterprise that recognizes 'we are all rave historians' (*Sydney Rave History*, Facebook).

Across such sites, we can note the deployment of terms such as history, archive and memory in titles, 'mission statements' and invitations to contribute as well as in the interactions of community members. We have echoed the slippage of this terminology, implicitly acknowledging and accepting the flexible parameters of such concepts as determined by these practitioners. Together, this slippage and variety of activity suggest something of the fluid, processual, practice-based aspects of memory visible in the digital world that offer insight for contemporary debates about its nature. For instance, in an excellent overview of current debates, Võsu, Kõresaar and Kuutma summarize Wulf Kansteiner's argument that while much attention has been accorded its mediation and production, the heterogeneous community of 'consumers of memory' have tended to be overlooked (Võsu, Kõresaar and Kuutma 2008:249). The world examined here problematizes the parameters of this oversight as online practices exhibit all of the characteristics of the convergence culture described by Henry Jenkins (2004), where the boundary between producer and consumer becomes blurred. In interactions around music and memory, engagement in memory work is *quantifiable* in terms of 'hits', 'views', membership numbers or 'likes' on Facebook. Even on this banal level, each consumer simultaneously confirms and makes a contribution to the process of memory-making, which is shared as communities are built. For more active users, their comments, uploaded materials and links make visible the co-construction of the meaning and value of music as well as the nature of memory. Production and consumption, the personal and communal, merge and reciprocate in the visible spaces of the Internet, affirming Plate and Smelik's suggestion that 'Memory is always re-presentation, making experiences as it were, present again in the form of images, sensations or affects. At the level of cultural memory, therefore, we are inevitably dealing with representations, performances and re-enactments' (Plate and Smelik 2009:4). This idea of performance is one that Ernst, via Panos Kouros, links to the idea of the anarchive, where the wealth of digital material that is constantly added makes for a fluid status, one that is characterized by 'a dynamic process of archive-making that evolves in the present, open for permanent re-editing and adding of new terms' (Ernst 2013:6). This is a fruitful way of thinking about the sites of digital memory examined here where much activity involves posting images, links, comments and so on and responding with evermore material. But what of the centre of gravity that galvanizes this activity: the fact of the music itself?

Even if one were to restrict a survey to Facebook alone and then to those pages devoted to music memory similar in nature to those we cite here, we estimate that the number would be in the thousands. Together, these confirm that music is an important aspect of presentation online, of a sense of the past, how it is recalled and for the role that individuals have played in its generation, circulation and consumption. To cite one instance that highlights this quality, at the Facebook group for New York's *Paradise Garage* one poster recalls how 'Paradise Garage made me realize that music was my life, no matter if it were house or club so to all my P.G. family and friends once we have entered those doors and received the P.G. experience we have never truly been the same'. Another recalls that 'Paradise Garage was my life. I learned to live and enjoy. Appreciate music and just dance' (*Paradise Garage*).

Such accounts are characteristic of memory sites and we find ourselves wondering about how they point to the ways in which individuals have something to say about music *qua* music for digital communities. For instance, while online activity does take its cue from a wider world of popular music culture as well as industry conventions, developed discussion of music in a manner familiar from the work of journalists and musicologists of any other analytical approach appears to be a minority pursuit in the many sites we have surveyed. At base, a common assessment one finds in response to the posting of a sound file, embedded YouTube performance or simple identification of a recording is the word 'tune!' that acts as both literal description and approving assessment. Nonetheless, we would suggest that an engagement with music in terms of opinion and analysis is writ large in the texture, scope and creativity of the memory practices of these sites.

One way of understanding this assessment and our direction here is to consider Morten Michelsen's questioning of a concept of music that concentrates primarily on the work and its structure, and imagines it as an 'object'. Instead, he argues for a conception of how music works that would acknowledge 'that there are many different concepts, notions and practices of music circulating in culture at any one time' (Michelsen 2004:25). In conceptualizing an aesthetics of popular music, Michelsen reaches beyond Kantian notions of 'the beautiful', 'the sublime' or 'judgements of taste', to a definition of sensory experience derived from Alexander Baumgarten. Here, music is understood as an experience constituted of more than the coherent object presented in any one piece or sound. Music incorporates parts of songs, albums, genres and 'objectified goods' that can be bought, sold and exchanged – as computer files, vinyl or sheet music as well as associated merchandise or intermediations from journalists for instance. Echoing Christopher Small's concept of 'musicking' (Small 1998), Michelsen suggests that it can also be understood processually, 'as the making, use and enjoyment of musical objects' (Michelsen 2004:26). Thus, his historical approach and the contexts in which it has had meaning address the fact that music may be understood in terms of 'fun or everyday transcendence in multiple ways' (Michelsen 2004:27). These insights suggest how we might conceive of online practices in the affective terms described by a range of scholars of popular music to comprehend the feelings that bond communities of interest around music and its memorialization.

Music, affect and online memory-making

We enlist a concept of affect here after Gilbert Rodman and Cheyanne Vanderdonckt as a means of conceptualizing the various emotional and psychological ways in which individuals respond to cultural phenomena, ways that are often felt – and so recalled in articulations of memory – at a physical level. This is a means of directing interest to 'the facets of people's cultural lives that cannot readily be reduced to (much less explained by) matters of semantics, semiotics, or ideology: where the central question is "how does it feel?" instead of "what does it mean?"' (Rodman and Vanderdonckt 2006:260). Certainly, a sense of affect is a means of pointing to the motivations of music memory sites, evocations of place and space, the attractions of community and feelings and emotions about the past. This is pithily expressed by the founder of *Sydney Rave History* who states of the project that 'It really is a labour of love'; and this is a labour that describes his own commitment and that of contributors: 'without members, like yourself, that are willing to share pics, stories, flyers etc this group would not amount to much. I am glad some people had the fore thought to document the time as it happened' (*Sydney Rave History*). Such expressions evince Lawrence Grossberg's description of the 'affective alliances' (Grossberg 1984:227) of music fans, an idea echoed in Baker and Huber's examination of physical DIY music archives where an enactment of social collectively and individual relationships with music and its artefacts characterize them as 'affective institutions' (Baker and Huber 2013:522).

A concept of the soundscape is helpful here in linking feeling, place, space and music and their memory. Our sense of this concept derives from the work of Emily Thompson (2004) where the idea defines an aural landscape that echoes and further anchors our understanding of Michelsen's work. Like a landscape, the soundscape is both physical as well as a cultural means of apprehending an environment. Thompson suggests that in cultural terms, soundscape involves 'scenic and aesthetic ways of listening, a listener's relationship to their environment, and the social circumstances that dictate who gets to hear what' (Thompson 2004:1–2). Sound in this vista is a matter of what has been heard as well as encompassing the practices that produced it, how and where it has been consumed as well as how it has informed affective experiences. Of course, in the memory of affective encounters with music, emotional experiences are both recalled and freshly minted in that process, conditioning perspectives on the past and what can or cannot be articulated.

Across online sites, the generic public places of popular music culture – the record shop, concert hall and night club – as well as the private space of home feature in evocative memories conjuring up a sense of soundscapes of individual and collective pasts. For instance, *Pompey Pop* is a site that commemorates the city of Portsmouth's music history. Posts recall the experience of hearing particular pieces of music and the contexts in which they were encountered. One recalls a sonic experience at a record store with his best friend: 'both of us squeezing into the listening-booth, and being blown away by the first Led Zep [Pelin] album – we were well impressed with the stereo effects coming through the tiny speakers!!' Another remembers listening with a friend 'to the latest releases in the booths in Ivan Veck's in Albert Road', mapping the streets and lost sites of local music culture: 'and there was another shop near the end of Queen's Road/Kingston Road that also had booths. Can't remember the name of it Happy days!' The joyful glow is extended to memories of the materiality of records as objects and the specific instances of how and when they were acquired: 'I remember on my way home from the Tech one day, I jumped off the bus, bought a copy of Eddie Cochran's Weekend, then managed to reboard the same bus! I was a fairly fit 14 year old, and most buses had open platforms. Oh what memories!!' (*Pompey Pop*). On Facebook, posters at *Birmingham Record Shops* seek names, location and memories about specific stores: 'What was the name of the record shop? […] They used to play the records so all the Bull Ring Indoor market could hear!!' Another recalls how one shop was 'right by my bus stop […]. Booming reggae while waiting for the number 47' (*Birmingham Record Shops*). Descriptions place such sites at the centre of personal soundscapes, where stores supplied music and formed an important social and cultural space; one poster recalls of his favourite store that he 'used to spend most saturdays hanging around there!'

Community discussion of *when* things happened, what was *where* and *who* did *what* and to *which* soundtrack can be remarkably specific or generalized in evoking how one felt and the wider affective associations and impressions of particular places. At the Facebook group *Birmingham Night Clubs in the 70's & 80's* for instance, a lengthy thread begins with an invitation from a female member to others to simply identify a song that they associate with particular clubs, responses evoking the 'essence' of place in naming or linking to representative tunes (*Birmingham Night Clubs in the 70's & 80's*). Communities affirm the value of those tunes and recall the rituals associated with them, of what was popular where, of the different tastes, crowds and ambiance associated with different places. At *Barbarella's Gang of '77*, a Facebook group devoted to the Birmingham venue associated with the city's punk scene, one woman notes amidst a list of gigs she attended that 'I remember they used to play "I feel love" Donna Summer at the beginning of the night […] What a time we had of it!!' Such associations extend into fond recollections of the regular rituals of nights out and the feelings they evoke. As she continues: 'We would walk home via the all night Cafe on Broad Street […] It was the best venue for it's time, dark and seedy and had just about every band that ever mattered play there!!!' Regular rituals are recalled in vivid and visceral fashion by others at the same site: 'Saw Generation X […] Billy idol lasted three phlegm showers and stormed off […] my girlfriend at the time got knocked out cold on the dance floor […]' Another recalls the same night: 'was at that gig […] Never forget watching Tex and a few other bouncers dragging a guy across the floor by his hair whilst kicking the shit outa him. What a great gig […]!' (*Barbarella's Gang of '77*). At Birmingham Music Archive, a thread concerning a recently demolished venue the *West End Bar* records impressions of the physical atmosphere and the excitement generated by this place. One male poster recalls the weekend rituals associated with this bar, of how he and his friends would 'change into our proper clubbing clothes […] My god thats when the night would get more interesting'. Another continues to sketch the musical feeling and ambiance of this space, where: 'The tunes in their would be banging. The atmosphere would [go] crazy […] when a dj would play a banging tune. The whole place would be having it'. The visceral interaction of bodies with music and each other has a material quality in this memory of a site that 'wasn't a very big place', in which 'you wouldn't get much space to dance your tits off without getting burnt by someones fag [cigarette] or dripped on by others sweat. even [*sic*] the walls and ceiling would be dripping' (Birmingham Music Archive).

The topographies of soundscapes are thus evoked in terms of physical associations, of feelings of space, of joy and sometimes (in retrospect) revulsion and even threat. At a Facebook group commemorating the past of London's *The Marquee*, one man notes his love for the place 'Even the disgusting bog [toilet]. Was so pleased when they lifted the punk ban'. He compares this with another venue and the palpable sense of threat from contemporaries: 'The Roxy was even shittier and you always had to dodge Teds [Teddy boy subcultural group] or the Millwall [Football fans] when you came out' (*The Marquee Club, Wardour Street*). Likewise, a woman at Facebook's *Crown Punks, Birmingham* group (For all old punks that frequented the Crown pub in Birmingham City Center from 1977 onwards) recalls the mélange of subcultural tribes, skinheads, punks and mods, who would congregate at the pub's upstairs disco, 'and you were never sure if that old floor was ever going to go through. If you came out of there without a bruise or a thick lip you hadn't had a good night' (*Crown Punks, Birmingham*).

Such accounts suggest how it would be reductive to assume that memories here are uniformly benign in tone. Furthermore, nor is each site, in its community relations and orientation to its central objects, organized in wholly affectionate terms. As Sara Ahmed has written 'To be affected by something is to evaluate that thing' (Ahmed 2010:31), and evaluations are part and parcel of music culture and there are plenty of disputes, discontent and negative assessments of music and practices registered in memory-making. Such evaluations spill over into assessment of one's peers and certainly, online communities are sometimes exclusive in nature. This quality ties memory-making to a history of taste and the policing of the boundaries of communities of interest in order to summon up and maintain a sense of their integrity. At Facebook's *Memories of Studio 54*, which concerns the notorious New York club, its creator warns that 'This group Is for DISCO ERA (1973–1985) music that would have been played at Studio 54, or other clubs during that period. ATTENTION NOT FOR PERSONAL ADS, OR MUSIC OF TODAY. Violators will be permemtley remove [permanently removed]' (*Memories of Studio 54*). In contrast to the openness of a group like *Shoom 88* cited earlier, 'closed' Facebook groups such as *Northern Soul. The Old Crowd* exhibit an exclusive camaraderie. It announces to any prospective members that 'This will only ever be a small group. Invite only. For my friends and their friends. For people I looked up to and respected. Covers mainly the time and era we were on the scene' (*Northern Soul, The Old Crowd*). Such sites draw our attention to the fact that collective memory is serviced by and services many more than those who were ever in the original audience for historical concerts or who attended clubs. As a result, the space of memory is a potential site of struggle in which individuals enlist their credentials and authority to determine who belongs to any community.

Whether understood as akin to the overt negativity of some online practices, a significant affective quality of the recall of the music and place of the past in communities is that of a sense of loss. As suggested above, communities of memory-making exhibit a quest for confirmation of the value and detail of past events as participants seek to explore what happened and where. That memories are sometimes 'missing' is blamed on age or intoxication in the original moment. One woman at a Facebook group for *Le Beat Rout*, the London club associated with the New Romantic movement of the early 1980s, poses the typical question 'Does anybody remember seeing […]' (*Le Beat Rout*). She bids members to write down as much as possible in light of her own failing memory while others apologize also for their own 'haze'. Sometimes, the actual details of musical references associated with particular places are lost; at the *West End Bar* thread, one man laments: 'I wish I knew the names of some of the tracks that were played there. I had a wicked tape that the dj recorded his set he'd done the one morning and I think I played it to death […] I remember what they went like singing them in my head' (Birmingham Music Archive).

A sense of loss is prompted too by the groups disbanding, the retirement or death of individuals – whether musical icons or peers – as well as the 'ending' of scenes and the closure of venues. A Facebook group for *The Roxy*, a centre for London punk in the 1970s, features questions from its members regarding what happened to the club site after its closure and laments how other valued sites have become commercialized 'plastic pubs'. When 'memories keep flooding back' in such instances, they are as bittersweet as they are joyful. Community members mark the physical loss of places and with them a sense that something essential to popular culture has disappeared with them. As one post at the site devoted to London's *Marquee Club* laments: 'Too many places are gone I'm afraid, all the scuzz and filth washed away [...] the fools don't know what they're missing' (*The Marquee Club, Wardour Street*). As we saw above, places that have been memorialized include the record stores that were once a central feature of popular music culture. Facebook pages and groups organized around such sites include: *Record Shop Archive; Birmingham Record Shops 1970–1990* and *I remember…at Bubble Records in Kent, WA*, which is announced as 'A collection of thoughts and rememberances from possibly the last, great, suburb record store in America'. Communities log the places in which music was acquired, judged and exchanged, mapping and recording the existence of everyday practices now virtually lost in the realm of music culture thanks to online ordering and downloadable music.

At *Birmingham Night Clubs in the 70's & 80's*, a sense of the parameters of the past invoked in memory and the current moment is conveyed in one post where a male community member ponders how 'There are so many of us remembering [...] the many nights we all enjoyed in our youth'. He seems himself to be unlike the majority as: 'Some like myself never stopped partying through life and still enjoy the great nights out some 30 years on! Lol. So who still goes out dancing and romancing like it's 1985?' (*Birmingham Night Clubs in the 70's & 80's*). This post succinctly highlights a further framework for thinking of a sense of loss around the inevitability of ageing and what it means for communities of memory-making around music cultures. While many have grown old with its culture (see Bennett 2013), and plenty consume contemporary releases and attend concerts, there is a sense that popular music is really something associated with one's youth. This idea is captured in self-deprecating manner by the blogger *Retroman* who describes himself as 'a man who really should have grown out of listening to "that sort of music" a long, long time ago' (*Retroman65*). Remembering the music of the past and its association with youth is to recognize and confront a dwindling of one's own involvement and determining cultural role. This involves a confrontation with memories in which a younger self is invoked, one long since submerged by maturity and the passage of time. The memories of shared soundscapes are thus viewed in terms of a site of a rite of passage, one that marks one's growth as an individual and entry into adulthood. This is a transition confirmed by the way in which a lost community reconvenes online as well as the memories that are generated by it. At the popular *Birmingham Night Clubs in the 70's & 80's*, this is apparent in threads concerning invitations to identify songs and sites associated with fleeting sexual encounters and meeting partners. One female poster prompts just such a thread by asking for information from the community on 'the crushes!!?? Unrequited love?

Angst? Heartbreak?' recollections of those for whom 'You can't even remember their name now???' (*Birmingham Night Clubs in the 70's & 80's*).

Finally, feelings of regret and loss are signalled in the very essence and purpose of memory sites even as they are imbued with expressions of delight and celebration. This is expressed at one generically oriented Facebook group in which an implicit judgment is conveyed in the title: *Back in the Days of Great Music*. The past is evoked as the place where music and culture mattered, where it was better than it is today. We suspect that such assessments have as much to do with regret for what has been lost in growing older and a feeling of the loss of community as in any qualitative change in music. At *Birmingham Music Archive*, one man recalls the manner in which one was lost in music at a club, of the communal spirit of dance, when 'U didnt care because everyone was having it'. Members of the clubbing community he recalls shared an affective spirit in which 'everyone was happy'. Indeed, the associations are such that 'even know when I hear tunes from back then it puts a smile on my face'. Indeed, in a paraphrase of a recurring assessment of the past online, he notes that 'them were the days', the power of which is such that the present cannot compare with these 'great memories' of 'Happy Days!!!!' (Birmingham Music Archive). A lament about his hometown's scene is one echoed across online sites of memory, explicitly and implicit in much of the activity and feelings that are articulated online. In short, these insist that things are not the same as they were and are sometimes bound up in a wish to 'relive just one more night from start to finish'.

Conclusion

In their discussion of the underground practices of bootleg recording and popular memory, Mark Neumann and Timothy Simpson reflect on the way in which publics are constructed as audiences and targeted as consumers by media and entertainment industries. In such circumstances, they suggest that individuals have little role in the construction of resultant narratives. Nonetheless, 'With little control over the mechanisms generating cultural stories, people still look to these media events as a potential source of connection with the present, a past, and each other' (Neumann and Simpson 1997:329). The evidence surveyed here demonstrates the ways in which individuals and communities of interest are constructing sites centred on the stories of popular music in which they have played a part. Community members evince powerful feelings about the place of music in their lives although these sometimes mitigate any transparent insight, grasp or explanation of a group's history to itself or outside observers. This is done on terms that matter to community members, even if ultimately the platforms on which they are founded are not within their ultimate control. After all, much of the material that anchors such sites is copyright protected while the intellectual property that might be generated by the collective endeavour of a Facebook group belongs to that company.

In the use of digital resources, the 'technologies of memory' of the Internet and the digitized anarchive of YouTube, etc., online practices demonstrate approaches to the past that suggest extensions of the empowering practices of community archiving, collective memory and public history (for a summary see Collins and Long 2014; Collins 2015). However, if such a pronouncement appears a little utopian in light of the comments on the ownership of memory signalled above, we should bear in mind too that the sites surveyed here allude to a wider set of practices that we have yet to comprehend. There is a need for a broader sense of the quantitative and representational qualities of such sites: sites associated with rock and its subgenres appear more prevalent than forms such as reggae and soul for instance. Likewise, the apparent demographics suggested by those who attend such sites, if not digital culture as a whole, pose questions about the nature of online participation in terms of age, gender, ethnicity and social class. Nonetheless, online sites provide genuine resources for community members in memory-making and affective exchange in which there are tangible expressions of feelings and connectivity to consider further in order to understand what matters to people, why and in what ways. As we come to the end of particular forms of popular music culture heralded by the digitization that facilitates this memory work and community building, with their wealth of posted personal materials, such sites may also offer resources for scholars of popular music culture – if we proceed in respectful fashion into this domain.

References

Ahmed, Sara (2010), 'Happy Objects', in Melissa Gregg and Gregory J. Seigworth (eds), *The Affect Theory Reader*, Durham and London: Duke University Press.

Anderson, Benedict (1983), *Imagined Communities: Reflections on the Origin and Spread of Nationalism*, London: Verso.

Ashton, Paul and Hilda Kean (2009), *Public History and Heritage Today: People and Their Pasts*, Houndmills, Basingstoke: Palgrave Macmillan.

Baker, Sarah and Alison Huber (2013), 'Notes towards a Typology of the DIY Institution: Identifying Do-It-Yourself Places of Popular Music Preservation', *European Journal of Cultural Studies*, 16:5, pp. 513–530.

Barbarellas gang of '77, Facebook, https://www.facebook.com/groups/35060574733/. Accessed 1 January 2014.

Bennett, Andy (2009), '"Heritage rock": Rock Music, Representation and Heritage Discourse', *Poetics*, 37:5, pp. 474–489.

——— (2013), *Music, Style, and Aging: Growing Old Disgracefully?*, Philadelphia: Temple University Press.

Birmingham Music Archive, *West End Bar*, http://www.birminghammusicarchive.com/west-end-bar/. Accessed 1 January 2014.

Birmingham Night Clubs in the 70's & 80's, Facebook, https://www.facebook.com/groups/birmingham.nite.clubs/. Accessed 1 January 2014.

Birmingham Record Shops 1970-1990, Facebook, https://www.facebook.com/groups/282165277076/. Accessed 1 January 2014.

Chun, Wendy Hui Kyong (2011), *Programmed Visions: Software and Memory*, Cambridge and London: MIT Press.

Collins, Jez (2015), 'Doing-It-Together: Public History-Making and Activist Archivism in Online Popular Music Archives', in Sarah Baker (ed.), *Preserving Popular Music Heritage: Do-It-Yourself, Do-It-Together*, New York and London: Routledge.

Collins, Jez and Paul Long (2014), 'Online Archival Practice and Virtual Sites of Musical Memory', in Les Roberts, Marion Leonard, Sara Cohen and Robert Knifton (eds), *Sites of Popular Music Heritage*, New York and London: Routledge.

Connell, John and Chris Gibson (2003), *Soundtracks: Popular Music, Identity and Place*, London and New York: Routledge.

Crown Punks, Birmingham, Facebook, https://www.facebook.com/groups/108486069179177/. Accessed 1 January 2014.

Discogs. About, http://www.discogs.com/about/. Accessed 1 January 2014.

Ernst, Wolfgang (2013), *Aura and Temporality: The Insistence of the Archive*. Text of the keynote lecture of the conference *The Anarchival Impulse in the Uses of the Image in Contemporary Art*, University of Barcelona, http://www.macba.cat/en/quaderns-portatils-wolfgang-ernst. Accessed 1 December 2015.

Grossberg, Lawrence (1984), 'Another Boring Day in Paradise: Rock and Roll and the Empowerment of Everyday Life', *Popular Music*, 4, pp. 225–258.

Hewison, Robert (1987), *The Heritage Industry: Britain in a Climate of Decline*, London: Methuen.

Huyssen, Andreas (2003), *Present Pasts: Urban Palimpsests and the Politics of Memory*, Palo Alto: Stanford University Press.

I remember…at Bubble Records in Kent, WA, Facebook, https://www.facebook.com/groups/169950922305/. Accessed 1 January 2014.

Jenkins, Henry (2004), 'The Cultural Logic of Media Convergence', *International Journal of Cultural Studies*, 7:1, pp. 33–43.

le beat rout, Facebook, https://www.facebook.com/groups/6736368692/. Accessed 1 January 2014.

Long, Paul and Tim Wall (2010), 'Mediating Popular Music Heritage: British Television's Narratives of Popular Music's Past', in Ian Inglis (ed.), *Popular Music on British Television*, Farnham: Ashgate.

Mabuhay Gardens – The Fab Mab, Facebook, https://www.facebook.com/groups/fabmab/. Accessed 1 January 2014.

Memories of Studio 54, Facebook, https://www.facebook.com/groups/483778518367961/. Accessed 1 January 2014.

Martin, Paul (2000), 'Sound Judgements: The Compact Disc Reissue Scene as Public History', in Hilda Kean, Paul Martin and Sally Morgan (eds), *Seeing History: Public History Now in Britain*, London: Francis Boutle.

Michelsen, Morten (2004), 'Histories and Complexities: Popular Music History Writing and Danish Rock', *Popular Music History*, 1:1, pp. 19–36.

Music of the 70s 80s 90s, Facebook, https://www.facebook.com/Music70s80s90s/info. Accessed 3 January 2014.

Neumann, Mark and Timothy Simpson (1997), 'Smuggled Sound: Bootleg Recording and the Pursuit of Popular Memory', *Symbolic Interaction*, 20, pp. 319–341.

Northern Soul, The Old Crowd, Facebook, https://www.facebook.com/groups/1381607472090814/. Accessed 1 January 2014.

Paradise Garage, Facebook, https://www.facebook.com/pages/Paradise-Garage/112841692063735. Accessed 1 January 2014.

Plate, Liedeke and Anneke Smelik (2009), *Technologies of Memory in the Arts*, Houndmills, Basingstoke: Palgrave Macmillan.

Pompey Pop (2013), *Thoughts on 'Next'*, http://pompeypop.wordpress.com/2013/01/21/next-2/. Accessed 1 January 2014.

Proyecto Memorabilia Caracas, Facebook, https://www.facebook.com/groups/caracasmemorabilia/. Accessed 1 January 2014.

Retroman65, http://retroman65.blogspot.co.uk. Accessed 1 January 2014.

Reynolds, Simon (2011), *Retromania: Pop Culture's Addiction to Its Own Past*, London: Faber & Faber.

Roberts, Les and Sara Cohen (2013), 'Unauthorising Popular Music Heritage: Outline of a Critical Framework', *International Journal of Heritage Studies*, 20:3, pp. 241–261.

Rodman, Gilbert B. and Cheyanne Vanderdonckt (2006), 'Music for Nothing or, I Want My MP3: The Regulation and Recirculation of Affect', *Cultural Studies*, 20:2–3, pp. 245–261.

San Pedro 4th Street Punkhouse Resurrectors, Facebook, https://www.facebook.com/groups/157709470931831/. Accessed 1 January 2014.

Shoom 88, Facebook, https://www.facebook.com/groups/2499552487/. Accessed 1 January 2014.

Small, Cristopher (1998) *Musicking: The Meanings of Performing and Listening (Music Culture)*. Middletown, Connecticut. Wesleyan University Press.

Songkick, *About Songkick*, http://www.songkick.com/info/about. Accessed 1 January 2014.

Sydney Rave History, Facebook, www.facebook.com/groups/sydneyravehistory. Accessed 1 January 2014.

Sydney Rave History, *Welcome to SRH!*, http://sydneyravehistory.com/about/. Accessed 1 January 2014.

The Goldmine Nightclub Canvey Island, Facebook, https://www.facebook.com/groups/10864370879/. Accessed 1 January 2014.

The Marquee Club, Wardour Street, Facebook., https://www.facebook.com/groups/49711815217/. Accessed 1 January 2014.

The UG – Hiphop – Archivist/Celebrate your History, Facebook, https://www.facebook.com/UgHiphopArchivist. Accessed 1 January 2014.

Thompson, Emily (2004), *The Soundscape of Modernity: Architectural Acoustics and the Culture of Listening in America, 1900-1933*, Cambridge: MIT Press.

Van Dijck, José (2006), 'Record and Hold: Popular Music between Personal and Collective Memory', *Critical Studies in Media Communications*, 23:5, pp. 357–374.

Van House, Nancy and Elizabeth F. Churchill (2008), 'Technologies of Memory: Key Issues and Critical Perspectives', *Memory Studies*, 1, pp. 295–310.

Vintage TV, *Who we are*, www.vintage.tv/who-we-are/about-us. Accessed 1 January 2014.

Võsu, Ester, Ene Kõresaar and Kristin Kuutma (2008), 'Mediation of Memory: Towards Transdisciplinary Perspectives in Current Memory Studies', *Trames*, 12:3, pp. 243–263.

Wall, Tim (2006), 'Out on the Floor: The Politics of Dancing on the Northern Soul Scene', *Popular Music*, 25:3, pp. 431–445.

Part II

Space

Chapter 6

Music as Cartography: English Audiences and Their Autobiographical Memories of the Musical Past

Sarah Cohen

I f asked to map and share memories of your own personal musical past, then how would you go about it? What would you present as a music-related memory and why, and how would these memories be presented and located? These questions, and the process of locating memories of the musical past, provide a starting point and basis for this chapter, which explores the relationship between music, space and autobiographical memory. Memory is a broad concept defined in various ways and encompassing discourses that are multiple and diverse, and in this case the emphasis is on memory as a social practice produced through social interaction, grounded in social situations and contexts, and informed by social and ideological conventions. The notion of memory as practice draws attention not only to the process of memory-making but also to memory as work, a common way of conceptualizing memory within disciplines such as social anthropology (e.g. Litzinger 1998; Krause 2005) that helps to emphasize the effort of memory-making (recalling, forgetting, inventing, re-inventing, organizing, sharing and so on), often in order to achieve particular results.

The chapter begins by explaining how audiences in England were invited to undertake such memory work, and to map and share memories of their musical and autobiographical past. Drawing on this research, the second section of the chapter considers how these memories were located: in other words, how they were spatially situated and related to a more defined and meaningful sense of place. Reflecting on this process, the third and final section considers what it reveals not just about the relationship between music, space and autobiographical memory, but also about the value and significance of music.

Gathering memories of the musical past

Between 2010 and 2013, I participated in a project entitled 'Popular Music Heritage, Cultural Memory, and Cultural Identity'. It was based on collaboration between researchers in England, the Netherlands, Austria and Slovenia, and on comparative research conducted in each of these four countries. In England, the research team consisted of me, a post-doctoral researcher, Les Roberts, and a doctoral student, Gurdeep Khabra, whose focus was on English South Asian popular music. The first phase of our research involved interviewing representatives from the music and media industries and the tourism and heritage sector, in order to examine their role in the construction of dominant histories and heritages of English popular music, whether through films, books, exhibitions and so on. The second phase involved research on audiences and *their* music histories and memories, research that provides a basis for this chapter. To begin with, therefore, I will briefly explain how this audience research was conducted and the different methods involved.

As part of our research, audiences were invited to complete a central questionnaire hosted on the main project website in Rotterdam and made available in the language of each of the four countries involved. In England, the questionnaire was largely circulated via social media networks, particularly Facebook, as well as a project website (less successful were our considerable efforts to direct radio listeners to the questionnaire through features on the project broadcast on BBC regional radio). After accessing the questionnaire, audiences were encouraged to answer a broad range of questions, including those concerning their social and musical background, their earliest and most precious musical memories, their favourite music and so on. They were also asked to indicate their willingness to be interviewed so that we could follow up on some of the responses, exploring them in more detail and depth through face-to-face meetings and conversations. By May 2013, we had received over 600 responses from England and explored 30 of them through recorded interviews with the individuals concerned. The interviews usually ran for a couple of hours and were conducted in various parts of the country and in venues chosen by the interviewees. There were roughly equal numbers of male and female interviewees aged between 20 and 70 years of age. Most were white and relatively well educated but they nevertheless varied considerably in terms of their music practices and the extent of their involvement with music, and were from diverse occupational backgrounds.

During our earlier conversations about ways of publicizing and promoting the questionnaire, I had suggested to Les and Gurdeep that we invite audiences to draw us a map of their musical memories. As part of a previous project on music and urban landscape, I had made use of this kind of conceptual, cognitive, hand-drawn mapping as a research tool (Cohen 2012a, 2012b). Such hand-drawn maps (also commonly referred to as 'sketch maps' or 'memory maps') have long been used by human geographers, social anthropologists and others to study how people describe places and remember what is where, their subjective sense of space and place, and differences between people in terms of their spatial knowledge and understanding (see, e.g., Lynch 1960; Tuan 1975; Ben-Ze'ev 2012). The maps were drawn during our conversations with the musicians concerned and took various forms. While some were rather like conventional cartographic maps, others looked more like pictures, diagrams or flow charts. Some were maps of music and place at particular points in time, but others were more temporal, charting the journeys of individuals and groups through time as well as across urban space (how and where the musicians had started out, where they had been and ended up and so on). These maps were not objective representations of reality but revealed something about the practices and perspectives of those who created them. Most importantly, the act of mapping prompted memories and stories about music, so I wondered if we could apply this approach to our research on audiences, inviting people to map their musical past, and using these maps to explore ways of conceptualizing autobiographical memories of and engagements with music.

A project website had been created to provide information about the research and a link to the questionnaire, and through it we also invited people to draw and submit their music memory maps. We uploaded our own maps onto that site, having created them in order to test out the potential of this approach and show how loosely we were defining the notion of a 'map'. These maps were strikingly different in form and approach. Mine had been produced in a rush and featured a blue biro scribble of circles, doodles and lines radiating out like spokes from the middle of a sheet of white, lined paper. It began with childhood memories of home and school and then moved through the decades in a clockwise direction, ending with the 1990s, by which time I had run out of space. Les' map had been much more carefully and intricately drawn and meticulously annotated. It featured a dense mesh of triangles, circles and squares, all hand-drawn onto A3 paper and shaded in yellow, green, purple red and blue, before scanning and editing with Photoshop. Les told us that although it had taken him longer than he had bargained for, he had found the mapping process to be a useful and thought-provoking exercise, and had ended up mapping memories of live music during one ten-year period and his twenties. Gurdeep's map also focused on memories of live music but was less populated and had been created using PREZI computer software, making it possible to zoom into it in order to reveal more detail. It took the form of a map of central and northern England that was coloured in blue and featured circles marking three cities in which Gurdeep had lived and participated in live music events, each containing text and images that provided further details of those events.

Locating memories of the musical past

As part of the audience research, autobiographical memories of the musical past were thus presented in various ways and through written questionnaire responses, face-to-face conversation and visual maps or diagrams. While comments on the questionnaire were generally and inevitably rather brief, some people nevertheless took the time and trouble to elaborate in response to the more open questions and provide answers that were surprisingly detailed, and the face-to-face interviews enabled people to elaborate further. During these interviews, memories still tended to be presented as brief and selective snippets of information, as if snapshots of or fragments from the past, but they nevertheless provided a basis for stories and anecdotes about music and the autobiographical past, a kind of storytelling that was also prompted by the process of creating a memory map. These stories involved recollections that were specific, vivid and detailed or more vague and generalized, and while some were well-rehearsed and deliberately narrated, others emerged unexpectedly through the process of conversation or map-making. This second section of the chapter considers in more detail how these memories were presented and, more specifically, how they were located and related to space and place. It does so by focusing on two particular maps and on audience responses to questions about their 'earliest' and 'most precious' music memories.

June's map and earliest memories of the musical past

I begin with June, a health worker in her late thirties whose memory map was rather similar to the one produced by Gurdeep, although in general there were striking differences between the maps gathered during the project, whether in terms of style or approach. Like Gurdeep, June had also used computer software to create her map and present her autobiographical memories of the musical past in the form of circles or ovals representing places in which she had lived at particular points in time. She had organized these shapes chronologically and according to age, beginning with memories of her childhood and progressing in a clockwise direction up until her thirties and the present. Unlike the maps created by Les and myself, featuring hand-written notes and a density of hand-drawn shapes and lines, June's map was relatively clean and simple. Within each oval she had listed the names of artists whose music she associated with memories of that particular time and place.

June provided us with a short written narrative that could be uploaded onto the project website to accompany her map:

> Participating in the research made me think about what music I had been listening to at different times of my life. When I started writing it down I realized how this grouped into stages beginning in my childhood, developing when I was a student and especially in my 20's when a lot of my friends were in bands and my social life largely revolved around

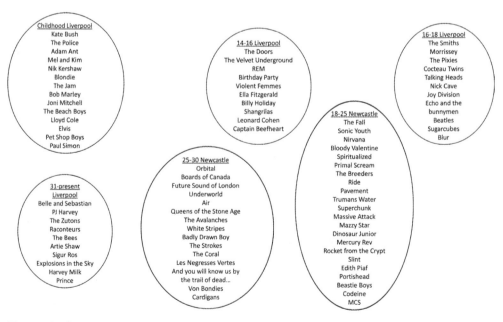

Figure 1: June's music memory map.

gigs and festivals. I noticed that I am listening to less new stuff now, I'm more likely to put something on I know and love. It will take going to a music festival such as ATP or a friends recommendation that I will listen to something different. Or Jarvis Cocker's Sunday Service on 6 music (I never had much time for Pulp but Jarvis is legend).[1] There are some things I won't think about for years but then something will remind me and I'll dig out a CD or get it from Amazon or Fopp. I think the music I listen to does say a lot about me and has been a central part of my social life and had a big influence on my friends and family. I like how music can bring people together to share experiences like festivals or just agree they like something on the radio [...] I guess music can create a sense of belonging and familiarity which is reassuring. People like to be reassured.[2]

In response to the question about her earliest memory of music, June wrote on the questionnaire, 'The only time I've ever seen my dad mad was [when I had been] getting his vinyl out and putting it on the living room floor and playing a game that involved jumping on it – I've never seen my dad so angry – "don't mess with my dad's records!"' On June's map, however, Kate Bush tops the list of artists connected to her Liverpool childhood, and she elaborated on this when we met up with her in person close to her place of work. Another early memory of music, she explained, was of being around five- or six-years old and listening as her mother played Kate Bush tapes. She had since grown up with Kate Bush, singling out her song 'Wuthering Heights' and how it 'still makes the hairs on my neck stand up'. In fact, almost all of the artists on June's childhood list are connected to the records her parents used to play before they got divorced, and she also presented a memory of the time they bought their first CD player and how they christened it by playing their first ever CDs (of *Carmina Burana* and an album by Sting).

The next oval along on June's map contains a list of artists associated with memories of key moments during her teens, such as 'dancing and drinking for the first time' and the loss of her virginity, which was something she referred to in writing on the audience questionnaire. In response to the question, 'What is your most precious memory relating to music (either from your youth or later in your life)?' she wrote, 'velvet underground and nico.[3] my dad had an original copy although the peel off banana was long gone. i lost my virginity to a boy who had the same version because that was a good enough reason as any!' When interviewed, she explained that she increasingly listened to music associated with those teenage years, revisiting songs via YouTube and then ordering them again on CD to replace the records she'd lost over the years. She also referred to songs and musicians that prompted memories of the past and her childhood, such as the Jam, and a Beach Boys album cover that 'reminds me of dad who had the record'. Her father had introduced her to a wide range of musicians and musical styles, and the two of them shared similar tastes in music. She described how they would collaborate on the compilation of the mix tapes to take with them on holiday, carefully selecting the records beforehand from her dad's extensive vinyl collection. Later, during her university years, she compiled mix-tapes for friends and established long-term friendships with people she met at gigs and festivals across various parts of the United Kingdom.

The stories June told about her memories of the musical past, and how her engagement with music had changed over the years, were unique to her. When reading through the hundreds of questionnaire responses and listening to the recorded interviews, what immediately becomes clear is the diversity of people's engagements with music and memory, something also evident from the interviews conducted for the 1980s *My Music* project in Buffalo, New York, when individuals between the ages of 4 and 83 were asked to explain what music meant to them (Crafts et al. 1993). Thus, some of those who participated in our research explained that music had not played a particularly significant role in their lives and was not especially important to them, while others described music *as* their life and explained how it had defined the kind of person they were.

Despite such differences, the research also pointed to certain common trends and conventional narratives across the audience responses. Like June, most were keen to emphasize the eclecticism of their music tastes and their engagement with a broad range of music styles and genres. Also apparent was how memories of music are inevitably related to many other things. When asked about their earliest memory of music, for example, individuals commonly presented a memory of listening to a particular song or genre of music, such as lullabies, nursery rhymes, hymns, hit singles and theme or advertising tunes. These memories were often related to the type of music media, recording formats and technologies involved, whether 45 or 78 rpm vinyl records; cassettes, VHS or reel-to-reels, Walkmans and CDs, radio and television or even a toy record player. In turn, these recordings and recording technologies were commonly related to the particular relative they belonged to, hence references to 'my dad's records', 'my brother's record player', 'my parents' music', 'my sister's radio', 'the music my mum played'.

In addition to this, 'earliest' music memories were related to a broad range of social activities and events, such as dancing and singing and the rituals and routines of domestic life. Hence, we were presented with memories of parents playing records on a Saturday and Sunday morning when they were both at home; mothers singing as they were ironing, cooking or doing other housework chores; songs heard or sung during family camping trips and fathers singing to their children when they were ill or to help get them to sleep. Alison's father, for example, was at the centre of her childhood memories of music, and she mentioned his love of music hall and how her earliest memory was of him singing the song 'My baby has gone down the plug hole' to her at bath-time. For Val, it was a memory of, 'going to a department store for tea-cakes with mum and listening to Petula Clark's "Downtown"'.

Unsurprisingly, as with this reference to a department store, people's earliest memories of music were related not just to certain activities and events (whether a special moment or regular routine) and the people and sounds connected to them, but also to the particular spaces and places involved. These earliest memories were occasionally related to infant school ('Singing puff the magic dragon in school and crying because the song was so sad'; 'Yellow submarine being played at infant school assembly'; 'Being asked to dance to bohemian rhapsody at primary school') but much more commonly to domestic spaces. There were memories of dancing to particular songs in parents' bedrooms, and of listening to mum's portable radio while playing in the garden in summer or to 'the records in nan's house' as she cooked the Sunday roast. The kitchen was commonly mentioned as the place where people had once listened to music with their mother or heard her singing. Jen's earliest memory of music was connected to the kitchen table upon which her parents sat her when she was a toddler, and how she 'would move about and polish' that table if they played a song she particularly liked. For someone else, it was a memory of 'Sitting on the kitchen windowsill listening to three lions during a world cup when I was about 6'.

The living room also featured prominently as a site attached to memories of dancing to music with parents or siblings; lying on the sofa listening to music at times of illness; sneaking into the cabinet where the records were stored to look at the strange sleeve designs or, as in June's case, jumping on vinyl records. For a surprisingly large number of research participants, however, their earliest memory of music was connected to the family car and to journeys that were special, such as those to holiday destinations, or more regular and routine. There were thus references to road trips accompanied by the Clash, Nat King Cole and Fleetwood Mac; travelling through the dark with the Moody Blues' 'Knights in White Satin'; bouncing round the back seat whilst listening to The Police and watching 'dad drumming the steering wheel along to Pink Floyd'. Lorna's earliest memory also involved Pink Floyd:

> When I was a child. I used to go hiking and camping in the countryside with my Dad. He had a mix-tape that he'd made from his vinyl records of his favourite songs and we used to play it in the car. I can remember most tracks vividly, particularly 'Time' by Pink Floyd. The introduction has some clock chimes and alarm clock sounds, and he used to warn me every time that it would startle me. and it never did because I knew it so well.

Ian's map and precious memories of the musical past

The second map (Figure 2) was created by Ian, a London-based business manager in his late fifties, and features a collage of ticket stubs from performance events that he had attended over three decades:

> Ticket stubs represent a great (and no doubt lazy) way for me to recall my musical journey. More often than not the tickets have the time, the date, the place and the principle [sic] reason of what I'm trying to remember all there right in front of me and therefore the hard work of recollection is all pretty much done. And yet, I find that once I start to put these random components together to form a memory map, the names and dates on the actual tickets themselves stay still and what is laying seemingly dormant beneath the surface starts to come to life. The different shapes, sizes and colours, the logos, the font's [sic], the quality of the paper all start to trigger more thoughts [...] A few of the gigs I have tickets for I can't even remember, a lot of the gigs I have tickets for I will never ever forget.

Figure 2: Ian's music memory map.

The idea of creating a map, Ian explained, had prompted him, 'to see what ticket stubs I had lying around the house and what gigs I had been to and still had the tickets for, and that was a real journey for me. I'd never done that before'. As he talked us through this map, Ian related tales of the events and locations involved, from the boring folk festivals he used to go to with his parents, to the dangerous and exciting rock gigs in London during the 1980s. There were memories of the time someone got knifed during a performance by the punk band the Redskins, and when someone threw a coin at the lead singer of the Smiths and he walked off the stage after only one song. However, there were also memories of all the car journeys: all the driving around to see bands in places where, as he put it, 'there was always the chance that something special might happen'. He described listening to music as he travelled along and how on one freezing cold January night he even had to sleep in his car. Best of all was a performance by Portishead at Glastonbury. The rain was heavy and they waited ages for the band to appear. It got late and they were cold and hungry but then the band came on, the sound was loud, the visuals were fantastic, and the performance 'utterly transcended the environment'. But it was the social interaction of live music that appealed the most. 'Sometimes', he explained, 'I can't even remember the band playing: it's the whole context around music that is significant for me'.

As part of the questionnaire, audiences were asked not only about their earliest but also their 'most precious' memory of music and most of the responses were related to live music, and memories of going to gigs or festivals. These memories were commonly described through rather conventional narratives. Like Ian and June, for example, individuals dwelt on memories of live music as a social experience, whether of being part of a crowd and out with friends, or of participating in the interaction between audience and performers. For many, such memories symbolized certain key moments or periods in their lives, whether the thrill of venturing into the city at night for the first time to go to a gig or club, or a time when they were free from the responsibilities of parenthood and able to go out and socialize with others on a regular basis. Live music thus tended to be remembered as an experience that was uniquely collective and participatory, as well as an emotional, physical and sensual experience related to a sense of occasion, excitement and anticipation, and to youthful pleasures and freedoms, trials and tribulations. These examples support Simon Frith's observation that, 'A live concert is not simply a transitory experience but symbolises what it means to be a music fan and can also represent a community' (2007:5, 7). This helps to explain, he continues, why live music 'remains vital for almost all music genres', while for those involved with rock, jazz and folk performance it is regarded as 'the truest form of musical expression' (Frith:8). For our audiences, live music mattered not only because it offers an experience that is collective and participatory but also one that is unpredictable and unique; and because it involved sharing music and emotion with others in the same place at the same time.

Memories of live music were commonly related to places that symbolized the experiences involved (whether performance venues, festival sites or the night-time city), as well as to the journeys to and from those places. The location and spatial aspects of live music events, such as the shape, layout and size of venues and proximity to the stage and performers, had apparently contributed to the atmosphere, making them more memorable. Thus, one person related his most precious memory of music to a festival held on a beach, while many likewise presented memories of performances at other significant venues and times, or even of events categorized as 'precious' because of the perceived insignificance of the venue:

Oasis at Wembley (just before it got ripped down) in 1999/2000. It was so exhilarating and terrifying being amongst so many other people all singing the same song [...] I looked around and there were thousands of people moving their hands in the same way, at the same time and it's an amazing feeling of belonging.

A Suzi Quatro concert, believe it or not. It was my first big concert and it was thrilling and amazing to be in such a large crowd of people who were all there to see the same performer. Adelaide is a small city in a peripheral, small country, and it was always amazing that a big star would visit.

As with Ian's map, the maps created by Les and Gurdeep likewise focused on live music and the spaces and places involved, which was something that took Les rather by surprise: 'This wasn't especially planned, but records/CDs, other than the act of buying them [...] did not really present themselves to me as memory' (Les).[4] The importance of the location of live music events in popular memory – the places in which live music is performed – has been noted by several scholars (Frith 2012; Turner 2003: vii; Forbes 2014; Cohen 2014). It was also noted by Gurdeep in relation to his map:

> The map I've come up with is based on the first thoughts that came to my mind when thinking about my significant musical memories. Without really intending it to, it seems mostly to be based around gigs or festivals that I've attended, and I've arranged it spatially using the different places I've lived or seen concerts in […] the memories certainly didn't come to me in a fixed chronological order – I would think of one particular memory, which then triggered me to remember something else in a completely different location and year.

Like Ian and Les, several interviewees expressed surprise that they remembered so little about the musical aspects of performance events, which is something that also struck John Street during his research on audience memories of Woodstock (2004:31), and Sheryl Garratt (1990:402) who reflects on her own memories of being a Bay City Rollers fan in the mid-1970s. As illustrated above, memories of listening to recorded music, or to music performed within the home, were similar to memories of going to gigs, festivals and concerts in that they too were connected to social events, interactions and relationships, and to a sense of social belonging. At the same time, however, these memories tended to be related to more private and personal spaces and to specific songs and musical sounds. Thus, the most precious memory of one questionnaire respondent was of,

> Listening to 'Life and Life Only' by Al Stewart, whilst driving a rollertruck in a bakery on 12 hour night shifts. Made me understand what soul memory and reincarnation were really about. I finally grasped the ennui and deep sadness that I had always felt. I became at one with it. it was me. not a 'wrong' me. but the authentic me.

Mapping music and memory

Having described research on audiences in England and how autobiographical memories of music were gathered and presented, this final section of the chapter draws together the threads of the discussion and makes two general points about the relationship between music, space and autobiographical memory.

Space, identity and vernacular memory

The first point is that, as illustrated by the maps and stories of June and Ian, autobiographical memories of music are embedded in the geographies of everyday life and enable a mapping of the musical past, becoming attached to space and places in ways that inform personal and collective identity.

During our research, we were continually surprised by the remarkably personal and intimate nature of the autobiographical memories we were presented with, but such memories are at the same time deeply social (Van Dijck 2006). For Andreas Huyssen, memory is a lived practice that is, 'active, alive, embodied in the social – that is, in individuals, families, groups, nations, and regions' (2003:28). Autobiographical memories of the musical past are thus shaped through social interaction and bound up with the collective. They are commonly shared with others and exchanged and circulated in multiple and diverse ways, providing a basis for establishing social relationships and groups. Paul Long and Jez Collins (this volume, Chapter 5), for example, describe online communities formed through the sharing of individual recollections of music, and in particular memories related to place. Referring to websites such as *Pompey Pop*, a site that commemorates the city of Portsmouth's music history, they note how, 'the record shop, concert hall and night club – as well as the private space of home, feature in evocative memories conjuring up a sense of soundscapes of individual and collective pasts'. There are many such websites devoted to memories and places of the musical past, hence Frith (2012) describes:

the remarkable blossoming of local music archive material on the web [...] Every British city, town and region, it seems, has people putting together exhaustive historical accounts of their local venues, bands and gig (most sites illustrated liberally with concert posters and ticket stubs). Such sites are a treasure trove of oral history; they provide not just factual information – who played where and when – but emotional insights too.

Collins (2013) provides a detailed description of the kind of memory work motivated by such sites, and how they attract ever increasing amounts of uploaded historical materials, including links to official band sites and other tribute pages; embedded video from YouTube and occasional streams of music; and digitized photographs, ticket stubs, posters and other ephemera from personal collections. These sites motivate a kind of online communication described by Collins as 'often scrappy in nature', involving comments made with little care or attention to language or even detail: 'Names, sounds, scenes and places are cited and users call on others to add detail for their own sometimes vaguely recalled fragments of experience'. This kind of prompting, he argues, produces conversational exchanges between individuals and within groups that give rise to 'multiple perspectives on the past'. Collins runs the virtual *Birmingham Music Archive*, which he established to counter the marginalization of Birmingham within dominant and 'official authorised' (Smith 2006) constructions of English music heritage. On its website, the archive is dedicated to 'Celebrating, Preserving and Sharing Birmingham's Music Heritage' (*Birmingham Music Archive*), illustrating how in England the term 'heritage' has been increasingly used to legitimize music and memory, although the language of heritage is used in many different ways and serves various interests. Hence, organizations across public, private and community sectors have sought to ascribe heritage status to music texts and artefacts and attach it to sites and monuments; and to use heritage to canonize the musical past and for place-branding purposes (Cohen 2013; Roberts and Cohen 2013).

Yet few of the individuals who participated in our research found the term 'heritage' particularly meaningful or relevant for popular music or their own personal musical past. For these participants, memory did not require authorization as heritage and many referred instead to notions of music 'inheritance' or to 'influences' they could trace back and forth, whether through their record collections or YouTube. This helps to highlight the work of memory, something emphasized by the character central to Nick Hornby's novel *High Fidelity* whose records were closely connected to past events and relationships, and who declares, 'Tuesday night I reorganized my record collection. I often do this at periods of emotional stress. There are some people who would find this a pretty dull way to spend an evening, but I'm not one of them. This is my life, and it's nice to be able to wade in it, immerse your arms in it, touch it' (1995:54). This kind of memory work clearly provides a seemingly tangible resource for identity-building – for the construction of autobiographical narrative and stories of self and others. During our audience research, the unfolding of these narratives, and the form and direction they took, were shaped by the specific social situations and interactions involved. At the same time, the emergence of familiar and repeated narratives of remembering throughout the audience research highlighted broader cultural and ideological conventions influencing what is appropriate to remember, how to present memories of music and 'what it means to be a self with an autobiographical past' (Fivush and Haden 2003:vii).

Just as few of our research participants referred to music as 'heritage', it was also notable that few related their autobiographical memories of music to a sense of national or even local identity, although these memories nevertheless tended to be spatially located. For Pierre Nora, 'Memory attaches itself to sites [*lieux de mémoire*], whereas history attaches itself to events' (1989:22), and 'crystallises and secretes itself' in place (1989:7). The autobiographical memories of our audiences in England had become attached to sites that were multiple and diverse, and had crystallized around spaces and places of variable scale: small domestic spaces, such as a kitchen shelf and table top and a garden shed, or a more diffuse and generalized sense of home; the private solitary space of the bedroom or the crowded festival site; mobile spaces, such as a rollertruck or the family car. The research on audiences thus revealed the material sites, contours and journeys that, in all their complexity and colour, define the spaces, landscapes and geographies of popular music memory; and it highlighted vernacular musical memories that differed quite strikingly from constructions of local and national 'heritage' (Roberts and Cohen 2013).

Throughout this research, memory was typically presented as experience, as is common in modern consumerist societies (Antze and Lambek 1996), an experience located and embedded in the musical geographies of everyday life and the rituals and routines involved. Drawing on the seminal work of Feld and other anthropologists or sociologists, such as DeNora (2000) and Bull (2000), Georgina Born argues that focusing on music experience, rather than on narrower categories such as music 'listening', allows 'questions of the encultured, affective, corporeal and located nature of musical experience to arise in a stronger way than hitherto' (2010:89). Thus, in his seminal study of the lives of the Kaluli people of the tropical rainforests of highland Papua New Guinea, Steven Feld (1982) shows how Kaluli music expression and experience is 'embedded in and constitutive of their cosmology, environmental ecology, social relations, rituals, and collective experience of emotion, space, time and labour' (Born 2010:82). Feld describes, for example, the paths taken by the Kaluli as they move through the rainforest: 'For the Kaluli, every place lies on a path (*tok*) so that the naming of places is always a part of a remembrance, in speech or song, of travelling the *tok* along which they lie' (Ingold 2007:88).

Music is similarly woven into many different aspects of the lives of audiences in England, as evident in the maps and autobiographical memories presented by June, Ian and others. Mediated through memory, music is connected to spaces and movements that are regular and routine, mundane as well as special (cooking, camping, going for a night out or on holiday and so on), and creates and recreates social and spatial boundaries (home and away, here and there, public and private and so on), enabling a mapping of the past. In an earlier article on music and autobiographical memory, I drew on Stuart Hall's work on diaspora to describe music as providing a meaningful map through which individuals and groups can locate 'themselves in different imaginary geographies at one and the same time' (Cohen 1995:287). Reflecting on his own autobiographical memories of music in Madrid, Francesco Cruces (2013) likewise points to 'the forcefully cartographic nature of such an exercise', describing how it involved 'narrating a city through music' and revealing the intimacies of urban life:

> those quotidian, apparently little things which are ultimately the stuff of which daily life is made. These dimensions (which we could loosely lump together under the labels of the domestic/private/intimate sphere) tend to be underrepresented by neglect, invisibility or even mystification, both in urban theory and in the very common sense of early modernity.

Ruth Finnegan (1989:323) makes a similar point in relation to the everyday rituals and routines of amateur music-making in an English town, describing this music-making as hidden from the view of urban planners and policy-makers, and conceptualizing it in terms of urban 'pathways':

> One way of looking at people's musical activities is therefore to see them as taking place along a series of pathways which provide familiar directions for both personal choices and collective actions. Such pathways form one important – if often unstated – framework for people's participation in urban life, something overlapping with, but more permanent and structured than, the personal networks in which individuals also participate. They form broad routes set out, as it were, across and through the city. They tend to be invisible to others, but for those who follow them they constitute a clearly laid thoroughfare both for their activities and relationships and for the meaningful structuring of their actions in space and time.

The work of Finnegan, Feld and Cruces, and the maps and stories of our research participants suggest that people's known and regular routes (pathways) across urban space in order to engage in music activity, and their embodied experience of going along from one place to another, can become imprinted in memory. For José Van Dijck (2007:78), the process of remembering music is simultaneously embodied, enabled and embedded:

> Autobiographical memories are embodied in the brains and minds of individual people, meaning that specific affects and emotions are attached to specific songs, a connection that is literally embodied in the body/mind [...] Moreover, musical memories are enabled through instruments of listening [...] Remembrance is also embedded, meaning that the larger interpersonal and intercultural worlds stimulate memories of the past through frames generated in the present.

Music as cartography

The second, concluding point is that the specificity of music as a social, spatial and sonic practice and experience informs its significance and value as cartography, and its ability to map the autobiographical past.

For our research on audiences in England, we explored memories and experiences of the musical past from the perspective of those involved, in order to produce fine-grained insights into the role of music in constructions of social memory, and the forging of identities through music and memory work. The narratives of these audiences highlighted the role and significance of music in memory and in everyday life. They showed how music provides a focus or frame for memories of a broad and diverse range of social activities (eating, worshipping, driving, walking, going to sleep and so on), as well as events that can be deeply personal, intimate and solitary but also public, shared and collective. For Cruces (2013), music also has the power to manage distances, whether by setting up symbolic frontiers inside a house or, on the contrary, by embracing the participants inside a common 'atmosphere' or 'ambience'. In addition to this, our research participants presented us with memories of music that had accompanied them as they journeyed along, a process enabled by music technologies such as the car stereo and MP3 player. Yet, music moves not only with people but also involves the movement of sound through time, and Tia DeNora argues that because music is a temporal medium heard over time, when reheard and recalled it provides a 'device for unfolding, for replaying, the temporal structure of that moment, its dynamism as emerging experience' (2000:67). She consequently describes music as a resource for memory retrieval and the construction of self-identity (2000:66). Certainly for those who participated in our research, songs and musical sounds were not just something to be remembered but had also prompted memory and emotion, reminding them of times of joy and happiness, illness and depression and of people they cared about. DeNora describes how this can happen unexpectedly and as a form of spontaneous memory that can catch people unawares (2000:63). Music artefacts also prompted memory, thus June's reference to the Beach Boy's album sleeve that reminded her of her dad, and Ian's festival ticket associated with his parents and their music tastes. Like Ian, most of our research participants kept items of music memorabilia associated with particular events, such as concert tickets and album sleeves. The value of such items, as Frith (2012) points out in relation to tickets, was determined not by their economic worth but by how the events had been experienced, and several interviewees questioned why anyone would collect items of music memorabilia that didn't have that personal connection but were instead attached to 'someone else's memory', someone else's experience.

As part of our research, we invited people to map their autobiographical memories of the musical past not just through written questionnaire responses and face-to-face conversation, but also through visual and literal 'maps', such as the ones created by June and Ian. While we used these maps as a methodological tool to prompt memories and stories of music, the individuals who created them commented on how the process of mapping had made them think about their musical past in new ways and from different perspectives. For some, it made them reflect on how their memories of music had crystallized around sites that varied in type and scale, whether cities and live music venues or domestic spaces such as the family home and car. In fact as illustrated above, music and memory were commonly related to space and place as well as to people and social events and relationships, music sounds and genres, music and media technologies, feelings and emotions, and particular times or moments. This drew our attention to the cartographic properties of both music and memory, and thus to what music and memory *do* rather than what they are, to the 'where' as well as the 'what' of music memory and to how and why music matters.

Acknowledgements

The research this chapter is based on was supported as part of the *Popular Music Heritage, Cultural Memory and Cultural Identity (POPID)* project by the HERA Joint Research Programme (www.heranet.info), which is co-funded by AHRC, AKA, DASTI, ETF, FNR, FWF, HAZU, IRCHSS, MHEST, NWO, RANNIS, RCN, VR and the European Community FP7 2007–2013, under the Socio-economic Sciences and Humanities programme. I would like to thank my co-researchers on the POPID team, particularly Les Roberts, and all the research participants who gave us permission to use their interview material and memory maps.

References

Antze, Paul and Michael Lambek (1996), *Tense Past: Cultural Essays in Trauma and Memory*, London: Routledge.

Ben-Ze'ev, Efrat (2012), 'Mental Maps and Spatial Perceptions: The Fragmentation of Israel-Palestine', in Les Roberts (ed.), *Mapping Cultures: Place, Practice, Performance*, Basingstoke: Palgrave Macmillan, pp. 237–259.

Birmingham Music Archive, http://www.birminghammusicarchive.com/about-us/. Accessed 20 March 2014.

Born, Georgina (2010), 'Listening, Mediation, Event: Anthropological and Sociological Perspectives', *Journal of the Royal Musical Association*, 135:1 (special issue), pp. 79–89.

Bull, Michael (2000), *Sounding Out the City: Personal Stereos and the Management of Everyday Life*, Oxford: Berg.

Cohen, Sara (1995), 'Sounding Out the City: Music and the Sensuous Production of Place', *Transactions of the Institute of British Geographers*, 20:4, pp. 434–446.

—— (2012a), 'Bubbles, Tracks, Borders and Lines: Mapping Music and Urban Landscape', *Journal of the Royal Musical Association*, 137:1, pp. 135–171.

—— (2012b), 'Urban Musicscapes: Mapping Music-Making in Liverpool', in Les Roberts (ed.), *Mapping Cultures: Place, Practice, Performance*, Basingstoke: Palgrave Macmillan, pp. 123–143.

—— (2013), 'Musical Memory, Heritage & Local Identity: Remembering the Popular Music Past in a European Capital of Culture', *International Journal of Cultural Policy*, 19:5, pp. 576–594.

—— (2014), 'Live Music, Memory and Local Identity', in Karen Burland and Stephanie Pitts (eds), *Coughing and Clapping*, Guildford: Ashgate.

Collins, Jeremy (2013), 'A Pile of My History, Found in My Parents Attic: Online Music Memories', *Unpublished Conference Paper presented at the Cultural Memory of Sound and Space*, University of Turku, Finland, 13–15 March.

Crafts, Susan. D., Daniel Cavicchi and Charles Keil (1993), *My Music*, New England: Wesleyan.

Cruces, Francesco (2013), 'Music as Intimacy: Variations on Music and the Urban Place', *Keynote presentation at the 17th Biennial Conference of the International Association for the Study of Popular Music*, Gijon, Spain, 28 June.

DeNora, Tia (2000), *Music in Everyday Life*, Cambridge: Cambridge University Press.

Feld, Steven (1982), *Sound and Sentiment: Birds, Weeping, Poetics and Song in Kaluli Expression*, Philadelphia: University of Pennsylvania Press.

Finnegan, Ruth (1989), *The Hidden Musicians: Music-Making in an English Town*, Cambridge: Cambridge University Press.

Fivush, Robyn and Catherine A. Haden (2003), *Autobiographical Memory and the Construction of a Narrative Self: Developmental and Cultural Perspectives*, Mahwah, New Jersey: Lawrence Erlbaum Associates, Inc.

Forbes, Kenny (2015), '"You Had to Be There": Memories of the Glasgow Apollo Audience', in Sara Cohen, Robert Knifton, Marion Leonard and Les Roberts (eds), *Sites of Popular Music Heritage*, London: Routledge.

Frith, Simon (2007), 'Live Music Matters', *Scottish Music Review*, 1:1, pp. 1–17.

—— (2012), 'Live Music and Memory', Live Music Exchange blog entry, http://livemusicexchange.org/blog/live-music-and-memory/. Accessed 20 March 2013.

Garratt, Sheryl (1990), 'Teenage Dreams', in Simon Frith and Andrew Goodwin (eds), *On Record: Rock, Pop and the Written Word*, New York: Pantheon, pp. 399–409.

Hall, Stuart (1995), 'New Cultures for Old', in Doreen Massey and Pat Jess (eds), *A Place in the World*, Milton Keynes: Open University Press.

Hornby, Nick (1995), *High Fidelity*, London: Victor Gollancz Ltd.

Huyssen, Andreas (2003), *Present Pasts: Urban Palimpsests and the Politics of Memory*, Palo Alto: Stanford University Press.

Ingold, Tim (2007), *Lines: A Brief History*, London: Routledge.

Krause, Elizabeth L. (2005), 'Encounters with the "Peasant": Memory Work, Masculinity, and Low Fertility in Italy', *American Ethnologist*, 32:4, pp. 593–617.

Litzinger, Ralph, A. (1998), 'Memory Work: Reconstituting the Ethnic in Post-Mao China', *Cultural Anthropology*, 13:2, pp. 224–255.

Lynch, Kevin (1960), *The Image of the City*, Cambridge: MIT Press.

Nora, Pierre (1989), *Realms of Memory: Conflict and Division*, New York: Columbia University Press.

Roberts, Les and Sara Cohen (2013), 'Unauthorizing Popular Music Heritage: Outline of a Critical Framework', *International Journal of Heritage Studies*, 20:3, pp. 1–21.

Smith, Laurajayne (2006), *Uses of Heritage*, Abingdon, Oxon: Routledge.

Street, John (2004), 'This is Your Woodstock: Popular Memories and Political Myths', in Andy Bennett (ed.), *Remembering Woodstock*, Guildford: Ashgate, pp. 29–42.

Tuan, Yi Fu (1975), 'Images and Mental Maps', *Annals of the Association of American Geographers*, 65, pp. 205–213.

Turner, Graeme (2003), 'Foreword', in Shane Homan, *The Mayor's A Square: Live Music and Law and Order in Sydney*, Newtown: Local Consumption Publications, pp. vii–ix.

Van Dijck, José (2006), 'Record and Hold: Popular Music between Personal and Collective Memory', *Critical Studies in Media Communication*, 23:5, pp. 357–374.

——— (2007), *Mediated Memories in the Digital Age*, Stanford: Stanford University Press.

Notes

1 A reference to Jarvis Cocker's music programme on the BBC radio channel 6 Music.

2 I have preserved the original wording of written text provided by this and subsequent informants and have not edited or reworded it in any way.

3 All quotations are presented verbatim, following the often ungrammatical conventions formed in digital cultures.

4 See also Cohen (2014).

Chapter 7

Serbia's Exit and Guča Trumpet Festivals as Micro-National Spaces:
Between Nation Building and Nation Branding

Jelena Gligorijević

The Exit and Guča trumpet festivals are two major music festivals in post-Milošević Serbia and they differ significantly from one another in terms of their conceptualization and music-stylistic output. Exit festival is a pro-western popular music event founded in 2000 in Novi Sad, the second largest city in northern Serbia, as a lengthy youth protest against the Milošević regime. Since then, it has evolved into the most highly acclaimed international rock music spectacle in south-eastern Europe. The Guča trumpet festival was established in 1961 in the village of Guča in the Dragačevo region of central Serbia with the aim of reviving the vanishing Serbian brass band tradition. Hence, its main focus and appeal reside in the brass band competition part of the programme, which includes a range of awards with the First Trumpet, First Band and Golden Trumpet being the most prestigious ones. Nowadays, the festival in Guča draws up to 600,000 visitors every year, and from 2010 onward, when the category of international competition was introduced into the festival programme, organizers immodestly called it 'the trumpet capital of the world' (Tadić et al. 2010).

Differing fundamentally in their musico-ideological content and aesthetic execution, the Exit and Guča trumpet festivals have been constructed in domestic academic,[1] media and vernacular discourses as representatives of two diametrically opposed evaluative orientations (embodied in the widely exploited concept of 'two Serbias') and, thus, two dominant cultural models at work in post-socialist Serbian society: namely, a pro-western and a populist. This gives us solid ground to think of these two festivals as relevant and legitimate sites for ongoing Serbian national identity imaginings and negotiations. Moreover, in this chapter I intend to explore and develop the idea of contemporary music festivals as micro-national spaces by using the Exit and Guča trumpet festivals as case studies.

To outline such concept, I largely draw on Lefebvre's (1974/2009) unitary theory on the production of (social) space and its post-Marxist, semiological and psychoanalytic underpinnings. More specifically, Lefebvre's theorizing on space allows for a context-sensitive and multi-layered analysis of ongoing Serbian national identity narratives in light of 'the multiplicity of spaces' that the Exit and Guča trumpet festivals instantiate. To begin with, both festivals should be defined in terms of a 'consumed space', which functions as a counterpoint to a production-based space and reflects people's nostalgic search 'for a certain "quality of space"', incorporating such elements as sun, snow, sea, antiquity, eternity, festivity, etc. (p. 353). The consumption of festival space is not univocal in its meaning, however, insofar as such space displays the potential of being transformed into a 'counter-space' by means of 'diversion' (i.e., by having the original space's function put to an alternative use); or a 'utopian space' by means of domination of the symbolic and the imaginary (i.e. by having the original space appropriated by the work of symbols); or an 'organic space' by 'looking upon itself and presenting itself as a body' (p. 274); or a 'masculine space' by means of demonstration of phallic power and so on.

In addition, my use of the term 'micro-national' is driven by two factors. The first is to emphasize awareness that the field of (Serbian) national identity and music is much larger and more diverse than the musical cultures promoted at the Exit and Guča trumpet festivals could ever entail. If we are to differentiate between 'ethnic, civic and economic constructs of nationality' (O'Flynn 2007:23), then it seems self-evident that the festivals' musical offerings comprise only a small proportion of the Serbian traditional/folk (i.e. ethnic) and popular (i.e. economic) musics, let alone the totality of the national music field. The other advantage of the concept of the 'micro-national' lies in both festivals' self-proclamation of 'statehood'; that is, in their self-promotion as two apparently autonomous spatial entities, operating as symbolic states in their own right during the festival days within (or despite?) the actual (Serbian) state's borders.

Indeed, the 'State of Exit' was born at Novi Sad's Petrovaradin fortress as a result of the marketing campaign for the festival production in 2003. The campaign's aim was to depict Exit festival as 'a meta-state' of all people of good will and vast optimism; as a zone of freedom, love, harmony, tolerance and peace, whose founders and supporters were determined to put up fierce resistance to visa restrictions, drug abuse and the society's various instances of corruption, violence and intolerance (Gruhonjić 2003). That the idea of the State of Exit has, however, gone well beyond the commercial scope of one short-lived advertising campaign can be illustrated by the way in which Miloš Ignjatović, a festival co-founder, reflects on the Exit festival in hindsight: 'Every festival [production] was a campaign. Exit […] is more than a festival, not only for us, for all visitors, because it's a statement, it's a state of mind, *it's the State of Exit actually*' (*The States of Exit* 2012, emphasis mine).

By the same token, the term 'Trumpet Republic' has been circulating for quite some time, chiefly to designate the region to which Guča belongs, as Nikola Stojić, a co-founder of the Guča trumpet festival, confirmed in a speech at the 42nd festival press conference. Speaking in the capacity of a Guča's Culture House president at the time, Stojić stated: 'These days you are in a special republic – during the festival, Dragačevo [region] becomes the Trumpet Republic' (*Trumpets' Republic* 2006).

To conclude then, both State of Exit and Trumpet Republic share similar aspirations to all instances of micro-nationalism that 'behave in a fashion deliberately imitative of a "true" state – they have governments, citizens, laws, territorial "claims", etc.' (Rasmussen n.d.). On top of this, both mini-states have launched their respective flags and emblems, along with the anthem *Sa Ovčara i Kablara/From Ovčar and Kablar Mountains* in the case of the latter festival.

Another conceptual frame of reference, which is central to this chapter and explains to a considerable extent the antagonistic relationship between the Exit and Guča trumpet festivals in Serbian public discourses, is that of 'Balkanism'. Balkanism is a relatively young and still not fully recognized academic field in its own right that differs from Orientalism (as a system of representations of the Orient) in at least two respects. For one thing, the specific geo-political position and socio-historical development of the Balkans, above all its exclusion from the European colonization project (unless such colonization is understood in metaphorical terms[2]), makes it incommensurate with what has been understood as the Orient's history and culture. Second, the Balkans bear no traces of the former grandiose eastern civilizations that could serve as a counterbalance and a redeeming antidote to the hegemony of western discourses (see, for instance, Bakić-Hayeden and Hayeden 1992; Todorova 1997; Fleming 2000). Either way, I would like to argue that the Balkan version of Orientalism in all its manifestations, oscillating between strategies of 'self-colonization' and 'self-exoticization' (Kiossev 2002 and Volčić 2005, cited in Kaneva 2012:7), plays a crucial role in what Naumović (2009) calls a 'political construction of [Serbian] quasi-ethnic identity split', whose two poles might be represented as well through the Exit/Guča dichotomy. Hence, special importance will be assigned to the West/East split and all familiar binaries stemming from it (e.g. Europe/the Balkans, modern/traditional, urban/rural, etc.) in the discussion on Serbian national identity and music that follows.

It is also equally urgent to address nation-branding discourses, which have begun to invade Serbian public space from 2006. This conceptual change in the understanding of the nation as brand has opened up another vista for alternative interpretations of the music festivals in question and their role in ongoing national identity narratives. More specifically, the festivals' gradual integration into the transnational music industry and cultural tourism market, respectively, as well as the moderate consolidation of Serbia's political scene through the disintegration and marginalization of the most hard-core nationalist political parties (especially from 2008), contributed to a more unified view of the Exit and Guča trumpet festivals as national brands having much in common, above all promoting a positive image of the country. Despite all the criticism that the nation-branding rationale, strategies and outcomes invite, this 'discursive formation' has in the case of Serbia's two major music festivals afforded a joint ideological platform from which to cast a new light on issues of national identity representation. Nation-branding talk may, indeed, serve as a springboard for the analysis of both festivals' transnational implications and internal controversies in turn.

The ultimate goal of this chapter is thus to show, following Lazić (2003), that both Serbian music festivals (particularly the trumpet one in Guča) are not only marked by the West/East split from within, but by a range of other conflictual arenas as well. I argue that exploring the liminal status of the Balkans/Serbia (see Fleming 2000; Živković 2001) through these two festivals might yield particularly fruitful results when it comes to understanding the very concept of national identity, marking a shift from a somewhat fixed, essentialized, romanticized and inward-projected notion of nation building, towards a more fluid, dynamic, pluralistic and outward-projected idea of national identifications (see Hall 1996).

To keep in line with all above-cited objectives, the chapter is divided into two sections. In the first, I explore in broad strokes dichotomies surrounding the Exit and Guča trumpet festivals presented in their most extreme forms. Of interest in the second section is the liminal status of both festivals, which I consider with respect to the musical component of their programming as well as some details of their promotion and self-perception, respectively.

The following inquiry is largely grounded in the broadly understood methodology of Foucauldian discourse analysis or 'critical reading' within the framework of post-Marxist cultural studies (Burr 2004; Storey 2012). Using the above methods, I conduct the analysis with reference to sources such as the festival(-related) fieldnotes, collected and produced over the years 2012 and 2013, and a small number of publications and documentary movies, as well as various media shows, reports and online forums on the music festivals in question.

Exit versus Guča: Counter-space versus organic space

As mentioned earlier, the Exit and Guča trumpet festivals can be understood as symptoms of the apparent split between two value systems (i.e. 'two Serbias') and therefore two dominant cultural models in Serbian society. To designate these two main evaluative orientations in recent Serbian cultural memory, Kuljić (2006:220) introduces the terms 'antifascism' and 'Hilandar' (a Serbian Orthodox monastery in Greece). In his words, 'Antifascism is a mark of rationalism, multiculturalism, brotherhood and unity, left[ist] position and anticonservatism. Hilandar is a mark of religion and national exclusivity and conservatism and the right[-wing] values'.

Clearly, Kuljić's interpretation fits neatly into the Orientalist model of the West/East split and a potentially endless list of binary oppositions associated with it. When applied to the Exit and Guča trumpet festivals, all such dichotomies point towards a clear demarcation line between the festivals' respective meanings and representations, situating them as extremes in a continuum (see Table 1).

Table 1: Binary oppositions surrounding the Exit and Guča trumpet festivals along the West/East split.

Exit festival	Guča trumpet festival
West	East
Europe	The Balkans
Modern	Traditional
Urban	Rural
Progressive	Conservative
Rock culture	Neo-folk culture
North	South
Austro-Hungarian heritage	Ottoman heritage
Antifascism	Hilandar

Translated into the Lefebvrian terminology of space production, the opposition between two Serbian music festivals can be considered on another level as distinguishing between a counter-space and an organically projected space. How this opposition works in each festival's micro-national universe I examine in turn in the analysis that follows.

Exit festival: A micro-national counter-space

In this section, I draw on Lefebvre's (1974/2009:349) concept of 'counter-space' to describe Exit festival as a micro-national space appropriated by a particular social group and put to a different use – one that offers a utopian alternative to the actual spatial/social reality. Such a 'diversion' of the 'real' space was especially evident in the founding year of the festival (2000), when it took on a prophetic role in the establishment of a new, post-Milošević democratic system, marking the very beginning of Serbia's second wave of transition. This was accomplished by means of at least two interrelated symbolic spheres: 'noise', embodied largely in rock music, and 'unbounded' space, located in the green area of the city's student campus adjacent to the Danube river bank; a space with no fences, walls or any sort of barriers, including financial ones (the event was free of charge). In short, a space re-appropriated by, and initially intended for, the local student population but open as well for up to 100 days of performative 'noise' to all youthful, like-minded, anti-Milošević-regime-oriented people. These two symbolic realms were underlined in addition by the festival's very name: 'Exit – Noise Summer Fest', and its initial idea to motivate young people to move from apathy to active participation in the upcoming general elections.

In the subsequent years, Exit festival officially 'continues to play an important role in the promotion of liberal values as well as in the determined fight against all sorts of xenophobia, primitivism and nationalism' (Kleut 2002). This time, however, such endeavours are pursued from within the system – or, to put it differently, carried out with the help of authorities across all levels of power (from municipality to state). This change was accompanied by the relocation of the festival in 2001 from the 'floating' space of the student campus area to the city's most prestigious and enclosed space of the Petrovaradin fortress. Although coded as a masculine space by definition, the fortress has lost some of its military associations by attaining the status of a historical monument as recently as the mid-twentieth century. The pacification of the fortress has also been effected through the appropriation of its originally military function for archival, artistic, scientific, educational, cultural and touristic purposes – not to mention the overall makeover of the fortress during Exit festival days with its 'wonderland' effects (interview with an American festival visitor, July 2012). By the same token, the trenches within which a majority of the festival's music stages are installed come to be experienced as something resembling a sonic womb.

Another reason for recognizing Exit festival as a counter-micro-national-space lies in its status as representative of a counter-culture proclaimed and believed in by the event's co-founders and organizers (*The States of Exit* 2012). According to them, the festival's major mission is not only to economically and culturally animate Serbian society, with a special focus on the local youth population, but also to 'civilize' it in its entirety. The task of 'civilizing' the nation is understood here very broadly, encompassing a variety of activities such as 'urbanizing', 'modernizing', 'institutionalizing', 'educating', 'individualizing', 'normalizing', etc., Serbian society. And such goals are to be achieved in synergy with quite a number of the companies that have over time sprouted from Exit festival as a result of the gradual growth, professionalization and diversification of activities in Serbia's initially niche market for event/creative industries.

Paradoxically, the festival's counter-space is discursively constructed as 'hard-core underground' (Pančić cited in Pintarić 2005:22) and, at the same time, as a symbol of normality. For a certain proportion of Serbian public, as the viewpoint of the RTV B92 general director Veran Matić confirms (*Exit News* 2002), Exit festival has, indeed, come to represent 'the strongest symbol of a return of normal life to this [Balkan] region'. By implication, the dominant cultural model (i.e. the norm) is deemed 'rotten' at its core and, therefore, in dire need of 'normalization' that the festival not only epitomizes but also restores in the long run. What once again crops up from these intertwined discourses of counter-culture and normality surrounding the festival are the ideological implications of the West/East split where the notion of normality is uncritically equated with the West/Europe as a utopian promise of a new paradise. Clearly, the equation of normal and civilized life with the West/Europe presumes that everything associated with Serbia and, more broadly, with the Balkans, comes across as abnormal, uncivilized, destructive and with no positive values to speak of.

The Guča trumpet festival: An organic micro-national space

According to Lefebvre (1974/2009), the idea of 'an organic space' is typically exploited by the societies that feel threatened and insecure about their own identity. As a result, representatives of such societies tend to explain themselves in physiological terms, by means of analogies with nature and the body. As Lefebvre clarifies further, 'The ideological appeal to the organism is by extension an appeal to a unity, and beyond that unity [...] to an *origin* deemed to be known with absolute certainty, identified beyond any possible doubt – an origin that legitimates and justifies' (pp. 274–275).

Likewise, the Guča trumpet festival should be understood and defined as an organic micro-national space, whose symbols of 'organic' nationhood project outwards the image of the nation as a static, invariable, ancient (if not eternal) entity with a basis in blood kinship and an ethnically 'pure' core. Or put into the language of physical analogies, such a concept of nation generates the image of an 'organism' whose head (i.e. the national elites), soul (i.e. the church), and body (i.e. the people) operate under conditions of perfect equality, unity and harmony. Let me illustrate now in more detail how each component of this organic unity functions in turn within the context of the festival's micro-national space.

The Guča trumpet festival has traditionally been 'home' to the representatives of Serbian political, economic and cultural elites from both ends of the political spectrum. Yet, the fact that the festival organizers and most dedicated supporters (among politicians, intellectuals, artists) are predominantly members of the right-wing, populist structures must not be overlooked. It goes without saying that the concept of organic nation, as Milosavljević (2002:38) notes, generates a belief that there are 'the ideologies (and the systems of governing) which are closer than others to a people's "spirit"' – namely, those taking on the form of '"authentic" governing regime, composed of people, church and elite, organised within the "natural" patriarchal order'. Indeed, both visual appearance and rhetoric of the authorities involved in the festival realization intend to 'naturalize' their relationship with the people by 'present[ing] themselves as folk culture devotees, people who are *of the people and with the people*' (Lukić-Krstanović 2011:276).

Orthodox Christianity in general and the Serbian Orthodox Church (SOC) in particular embody the next pillar within the organic nation's 'elite-church-people' trinity. Representing an important marker of Serbian national identification, the SOC and Orthodoxy came to exert a growing influence in Serbian society after the collapse of Yugoslavia. Their actual and symbolic presence can be traced to the space of the Guča trumpet festival as well. For instance, the very opening of the 40th festival anniversary featured the commemoration of 2000 years since the founding of Christianity. Likewise, from 2000 on, concerts of Serbian sacral music and exhibitions inspired by religious motives have regularly formed part of the festival programming. The high status of the SOC can be witnessed as well in its power to impinge on the festival timeframe as the former coincided with the fasting period (since 2002). Also, the festival ceremonial programme frequently involves the presence of SOC representatives, some of whom would deliver dirges or blessings dedicated to the persons and events of great importance to the national history or the festival itself (see Bojanić 2002; Timotijević 2005; Tadić et al. 2010).

In fact, Serbian Orthodoxy, including the system of theological ideas and the various elements of Orthodox culture associated with it, is considered one of three instances of the vernacularly understood notion of tradition. The other two correlate to the systems of representations arising from the fields of Serbian national history and Serbian folk peasant tradition, respectively (Naumović 2009:134). Unsurprisingly, all three components of Serbian tradition have been successfully integrated into the very ideological agenda of the Guča trumpet festival. Its overall conception rests, indeed, on the values, ideology and aesthetics of the Serbian peasant-warrior.

On the one hand, the Serbian trumpet practice continues to serve as a stage for the inscription and projection of many historico-mythological narratives of the nation and the 'exclusive pseudo-characters' ascribed to it, such as victimization, heroism and freedom fighting (cf. Milosavljević 2002:131–155). Clearly, the trumpet's status as a symbol of Serbia's numerous 'liberation' wars (pursued from the nineteenth century until the end of the Second World War) emanates from its military origins. It does not come as a surprise then that the festival opening rituals evoke strong military connotations, albeit combined with ceremonial procedures inherited from socialist times (cf. Lukić-Krstanović 2006:190). Nor is it surprising that the official festival programme includes the museum exhibitions in which the Serbian 'glorious' war-waging past can come to the fore (covering, for instance, topics from the First and Second Serbian Uprisings, the Goračić Upheaval or the Second World War).

On the other hand, there are narratives surrounding the Guča trumpet festival that place more emphasis on the integration of Serbian trumpet practice with the people's everyday life (see, for instance, Guča Culture House 2007:24–25; *Trumpets' Republic* 2006). In fact, the festival's rural origins, setting and iconography all work together to evoke and essentialize a sense of the people's aura. Given that the peasantry used to constitute 'the most numerous and autochthonous portion of Serbian society', as Naumović (2009:88–89) notes, symbolic linkage between rurality and the nation (i.e. 'the People's will/voice') is made to seem natural. He further points out that the great symbolic power of peasantry is, in general, typical of the societies lagging behind in modernization – hence its heavy exploitation at the Guča trumpet festival as a source of legitimacy for those in power. No wonder that more than once it has been stated that those who do not understand the festival do not understand Serbia either. Nor are descriptions of the festival as the 'heart', 'soul', 'spirit', 'essence' and similar incarnations of the Serbian folk, unexpected.

Among different traditional forms of cultural expression, Serbian folk music in general and the Serbian brass band tradition in particular hold a prominent place in the ongoing debates on articulations of Serbian national identity. Relevant here are two crucial interpretations of the brass band music's status as an authentic Serbian musical tradition. On the one hand, Lajić Mihajlović and Zakić (2012:227) argue that there is its actual continuity as a traditional musical practice dating back to the first half of the twentieth century. On the other, Lukić-Krstanović (2006:189, 191) takes the Guča trumpet festival itself as the most certain factor behind the installation of this musical practice. This, by extension, means that Serbian brass band music can be interpreted as an 'invented tradition' given that the question of its genesis remains vague and unresolved. Either way, within the scope of the festival-related 'organic' nationalist discourse, not only is this musical tradition regarded as an incarnation of the Serbian people's 'soul', but a claim over its authenticity figures as well as a guarantee of 'the salvation of the folk's soul' (cf. Naumović 2009:111). The authenticity issue of Serbian brass band music is therefore always raised whenever 'foreign' or 'external' musical elements and influences have been acknowledged as 'contaminating' traditional (trumpet) music. In all such instances, the idea of what Regev (2007:126) calls 'aesthetic cosmopolitanism and cultural (ethno-national) uniqueness' is clearly understood through the lenses 'of early to high modernity, when the invention of national traditions and imagining of nations were characterized by a quest for essentialism and purism'.

Exit and Guča: Micro-national spaces of liminality

The exploration of the Exit and Guča trumpet festivals as 'consumed spaces' in the era of 'neoliberal corpo-nationalism' (Surowiec 2012:140) will be excluded from the analytic purview of this chapter for reasons of the limited objectives it can accomplish within these pages. It is, however, necessary to acknowledge that a social change involved in Serbia's politico-economic transition has undoubtedly left its mark on the 'discourses about space and about things and people in space' (Lefebvre 1974/2009:281). Nation-branding talk plays a significant part in this discursive shift, and its effects have already been critically assessed in the cases of two Serbian music festivals (Mijatović 2012:213–235). However, it is not my intention to consider here the processes of spectacularization, commercialization and corporationalization that both festivals have undergone and that have surfaced in public discussion domestically thanks to the festivals' joint-status as Serbia's two leading national brands in culture and tourism. I would rather focus on those effects of nation-branding talk that have allowed for moving beyond the West/East split in the perception of these two festivals vis-à-vis the question of national identity articulation. More specifically, I approach the analysis of both festivals as micro-national spaces of liminality that are not only marked by the West/East divide from within, but by many other internal tensions as well.

One way to look at the in-between status of post-Milošević Serbian society is to tackle some of Serbia's ethnic (self-)stereotypes and the ways in which they have been embedded into various accounts of the Exit and Guča trumpet festivals. Following Živković's (2001) categorization of possible responses to stigma in Serbian society, I would like to argue that the strategies involved in both festivals' self-representation along national lines are characterized by strong ambivalence.

To begin with, Exit festival is discursively constructed as a micro-national counter-space, using a pro-western cultural model (called 'counter-culture' by the festival organizers) as a means of urbanization and modernization of Serbian society. Such an approach is a clear-cut example of internalization of western dichotomies and values, which, by extension, leads to the evaluation of one's own group and other society members through the lenses of the accepted stigma (see Živković 2001:105). Then again, Exit festival introduces at the same time into its organizational activities and self-narrativizing strategies selected elements of Serbia's ethnic (self-)stereotypes, such as those of hospitality and victimization, which are by definition evocative of imaginings of the Balkans/East.

One of the most widespread (self-)stereotypes about Serbs is, indeed, that of 'hospitality', portraying the nation as generally warm, kind, sociable, generous and welcoming. The institution of the Serbian host, be it related to family, nation or any other type of social groupings, forms a part of such (self-)stereotyping and is symptomatic of the society's deeply patriarchal origins. Within Exit's organizational structure, the 'hosting team' has been introduced to take care of the festival performers and visitors' needs during their entire stay in Serbia. To paraphrase Dušan Kovačević (Buha Milović 2008), one of the festival founders and general managers, such an approach has been described by the festival guests as something unique that can be experienced nowhere in the West, and it has developed into a distinguished Exit-related brand in its own right.

By the same token, the story about Exit in the narratives of those who have been in charge of its development deploys as well the recurrent Serbian self-stereotype of victimization. The latter implies that Serbia's century-old tragic destiny, which continues to be imperilled by other nations' attempt at suppression, is precisely what has made Serbs exceptional (see Milosavljević 2002:132–138). Considering Exit festival's critical approach and strong opposition to Serbia's recent warmongering past as well as to its nationalist and xenophobic sentiments enduring to the present day, such a self-stereotype reveals itself in the festival's self-narration through the characterization of toughness that comes along with the collective experience of adversity and oppression.[3] Given that the group in question feels anyway hard done-by for one reason or another, I understand any such expression of toughness as part of the victimization (self-)stereotype or, in this particular case, what Živković (2001:86) calls a 'Turkish stake' (a reference to impalement as a brutal form of execution performed by Ottomans) to designate the victim's 'claims over the wisdom originating from the[ir] agony and moral superiority'. Indeed, the implication of the 'Turkish stake' mode of ethnic self-characterization can be especially grasped in the following statement by Rajko Božić, an Exit strategic PR manager and State of Exit Foundation's board president:

> I'm quite sure that somebody facing difficulties on this scale in the Netherlands, in the UK, the US, or in Sweden, for that matter, would abandon this festival after four years, and we're still doing it. Probably these unrealistic expectations to make your dream here and now, it's a result of the war years we lived.
>
> (*The States of Exit* 2012)

The narratives surrounding the Guča trumpet festival are likewise infused with the same type of ethnic (self-)stereotypes but articulated within the horizon of nationalist discourse. More specifically, the Serbian self-stereotype of victimization is exercised in the festival's self-narration as part of the nationalist rhetorical arsenal to glorify the national history and culture. The original patriarchal sentiment and a sense of collectivity are preserved as well in the role of the festival 'host', which was added to the list of festival rituals back in 1995. In contrast to Exit, the hosting role is assigned here to (male) representatives of the (inter) national elite chosen to welcome the festival visitors at the very opening of the event and/or at the finals of the brass band competition. Within the perspective of an organically projected micro-national space, the role of host performed at the festival seems to replicate well the relationship between the nation state as 'home' and the national elite as 'host' (cf. Milosavljević 2002:37), reinforcing the view of the Guča trumpet festival as a state (i.e. the Trumpet Republic) in its own right. Predictably, the honour of the festival hosts was given from 2004 through to 2011 to the leading political figures from the conservative nationalist parties. In doing so, the festival organizers clearly show no intention of giving up their strong political ties with influential Serbian politicians (and, thus, their own particular interests); nor do they appear willing to change the festival's populist agenda and rhetoric. In consequence, the ethnic (self-)stereotype of Serbian hospitality fails to go beyond the limited scope of its traditionally conservative and male-dominated implications.

Discourses on the Guča trumpet festival incorporate and feature some other ethnic (self-)stereotypes coded as Balkan/eastern, too. This is most vividly articulated through the construct of 'madness' emerging from both *emic* and *etic* media representations of the festival (Gligorijević 2012:10). Here, the local response to stigma and negative stereotyping undergoes an inversion process and becomes re-interpreted in an affirmative way, depicting the demonized Balkan characteristics as somehow more authentic, real and vital than those that are associated with the western world.

Yet, this strategy of positive 'self-exoticization', as Živković (2001:105) calls it, is not exercised without ambivalence. Various reports on the Guča trumpet festival show that many different occurrences of the internalized western gaze and valorization practices are put into effect as well. This is, on the one hand, performed through the so-called 'aesthetics of distancing' by those festival visitors who are able to recognize positive values in the Balkans mainly thanks to the possibility of staying away from its 'dark' reality (Jansen 2001:60–63); or, alternatively, through the process that Čolović (2006) describes as the 'internal exoticisation of the ethno sound', which allows the festival visitors to experience the (post-)traditional sound of their own musical culture as something sonically remote, archaic, marginal – in a word, exotic.

On the other hand, internalization of western views vis-à-vis the Guča trumpet festival can also be detected in an ambivalent stance, which the Serbian population assumes towards the Romany minority and which can be described in terms of a familiar 'mixture of extreme disparaging and romanticising' (Živković 2001:98).[4] As for the former (i.e. the disparaging attitude), it is important to stress that within the Serbian/ex-Yugoslav context, the expression 'Gypsies' has often carried a pejorative meaning, operating 'as a metonymic signifier for everything considered to be a weaker, debased item in dichotomies' (Živković 2001:89). This explains convincingly the popularity of the Serbian public standpoint, whereby Emir Kusturica, a Serbian director whose internationally acclaimed movies have made Serbia's Gypsy brass band music widely known and appreciated, is to be blamed for creating abroad a misleading image of Serbs as Gypsies (cf. Jansen 2001:54). What is revealed here is, of course, a scornful attitude towards Romanies, whose status as Other in Serbian society (and beyond) can also be recognized in the ever-present polarization and tension going on between the festival's 'white' (i.e. Serbian) and 'black' (i.e. Romany) competing brass bands. Despite the festival's official politics of multiculturalism and inclusivism, the evidence of discrimination against 'black' bands has already been documented on several occasions (see, for instance, Lukić-Krstanović 2006; Arsenijević 2012; Lajić Mihajlović and Zakić 2012). According to Goffman (1963:107, cited in Živković 2001:99), this is the mechanism by means of which one social group (i.e. Serbs) renders itself 'normal'/'ordinary' and, thus, superior when compared to those (i.e. Romanies) whose stigmatized status and 'extraordinariness' are displayed even more dramatically.

For a brief analysis of the Exit and Guča festivals' musical programme within the perspective of micro-national spaces of liminality, I will address some of their internal tensions by deploying once again Regev's (2007, 2011) theory of aesthetic cosmopolitanism and cultural uniqueness. In his own words:

> Aesthetic cosmopolitanism is the contemporary cultural condition in which the representation and performance of national uniqueness is largely based on art forms and stylistic elements deliberately drawn from sources exterior to indigenous traditions.
>
> (Regev 2011:110)

Here it is also important to call attention to the dividing line Regev (2011:110–111) draws between 'inadvertent' or 'banal cosmopolitanism' as a widespread and unintentional consumption of those standardized cultural products amalgamating local expressive forms and elements with transnational stylistic trends and technologies; and 'advertent' or 'reflexive cosmopolitanism' that consciously seeks to replicate, incorporate and build on the latest transgressive forms of transnational culture within the specific local, ethnic and national contexts. Regev's theoretical model can, indeed, explain well the enduring tensions inherent to any one domain of human activity, including those in the cultural field articulated through all-too-familiar 'high/low', 'art/commerce', 'underground/mainstream' binaries; and so it does with respect to the tensions displayed at the level of the official music programming at both Serbian festivals.

On the one hand, the Guča trumpet festival is characterized by the tension between a competition and a manifestation part of the programming,[5] in particular between competing domestic brass bands and (inter)national neo-folk/WM stars, where the latter are accused of not only financially profiting at the expense of the former, but also of compromising the original idea(l)s and authentic values of the festival. Exit festival's musical programme is, on the other hand, split between pleasing the cultural needs of a wider audience (as most evident in some highly commercial and popular DJ sets featured at the festival's Radio AS FM Stage or Dance Arena), and meeting the expectations of the festival crowd with a more specialist and/or innovation-oriented taste (as exemplified in the underground-flavoured and experimental agenda of the festival's HappyNoviSad Stage or Suba Stage).

Nonetheless, Regev's theory of aesthetic cosmopolitanism and cultural uniqueness fails to accommodate some other occurrences that are also taking place at these two Serbian music festivals. In the case of Guča, it does not seem to be nuanced enough to recognize a distinction between the musicians who are perceived as genuine (authentic) representatives of traditional (brass band) music and those who are said to capitalize on its elite appropriations. A good case in point for the latter is a well-established love-hate relationship of the domestic population to the Bosnian Serbo-Croat, Goran Bregović, as a globally recognized soundtrack and World Music artist. Namely, some appreciate his international achievements and his capacity to make Balkan music famous, whereas others openly accuse him of music plagiarism.

The case of Exit festival shows in addition that the artistic contribution of peripheral countries such as Serbia to the transnational contemporary music culture does not necessarily have to adhere to the idea(l) of 'ethno-national difference' in order to be acknowledged in the global cultural arena – although this is, admittedly, a desired and well-expected route to follow. Such a contribution can also be made along the lines of affinities, or what Slobin (1993:68) calls 'affinity interculture', which implies a cooperation and exchange of musicians and musical experiences across national borders on the grounds of shared musical sensibilities and within the scope of transnational contemporary musical idioms. The partnership between the British festival Bestival and Exit, established in 2012 within the Association of Independent Festivals' initiative called 'Twin Festivals', could serve here as a relevant illustration. The aim of this partnership is to enhance cultural cooperation between the two festivals through exchange of their respective festival experiences, general ideas, musicians and even audience members (*Exitfest.org* 2012).

Conclusion

This chapter has sought to show that the analysis of two major Serbian music festivals, Exit and Guča, as micro-national spaces might be a helpful way of understanding the ways in which the national identity has been articulated in post-Milošević Serbia. The outcomes of such an analysis confirm that the West/East split continues to underline much of the public debate surrounding the two festivals, where the notion of the West, and all values associated with it, comes into being through Exit festival's 'counter-space' and constitutes itself in the opposition to the Guča festival's 'organic space' as an epitome of the East. However, the proclamation of both festivals by the domestic political and, partly, cultural elites as Serbia's two leading and unique national brands in culture and tourism has bridged a glaring gap between them by foregrounding the festivals' recently formulated joint-agenda – their survival on the market in times of what Surowiec (2012) calls 'corpo-nationalism'. Although not addressed in this chapter in detail, the shift of public focus away from the discussion instilled by the West/East split towards the festivals' transnational, corporate and marketing aspects has somewhat given way to the public construction of Exit and Guča as 'consumed spaces' within which the nation is imagined as a brand. Instead of looking critically at nation-branding talk pertaining to the festivals, which is undoubtedly much needed, this matter has been approached as both festivals' middle ground from which to question their internal controversies. The analysis of certain aspects of the festivals' marketing and programming strategies has, indeed, tended to confirm Lazić's (2003) findings valid – namely, that Serbian society dwells somewhere in between the two poles of the West/East split.

In the case of Guča, this can be convincingly illustrated with reference to Boym's (2001, cited in Buchanan 2010:129) two-part notion of 'reflexive' and 'restorative nostalgia' developed in her study on the power of remembrance in post-communist Eastern European identity construction. A key difference between these two types of nostalgia lies in the drives behind each. The former is fascinated with the idea of distance, be it temporal or geographical, and therefore with sentimental explorations of the past as a vast field of possibility for one's imaginings in the present times. The latter is, in contrast, largely occupied with the projects of national past and identity revisions that revolve around 'an ahistorical discourse of origins, authenticity, truth, tradition, and ethnic and cultural purity' (Buchanan 2010:129). Indeed, the chronicled projections of restorative nostalgia onto the Guča trumpet festival's space coincide well with the re-discovery process of 'ethnicity' in culture within Serbia's post-socialist context. This is most clearly revealed in the anxious narratives generated around the issues of the Serbian brass band tradition's origins, authenticity, homogenization and commodification.

Conversely, the instances of reflexive nostalgia can be traced in those narratives on the Guča trumpet festival that celebrate the ideas of intercultural exchange, equality, harmony, tolerance, unity, hybridity and neoliberal multi- and trans-culturalism. Their sources originate from the closely intertwined and celebratory discourses surrounding global World Music (WM) and New Age practices. Both are principally committed to the search for new forms of spirituality and the universal values of humankind, which WM is believed to embody by 'allegedly offering authentic and universally appreciated experiences of the human soul and the world of nature' (Čolović 2006). Another fascination they have in common is the sound of 'exotic' musical cultures – in short, all the properties that Serbia's (post-)traditional brass band music is deemed to have.

In contrast to the Guča trumpet festival, Exit is largely defined through the lenses of internalized western values and dichotomies, and as such is more inclined to fulfil and instantiate the collective and individual reflexive nostalgic needs; in fact, it does so even when promoting domestic WM bands. Not only do the festival organizers openly acknowledge Exit's 'inauthentic' status, as the festival has developed by implementing the transnational model of other massive pro-western popular music festivals across Europe, above all Budapest's Sziget festival, into the local context. They also do not seem to be concerned with any sense of authenticity loss and related questions of origins, cultural purity and/or ethno-national uniqueness. On the contrary, the widely shared image of Exit as a 'copy' is rather seen as a guarantee of its capacity to stay in line with other highly praised, gigantic European music festivals, as well as a great opportunity for more equal participation on the global cultural market within the scope of western standards and sensibilities. The liminality of Exit's micro-national space emerges rather in the tensions arising from the festival's promotional and self-narrativizing strategies – where ethnic (self-)stereotypes are entertained with ambivalence – as well as from contradictory details of its musical programming.[6]

Yet, it is crucial to bear in mind that if analysed solely at the level of the hybrid nature of cultural interaction and production (see, for instance, Lajić Mihajlović and Zakić 2012), the discourses of multi-/trans-culturalism and hybridity might obscure the actual situation on both festivals' ground vis-à-vis the issues of capitalist exploitation, western 'colonization' of the Serbian cultural space, racial/ethnic/gender/sexual discrimination, internal power struggles and so on – which all, admittedly, require further analysis. Then again, in post-Milošević Serbia, burdened by the recent experience of several civil wars, poverty, exclusion, violence, intolerance and total corruption, the cultural expressions of reflexive nostalgia that are put on display within the Exit and Guča trumpet festivals' micro-national spaces would secure at least a move away from the purist and exclusivist ideals of nineteenth-century nation-building projects towards more fluid, flexible and outward-projected models for national identification.

References

Arsenijević, Vladimir (2012), 'Trubačka diskriminacija/Trumpet Discrimination', *Jutarnji list*, 1 September, http://www.jutarnji.hr. Accessed 4 December 2013.

Bakić-Hayeden, Milica and Robert M. Hayeden (1992), 'Orientalist Variations on the Theme "Balkans": Symbolic Geography in Recent Yugoslav Cultural Politics', *Slavic Review*, 51:1, pp. 1–15.

Bojanić, Živko M. (2002), *Guča, svetska prestonica trube/Guča, the Trumpet Capital of the World*, Beograd: Udruženje nezavisnih izdavača knjiga.

Buchanan, Donna A. (2010), 'Sonic Nostalgia: Music, Memory, and Mythology in Bulgaria, 1990-2005', in Maria Todorova and Zsuzsa Gille (eds), *Post-Communist Nostalgia*, New York and Oxford: Berghahn Books, pp. 129–154.

Buha Milović, Dejana (2008), 'Hulahop/Hula-Hoop', an interview with the Exit festival's co-founders Dušan Kovačević and Dorijan Petrić, *B92*, 5 July, http://podcast.b92.net/hulahop. xml. Accessed 25 August 2013.

Burr, Vivien (2004), *Social Constructionism*, 2nd edition, London and New York: Routledge.

Centar za kulturu, sport i turizam opštine Lučani [Guča Culture House] (2007), 'Guča – limena duša Srbije/Guča – The Brass Soul of Serbia', 2nd ed., Beograd: Princip Bonart Pres.

Čolović, Ivan (2006), 'Etnomanija/Ethnomania', *Peščanik*, 30 June, http://pescanik.net/2006/06/etnomanija. Accessed 5 April 2013.

Exitfest.org (2012), 'Exit Festival Announces Twinning with Bestival', 19 April, http://www.exitfest.org/en/news/exit-festival-announces-twinning-bestival. Accessed 3 February 2013.

Fleming, Katherine E. (2000), 'Orientalism, the Balkans, and Balkan Historiography', *American Historical Review*, 105:4, pp. 1218–1233.

Gligorijević, Jelena (2012), 'World Music Festivals and Tourism: A Case Study of Serbia's Guca Trumpet Festival', *International Journal of Cultural Policy*, http://dx.doi.org/10.1080/10286632.2012.743531. Accessed 14 May 2014.

Goldsworthy, Vesna (1998), *Inventing Ruritania: The Imperialism of the Imagination*, New Haven and London: Yale University Press.

Gruhonjić, Dinko (ed.) (2003), *State of Exit: specijalna publikacija EXIT 03: akademski program/ State of Exit: Special Publication EXIT 03: Academic Programme*, Novi Sad.

Hall, Stuart (1996), 'Introduction: Who Needs "Identity"?', in Stuart Hall and Paul Du Gay (eds), *Questions of Cultural Identity*, London: Sage, pp. 1–17.

Jansen, Stef (2001), 'Svakodnevni orijentalizam: doživljaj "Balkana"/"Evrope" u Beogradu i Zagrebu'/'Everyday Orientalism: Experiences of "the Balkans"/"Europe" in Belgrade and Zagreb', *Filozofija i društvo*, 18, pp. 33–71.

Kaneva, Nadia (2012), 'Nation Branding in Post Communist Europe: Identities, Markets, and Democracy', in Nadia Kaneva (ed.), *Branding Post-Communist Nations: Marketizing National Identities in the 'New Europe'*, New York and London: Routledge, pp. 3–22.

Kleut, Jelena (2002), 'Interaktivne diskusije/Interactive Discussions', *Exit News*, 6 July.

Kuljić, Todor (2006), 'The New (Changed) Past as Value Factor of Development', *Sociologija*, 48:3, pp. 219–230.

Lajić Mihajlović, Danka and Mirjana Zakić (2012), 'Dragačevski sabor trubača u Guči: mesto umrežavanja muzičkih kultura/The Dragačevo Assembly of Trumpet Players in Guča: A Meeting Point of Many Musical Cultures', *Zbornik Matice srpske za društvene nauke*, 139, pp. 223–236.

Lazić, Mladen (2003), 'Serbia: A Part of Both the East and the West', *Sociologija*, XLV:3, pp. 193–216.

Lefebvre, Henri (1974/2009), *The Production of Space*, Trans. Donald Nicholson-Smith, Malden and Oxford and Carlton: Blackwell Publishing.

Lukić-Krstanović, Miroslava (2006), 'Politika trubaštva – folklor u prostoru nacionalne moći/ Politics of Trumpethood – Folklore in the Space of National Power', in Zorica Divac (ed.), *Zbornik radova Etnografskog instituta SANU*, 22, pp. 187–205.

——— (2010), *Spektakli XX veka: muzika i moć/Twentieth Century Spectacles: Music and Power*, Beograd: Etnografski institut SANU.

——— (2011), 'Political Folklore on Festival Market: Power of Paradigm and Power of Stage', *Český lid*, 98:3, pp. 261–280.

Mijatović, Branislava (2012), 'The Musical (Re)branding of Serbia: "Serbia Sounds Global", Guča, and Exit', in Nadia Kaneva (ed.), *Branding Post-Communist Nations: Marketizing National Identities in the 'New Europe'*, New York and London: Routledge, pp. 213–235.

Milosavljević, Olivera (2002), *U tradiciji nacionalizma – ili stereotipi srpskih intelektualaca XX veka o 'nama' i 'drugima'/In the Tradition of Nationalism – Or Stereotypes of Serbian Intellectuals about 'Us' and 'Them'*, Ogledi br. 1, Beograd: Helsinški odbor za ljudska prava u Srbiji.

Naumović, Slobodan (2009), *Upotreba tradicije u političkom i javnom životu Srbije na kraju XX i početkom XXI veka/The Instrumentalisation of Tradition in Serbia's Political and Public Life at the Turn of the Twenty-First Century*, Beograd: Institut za filozofiju i društvenu teoriju.

O'Flynn, John (2007), 'National Identity and Music in Transition: Issues of Authenticity in a Global Setting', in Ian Biddle and Vanessa Knights (eds), *Music, National Identity and the Politics of Location: Between the Global and the Local*, Abingdon, Oxon: Ashgate, pp. 19–38.

Pintarić, Drago (ed.) (2005), *Petrovaradin tribe: raziskovanje fenomena Festivala EXIT = istraživanje fenomena Festivala EXIT = reflections on the phenomenon of music Festival EXIT* (conference publication), Ljubljana: KUD Pozitiv.

Rasmussen, Peter Ravn (n.d.), 'What is micronationalism? An introduction' (last updated on 20 July 2001), http://scholiast.org/nations/whatismicronationalism.html. Accessed 8 November 2013.

Regev, Motti (2007), 'Cultural Uniqueness and Aesthetic Cosmopolitanism', *European Journal of Social Theory*, 10:1, pp. 123–138.

——— (2011), 'International Festivals in a Small Country: Rites of Recognition and Cosmopolitanism', in Liana Giorgi et al. (eds), *Festivals and the Cultural Public Sphere*, London and New York: Routledge, pp. 108–123.

Sejdinović, Nedim (2002), 'Povratak u život/Return to Life', *Exit News*, 8 July.

Simić, Marina (2006), 'Exit u Evropu: popularna muzika i politike identiteta u savremenoj Srbiji/ Exit to Europe: Popular Music and Identity Politics in Contemporary Serbia', *Kultura*, 116– 117, pp. 98–122.

Slobin, Mark (1993), *Subcultural Sounds: Micromusics of the West*, Hanover and London: Wesleyan University Press.

Spasić, Ivana and Tamara Petrović (2012), 'Varijante "Treće Srbije"/Variants of "Third Serbia"', *Filozofija i društvo*, XXIII:3, pp. 23–44.

Storey, John (2012), *Cultural Theory and Popular Culture: An Introduction*, 6th edition, London: Pearson.

Surowiec, Pawel (2012), 'Toward Corpo-Nationalism: Poland as a Brand', in Nadia Kaneva (ed.), *Branding Post-Communist Nations: Marketizing National Identities in the 'New Europe'*, New York and London: Routledge, pp. 124–144.

Tadić, Adam et al. (2010), *Guča: pola veka Sabora trubača u Guči (1961-2010)/Guča: Half a Century of the Assembly of Trumpet Players in Guča (1961–2010)*, Guča and Beograd: Centar za kulturu, sport i turizam opštine Lučani 'Dragačevo' and Princip pres.

The States of Exit (2012), [Documentary], Directed by Kevin Boitelle and Sander van Driel, The Netherlands: An 'Opslaan Als' Production, DJBroadcast.

Timotijević, Miloš (2005), *Karneval u Guči: Sabor trubača 1961-2004/Carneval in Guča: The Trumpet Festival 1961–2004*, Čačak: Legenda and Narodni muzej.

Todorova, Maria (1997), *Imagining the Balkans*, New York and Oxford: Oxford University Press.

Trumpets' Republic (2006), [Documentary], Directed by Stefano Missio and Alessandro Gori, Italy: il documentario.

Vuksanović, Divna (2007), 'Kultura i medijske politike u Srbiji: *strabizam* kao simptom muzičkog poretka jedne države/Culture and Media Politics in Serbia: *Strabismo* as a Symptom of State's Musical Order', the scholar forum *Kulturna politika u Srbiji*, Tara, Serbia, 31 August– 1 September, Belgrade: NSPM (New Serbian Political Thought).

Živković, Marko (2001), 'Nešto između: simbolička geografija Srbije/Something in-between: Serbia's Symbolic Geography', *Filozofija i društvo*, 18, pp. 73–110.

Notes

1   For more on the Exit and Guča festivals (albeit rarely ever as a topic in its own right) as symptoms of the ideologically charged polarization of Serbian cultural life and society on the whole, see Simić (2006), Vuksanović (2007), Lukić-Krstanović (2010), Mijatović (2012) and Spasić and Petrović (2012).

2   See Goldsworthy (1998).

3   This is clearly one way to authenticate the group's identity and experience, and is typical of many cultures with a fundamentally underdog mentality (as is the case with Finnish *sisu*, or the working-class ethos of northerners in Britain).

4   In addition, the Serbian attitude towards Romanies is also often fused with the self-deprecating strategies in the national self-narration in which Serbs think of themselves as

Gypsies (Živković 2001:98); or with the self-praising strategies that allow Serbs to perceive themselves as a very tolerant people living in perfect harmony with Gypsies (Jansen 2001:54–55).

5   The former is focused on selected Serbian folk brass bands (within the senior, junior and pioneer categories) that are competing among themselves for a range of awards, whereas the latter is organized around a display of overall national folk production (within music, visual arts, literature, crafts, customs, etc.), as well as several concerts of both national and international brass bands and popular musicians.

6   There is, of course, other evidence for both festivals' liminal status, but it is omitted from the analysis because of the chapter's limited space.

Chapter 8

Here, There and in between: Radio Spaces before the
Second World War

Morten Michelsen

It is not possible to have sound without space. Sound presupposes space in order to unfold, and as a consequence spatial qualities are integral to sound and to the study of sound. Studying mechanically and electro-acoustically relocated sounds (also known as transphonia, see Uimonen 2013:33) is somewhat different from studying live sounds because acousmatic sounds contain the only indications of the spaces in which the sounds unfold. But as space is a prerequisite for sound, sounds will always hold at least some information about their inherent spaces. Through the years radio has offered a wealth of spaces represented in and through sound. Some have been created meticulously by radio producers and sound engineers, others in the minds of listeners. Some spaces have been reproduced as carefully as possible, for example, in order to create the illusion of listening in a concert hall, while others have been created from scratch and do not resemble any spatial experiences known to man, for example, in radio feature experiments. Such aural representations of (more or less) three-dimensional Euclidian spaces as well as verbal commentary have contributed to the huge palette of imaginary spaces brought forth by radio. Radio has contributed to the ongoing production of social spaces as well by becoming an integrated part of most homes in the western world during the decade and a half before the Second World War. Suggestions on how to organize your private and public life came forth from the loudspeakers either directly in instructive programmes for men, women and children or indirectly through the choice of music, the organization of the programme flow and of the staging of sound.

Recently, the concept of staging has become an important tool for the analysis of sound. In his study on the staging of the voice in rock music recordings, Serge Lacasse defines vocal staging as:

> any deliberate practice whose aim is to enhance a vocal sound, alter its timbre, or present it in a given spatial and/or temporal configuration with the help of any mechanical or electrical process, presumably in order to produce some effect on potential or actual listeners.
>
> (Lacasse 2000:4)

Here, I will extend his definition to encompass all sounds that have passed through this practice. In his thesis, Lacasse develops the analytics of this staging in great detail while a more pedagogical model can be found in Michelsen (2012). The concept of staging has been developed on the basis of a stereo signal, but as Peter Doyle (2005) shows it still makes good sense to analyse mono signals with regard to spatial qualities and thus, also recordings of radio broadcasts from between the wars.

In a recent text on music, sound and space, Georgina Born has noticed a specific trait concerning the historical development of the technologies making transphonia possible (telephone, gramophone and radio), namely that they are 'both interiorising, in the domestic provenance of early sound media and the inter-corporeal, prosthetic uses of telephony, and exteriorising, in those media oriented more to engendering collective forms of life and work' (Born 2013:3). The then new technologies made possible a new sensation of privacy and intimacy when, say, the telephone aided the transmission of a speaker's articulatory sounds to the listener's inner ear and at the same time, it became possible to transport music to public places like the factory using gramophone or radio.

Born continues by arguing for three distinct lines in music/sound/space research. The first is concerned with space in (art) music as it appears in a (more or less metaphorical) pitch space. The second springs from multichannel recording studios and is mainly based on the illusory space created by the stereo signal, but also on a wealth of outboard devices like digital delays. By now, research in both traditions is well established. The third one has developed around sound art and electronic music. In this tradition, conceptions of space reach beyond sound as separate objects and investigate the space in which the sound sounds, and to some extent determines the sound. Summing up these three, Born writes that:

> [...] in all three lineages of cognising spatiality in music and sound [...] space is regarded as an element of the creative imagination and as an artefact of musical and artistic practice: space is both *produced* and *transformed*. But only in the third lineage is the ineluctably *social* nature of these processes to the fore; space is conceived as multiple and constellatory, as mediated and mediating.
>
> (Born 2013:20, italics in the original)

In the following, I will draw on all three lineages but with a special interest in how the actual sounds and musics are intertwined with the articulation of related social spaces. The complex nature of space (and place) that Born highlights is important as well: space is never something in itself but always constellatory and multiple (e.g. representations of social and physical spaces intermingle constantly) and it is mediated and mediating (including time, sociality and subjectivity in a great, relational matrix). As a conceptual dyad, space and place are not dichotomously ordered. Instead, it names a continuum from place to space, which might be understood along the lines of trajectories from, say, the more concrete to the more abstract, from the stable to the mobile, from the affective to the non-affective, from what is close by to what is faraway (see Forman 2002:25–31). A precise border between the two cannot be established. It is dependent on the actual analytical projects.

Jody Berland states that 'radio has unique capacities to map our symbolic and social environment' (1990:191), and since its early beginnings radio has contributed to a reordering of place and space. In the following, I will argue for conceiving of radio spaces within a tri-partite structure. First, I will comment upon radio 'hereness', that is, how radio helped redefine the home when it became equipped with loudspeakers and contributed to the re-evaluation of the family by defining age-, gender- and class-specific roles as well as the auditive layout of the home. Second, I will look at radio between here and there, that is, how radio combined places, especially the home and faraway places, by transmissions from dance restaurants or concert halls or reports from public events. Sometimes, the faraway places could be transported into your living room, sometimes the listener could be transported to the faraway place, sometimes the two places melted into abstract spaces. Third is radio 'thereness'. I will discuss how radio structured spaces or maybe even created new ones. 'The Ether' was one popular term for the abstractness of broadcast sound, and radio did create more or less imaginary, 'ethereal' spaces. The national state of 'Denmark' as an imagined community was one, the illusory depth of the sound stage and the bodiless radio voice were two others. While radio places remain fairly concrete and geographically defined, the idea of radio spaces refers to a wide variety of phenomena ranging from the more concrete ordering of objects in Euclidian space over trajectories in space, to purely metaphorical uses.

The following discussion is based on the contents of a recently established Danish radio research infrastructure. This database (www.larm.fm) contains daily programme schedules (text files) from Danish national radio's day one and all surviving radio programmes (sound files) together with detailed annotation tools. I will also draw on old Danish radio magazines and DBC yearbooks together with the many international, radio-historical publications on primarily German, British and North American radio from the last decade and a half.

Radio in private places (radio 'hereness')

The interbellum years marked a new stage in the development of modernity in Europe. Democracy, communism and fascism competed for sovereignty in several countries, while voting rights were bestowed on still larger parts of the populace in others, and the Nordic countries began developing their versions of welfare society. Most intellectuals at the time regarded the cultural development as a bow to mass culture, which was synonymous with Americanization. The human body got a second life, so to speak, as fashion highlighted rather than concealed it and sports and outdoor life became acceptable leisure activities. This became related to questions of sexuality, birth control and abortion, topics that it became possible to debate publicly. What was for many years called modern music (and modern art) broke through, as did different varieties of jazz and US-inspired dance crazes. Records and movies stabilized themselves as the central media for mass entertainment while the new medium of radio soon outdid the others with regard to effectiveness in mass communication by combining the qualities of the phonograph (reproducing sound), the telephone (live transmission of sound) and the wireless telegraph (transmission without cables) with an audience of a hitherto unimagined size.

In Denmark, the parliament chose a radio model that was to become the most accepted in Europe, a state monopoly led by an independent board and controlled by parliament legislation. Statsradiofonien (the Danish Broadcasting Corporation, in the following the DBC) began operating on 1 April 1925. In the following 15 years, radio went from being a technological gadget to being a part of the everyday for most citizens, and it became probably the single most dominating, cultural factor. Contrary to most European broadcasting houses, a musician was appointed manager. Emil Holm was a former opera singer with organizational clout. He held the post from 1925 until his retirement in 1937.

In the 1920s and the 1930s, radios sounded in people's homes, and broadcasting corporations addressed their listeners supposing them to be there. Only very seldom did they sound in cars or on the beaches due to the prohibiting costs of transportable radio sets. Until loudspeakers were introduced in the second part of the 1920s, listening was a 'secret' activity because you needed headphones in order to hear anything. The loudspeakers made listening a potentially shared activity for the whole family, be it voluntary or forced. Together with the headphones, the crystal sets soon became obsolete, and slowly radio moved from being a boy's toy stressing technology and exploration to being a medium for the family as the technology became encased in more or less elaborate wooden cabinets designed as living room furniture.

Radio's development changed fundamentally the auditive space of many homes. Some had previously had a gramophone that contributed to the home acoustic atmosphere, but radio offered a continuous live sound consisting of music and talk – a much more intrusive phenomenon acoustically speaking. Musicologist Vesa Kurkela describes the situation in late 1920s Finland like this:

> [...] the new radioscape [...] brought public sounds to private life and foreign culture into the living rooms of ordinary citizens. The new radioscape was very different from the traditional soundscape of the home with its domestic sounds. Radio brought many new voices to private and everyday life. Many of these sounds were considered unpleasant and irritating.
>
> (Kurkela 2010:72)

The modern medium helped to (re)define the spatial proportions of the home, basically by sounding for shorter or longer periods of time. The sounding radio told about the dimensions and the furnishing of the living room, its furniture, carpets and curtains. Late-Victorian interior decoration muffled the sound and prevented any reflections while modernist homes with harder surfaces and less furniture supported reflections making both sound and room livelier. Also, the radio signal told you how far away you were from the living room because of the muffled sounds penetrating the thin walls between living room, bedroom and kitchen. In many homes, whether working-class two-room apartments or spacious bourgeois detached houses, radios became main nodes thanks to their location as living room centrepieces. Radio sounds may fill the home with a continuous stream of sound and create a unified ambience and a sense of physical and psychological cohesion. Simultaneously, radio sounds may shut out other sounds from the streets, from the backyards or from the people and radio sets in the neighbouring apartments. The continuous sound may create the illusion that you are alone or alone with your family, temporarily shut off from the rest of the world by way of sounds imported into your home – from the rest of the world, although not from your immediate surroundings.

What was to become the basic programme flow can be traced already by 1927 in the daily programme schedules even though it only became (almost) continuous by the early 1930s when the radio day began at 7:00 am with physical training followed by various, intermittent broadcasts for special groups before noon (school children, religious people, farmers). After noon, the continuous sound began with two concert programmes between noon and 4:30 pm followed by half an hour of children's radio. Five to eight pm was information time with lectures, news and similar information services including some music. In what was supposedly prime time from 8 to 10 pm there were hardly any general programme rules. It could contain anything between one and four programmes, for example, concerts, plays, gramophone programmes, lectures or features. Early in the decade, music transmissions could last until 2 o'clock in the morning, while broadcasting closed with news and 45 minutes of dance music transmission before closing at 11 pm in 1939. It is interesting to notice that before the war, news programmes were not used as one of the most important flow structuring devices. Only by 1939 could you count four daily news programmes: around noon and at 6, 7 and 10 pm.

Such schedules made it possible for housewives to concentrate their most bustling work in the morning and do the less noisy work in the afternoon to a nice selection of light music sometimes followed by a practical lecture called 'Women's 30 minutes' addressing topics related to house work. When the kids returned from the playground, the DBC addressed them for half an hour with a mix of instructive and amusing topics. The information slot was designed for the concentrated listening of the returning man of the house, while prime time offered serious or quality entertainment ranging from cabarets to modern art music concerts. If wife and husband wanted they could end the evening with a foxtrot or a waltz transmitted from one of the city's fancy restaurants. In this way, radio both represented the family and its private life as a whole and addressed each of its three elements (kids, mother, father) at different times, thus contributing to the auditive structuring and instruction of the ideal (middle-class) family.

In an article on the early BBC, Simon Frith argues that the corporation's answer to the threatening North American mass culture was to construct a British mass culture related to the principle of public service articulating the values of the emerging middle-class and a middlebrow culture. He describes working-class entertainment as 'collective, disorderly, immediate – "vulgar" by definition' – while middle-class entertainment was 'orderly, regulated and calm', 'it was this aesthetic that informed the BBC's understanding of listeners' leisure needs' (1983/1988:32). To Frith, it was not really a battle between high and

1929		1939	
		07:00	Time signal
		07:00	Morning exercises for women
07:30	Morning exercises	07:15	Morning exercises
Break		Break	
		08:30	Morning service from the Copenhagen Cathedral
		08:55	Morning weather
		Break	
		10:15	Radio for school children
		Break	
11:00	Morning weather	10:58	Extended early afternoon weather forecast
Break		11:10	Fish prices
		Break	
12:00	Time signal and the Copenhagen Town Hall carillon	12:00	Time signal and the Copenhagen Town Hall carillon
12:00	Music transmission from restaurant or hotel	12:00	Concert
Break		12:30	News (midway through the previous programme)
		14:00	Gramophone programme
15:00	Afternoon concert	14:30	Concert
17:00	Children's radio	16:30	Children's radio
Break		17:00	Lecture or reading
		17:25	Extended late afternoon weather forecast
17:40	Stock exchange report	17:40	News
17:50	Lecture/language tuition	17:50	Gramophone programme
18:20	Lecture/language tuition	18:15	Lecture
18:50	Weather	18:35	Language tuition
19:00	News	19:00	Time signal
19:15	Time signal	19:00	News
19:16	One or two lectures	19:30	Debate
20:00	Concert/play/music programmes/lectures/features (most often three to four separate programmes)	20:00	Concert/play/music programmes/lectures/ features (one to four separate programmes)
		22:00	News
		22:15	Weather for fishermen
		22:20	Dance music
23:00	End of broadcast or transmission of dance music	23:00	The national anthem
24:00	Time signal and the Copenhagen Town Hall carillon (midway through the previous programme)		
00:30	The national anthem		

Figure 1: Average programme schedule, first seven days of November 1929 and November 1939.

low or between classes, but the definition of a place in between where public service and entertainment became one:

> The BBC was central to [...] the creation of mass, British, *middle-brow* culture. [...] Light entertainment, in particular, was defined in terms – balance, access, community – that cannot be separated from an account of the audience gathered round an essentially middle-class hearth. Balanced entertainment thus meant not pluralism, numerous different sorts of humor and music, but relaxation, programmes guaranteed soothing ('wholesome') by their exclusion of all excesses.
>
> (Frith 1983/1988:41, italics in the original)

The idea of the family was central to this middlebrow culture, and radio was identified as a natural centre for the family to gather around. In Great Britain, it was often compared to the old hearth, and one BBC official even stated that '[b]roadcasting means the rediscovery of the home' (C. A. Lewis, BBC's first programme organizer, quoted in Frith 1983/1988:32). Focusing on the psycho-social aspects of this acoustic situation, radio historian Kate Lacey states that the new auditive home culture was in constant flux and supported the flow of the ideal (middle-class) family (Lacey 2000:287). In sum, radio – be it the BBC, the DBC or most other state-licenced, European broadcasting corporations – offered a 'common' culture based on middlebrow family values to anybody who would listen.

Although radio heads like the BBC's John Reith and the DBC's Emil Holm wanted listeners only to listen in a concentrated way, they were well aware that most listeners listened distractedly or, as they called it, used radio for tap listening. Hardly anybody in official positions acknowledged this. Radio employees and radio journalists kept up appearances in hard-core discourses focusing on the best that culture had to offer this ideal listener, but everyday radio programming was rather different (as shown in Figure 1). Tap listening made it possible for listeners to avoid this hegemony and maybe even gain a certain amount of control over the medium because they used it as they saw fit, maybe concentrating on the crooners and using Mozart as muzak. They also controlled the volume knob, deciding if the sound should be heard softly in the background or if it should dominate the acoustic space. Turning off the radio was an option as well, but not one used very often.

Music was part of the structuring, the instructions and the negotiations contributing to the modern middle-class family's education as mature emotional beings. The DBC and other national broadcasting corporations tempted the sentiments with the sounds of light music and modern dance music derived from North American styles. This repertoire took up around 85% of the music programmes in the DBC from 1925 to 1940.[1] Music's many age-old functions, including as a means for identity work, for establishing and transcending social borders and for creating communities worked as well when mediated through radio. But mediation also brought forth new aspects of music and uses of music. One is quantitative. The oft-repeated phrase, 'never has so much music been available', was as relevant then as it is today. And one might add: 'to so many'. Another aspect is that listening may take place in the privacy of your own living room. Music was of course part of the home soundscape before radio, but intermittently because somebody had to sing, play or put a record on the gramophone. Now you could perform music-social climbing or slumming in private.

According to staff members in radio corporations, one of popular music's most important functions was to facilitate relaxing after a hard day's work (e.g. Kappel 1948:65 [DBC]; Matheson 1933:160 [BBC], quoted in Frith 1983/1988:32). Another was, of course, as a tool for raising the cultural level of the populace: from popular music to the great masters (i.e., unpopular music). Such intentions were common among policy-makers, but it is important to notice that the popular music repertoire also held other promises. The large repertoire of old and new instrumental dance music was in many ways related to the body, it was music made understandable as bodily movement, to some merely as the possibility of movement, to others as a concrete *Aufforderung zum Tanz*: to dance along alone or with a partner in your living room. Danish dance band conductor Jens Warny actually suspected that most listeners danced to his radio transmissions from the restaurant Nimb (ml 1928:13). The many isolated opera and operetta arias, which might be considered light music as much due to their programme context, were epitomes of music as formalized expression of feelings. They offered possibilities for temporary identifications with the singer, the emotions expressed or just the heightened state of sensibility. You could of course choose also to posit yourself as the temporary object of the affections expressed. As crooning (see below) slowly became accepted as yet another radio voice, it offered new ways of situating yourself as the addressee of the song.

In such ways, radio contributed to a reordering of the home as a specific place. It made the rooms audible, so to speak, it supported a specific family structure and the spatially defined hierarchies concerning gender and class as performed in the home. Radio helped articulate what was between high and low, maybe even dodging that spatial metaphor. Musically, it was not accordion-driven rowdiness, or contemporary art music, but a bit of old art music and a lot of light music and modern North American-derived dance musics that were used to articulate the sound of the emerging middle class in their own place, in the privacy of their own living rooms.

Radio combines places (radio in between)

Radio programmes had (and have) different acoustic ambiences, partly due to transmission equipment, partly because the actual broadcasts 'mirror' different spatial characteristics determined by the spatial qualities of the space from which the broadcast takes place and by microphone types and placements (and when listening today, the recording and reproduction equipment bringing the sound of the broadcasts to us). Emil Holm was very aware of this and spent much time designing recording studios, moving the musicians around within the studios and walking around among the orchestra players during rehearsals in order to readjust the microphones. One of his most important collaborators was his wife (a musician as well). She sat at home next to the radio set, listened and reported back to him the changes in sound (Granau 2000:48–50).

That early radio could transmit different acoustic spaces is demonstrated by the oldest surviving DBC recording, the first so-called 'listening picture' demonstrating the production of beer at the Tuborg brewery. Going from location to location, the ambience changes significantly. Some are rather muffled while others are cavernous. Even though it is a mono recording, the depth of the sound stage (i.e. the perceived distance between foreground and background noises) is quite clear as well.[2] In the few surviving clips featuring radio announcers, their voices sounded in quite deadened acoustics, that is, the 'voice of the radio station' sounded without many traces of the space wherein it spoke. On the other hand, the surviving music broadcasts have clear spatial characteristics with the musicians being placed towards the back of the room. In the recording of the first movement of Dvořák's cello concerto in B minor broadcast 13 October 1932, the soloist (Gregor Piatigorsky) is placed distinctly in front of the orchestra. As it is a live concert, the radiophonic balance between soloist and orchestra has been obtained by balancing the microphone inputs.

This means that for the listener, two sets of auditive information about space are coterminous: the actual room wherein the listening takes place and the room or space broadcast from. I have found no indications that this is a problem in an auditive sense, we can be both here and there at the same time. Or rather, depending on the listener and the way she is listening in concrete situations, the 'radio space' is probably superimposed more or less on the actual space and may be dominating in concentrated listening situations, be it sports, music, drama or news. In distracted listening situations, it might be more precise to talk about radio as auditive post cards – small tokens of other places. In this way, radio represents both a here and a there, and it combines them in endless variations, sometimes stressing the overlap, sometimes stressing the difference. Granted that the two spaces do not melt together, radio brings the listeners into contact with other spatial qualities, with other spaces and maybe even with other cultures. The family mentioned earlier comes closer to publicly known figures like radio announcers, politicians and musicians because their instruments and voices are not faraway. This goes for events as well:

> The radio offered access to a public world, compressing the distance in space between the listener and the event, and at the same time making the perception of that event accessible to a numberless audience of listeners, and celebrating the distance overcome in transmitting those events into the home.
>
> (Lacey 2000:285)

Here, the here and there are almost blended in an experience of community. But at the same time (or in the next moment), radio reminds you that the distance is still there: the presence of the prime minister's voice is also a reminder of his actual, physical inaccessibility, just like travel programmes, which give you a sense of being and not being there at the same time. Distance is present but also the hope of overcoming it. Questions of distance were negotiated in the daily programme flow and the actual programmes as well. Radio stations always found it important to announce if the programmes were produced in house or if they were outside broadcasts. The DBC labelled the latter transmissions, that is, the signal was received in the broadcast building from somewhere and retransmitted to the listeners. It was important to the early listeners as well:

> Transmissions have caught the listeners' special attention. It is as if the events move much closer when the broadcasts are transmitted directly from theatre, meeting room, football ground or other places where the events of our times take place. The radio waves bring us within close range of the special mood of place and event. This is why the large majority of listeners ask: let us hear transmissions, good transmissions, instructive transmissions.
>
> (Anon 1927:1, quoted from Poulsen 2006:190, my translation)

In opposition to transmission's 'there', in-house productions located the sound 'here'. Due to the very damped acoustics, the announcer's voice sounded rather close and without any clear sense of spatial position. The announcer was the primary marker of 'radio hereness', be it in the broadcasting house or in your living room. In this way, the sense of place is diminished and despite being placed at specific street addresses it is arguable that the radio studio was not localized in an actual or genuine sense. Partly due to this lack of spatiality, radio became an abstract place, the place of ether and radio waves, from whence named voices without bodies sounded.

To many, concentrated listening to preferred music in the Schaefferian manner of reduced listening (1966:267) may be one of the best ways to ignore the distance between sound sources and listeners. The medium appears to become transparent. This way of listening has been defended in authenticity discourses that are at least as old as mechanical or technologically mediated music. The main thrust of most of these discourses is towards ignoring or transcending the mediation taking place and focusing on the sounds produced by the musicians and explaining them as the direct expression of the musicians and/or the composers. Counter-discourses have arisen from time to time, one example being the Danish debate on mechanical music (radio and gramophone) in 1931. The most eloquent of the opponents, Karl Larsen, claimed that radio had ruined the natural sound of music, the sense for musical quality and musical life in general (Larsen 1931:17–25). Despite such voices, the domestic, cabinet-encased radio became transparent to many.

Yet another perspective acknowledged the medium and what it did to music. A contemporary commentator with a university background (*magister artium*) demonstrates the complexity clearly in this paragraph:

> Sitting [...] in your living room wearing headphones one's mind is turned towards something different from the ordinary, natural surroundings. You build a world, created by the sound impressions. On the one hand this weird sound world, this figment of the imagination, rests within your head; [...] on the other, it takes place in a large room which changes and undulates. Yes, even with a loudspeaker is it as if it does not take place here in the living room; because all the living room's tales and the riches created by us are

less important than the world built for us through sound. It may turn into an interplay where you at one moment notice how the radio studio treats the sound (its acoustics), at another notice the fate of the sound in the room where the loudspeaker is placed. By and large, though, we build both scenery and orchestra in our sound fantasy world.

(Hansen 1928:6, my translation)

Although Hansen is lyrical in this passage, he accepts three partly interweaving spaces, two concrete (the private living room and the semi-public radio studio) and one imaginary (the personal sound fantasy). We observe what Georgina Born has described as '[…] the capacity of music and sound, through their technological mediation, both to produce or initiate and to reconfigure public and private spaces' (Born 2013:24).

Another reconfiguration was that of the singing voice moving slowly from bel canto-derived voice production to technologically aided crooning. According to Allison McCracken (US), radio became crooning's primary medium as it made possible a certain intimacy between the singer and his audience. Its popularity also suggested new concerns. As noticed with the radio announcers, the crooners' voices also appeared as a 'disembodied, artificially amplified male presence' (McCracken 1999:365–366). And this new semi-parlando vocal style made it possible to integrate a huge series of paralinguistic sounds (sighs, small giggles and laughs, frowns) suggesting a much more intensive emotional life on the part of the singer than hitherto. It was, however, not popular with radio management. The BBC considered banning crooning, but ended up not doing it (Scannell and Cardiff 1991:189). Danish Holm called such 'microphone singers' '"Singers without voices," who place themselves next to the microphone and claim that they possess a singing voice while it would be impossible to hear them in an ordinary concert hall' (Holm 1939:183, my translation). The point is that the ideal of the soft-spoken, disembodied, male voice representing the institution as speakers also worked in music, overcoming distance 'better' in many ways, among other things because the singers added a heightened level of emotionality. Even if accepting the crooners' overcoming of distance due to the auditory signal, listeners could in another sense create or uphold a distance towards those singers they did not like and whose imaginary spaces they did not want to be part of.

In this context, radio blurred the border between close and faraway, between private and public. Radio barged into your living room, sometimes in the manner of a public announcer, sometimes in the manner of an intimate friend. The earlier, clear division between the two was questioned and the two were often mixed, perhaps as in the paradox of the musical experience in the privacy of a public concert hall.

Radio orders and reorders space (radio 'thereness')

As indicated, radio may to a certain extent order place, be it private or public. But it also orders more general, spatial levels – the nation or even the world – for the listeners according to radio's logic. In the first couple of years, the DBC mapped Copenhagen's musical life and musical spaces onto the living room, so to speak. Concert halls and concert societies, the opera house, variety, operetta theatres and restaurants with performing bands became well known to the public and nodes in a Copenhagen music-spatial grid. As transmission technologies developed, the grid became extended both towards national and international levels. Nationally, a newly developed radio studio system came to include 10–15 provincial cities, which then each had a studio for reporting and delivering talks. Transmissions from provincial restaurants and orchestral concerts also became an integral part of programming. Internationally, the transmissions came in mainly from the European capitals, especially Berlin, London and Stockholm. But retransmissions via London from, for example, the United States were not uncommon.

At a national level, the DBC (like most national broadcasters) contributed to an intensified sense of nationality, of belonging to the nation. As radio spread, it reinforced a centre/periphery structure with the capital as the absolute centre. Both the actual street address and the radio studios of the broadcasting house were located in central Copenhagen. Language of course was the most obvious mark of national belonging, but the dialect used in and between many programmes had a second connotation as well: Copenhagen. Musical time markers also had this double set of connotations. The national anthem (most of the time 'Der er et yndigt land/There is a lovely land') was played every night after the regular programmes, and the pause signal, the first station indicator (jingle), which came about in 1931, was the allegedly oldest notated, Danish melody ('Jeg drømte mig en drøm'/'I had a Dream'; Sangild [2013]). The hymns sung at the daily services and at the weekly high mass functioned as musical symbols of national coherence as well. On the other hand, the Copenhagen Town Hall carillon was the most repeated time signal being played at noon, 6 pm and midnight every day. As places for transmissions multiplied, they balanced the centre/periphery structure to some extent, but it did not change it in any way, partly because even though transmissions became more common, the amount of radio hours grew exponentially making most of the programmes Copenhagen-centric anyway.

Musical life in general was remapped partially thanks to radio (and talking pictures and the gramophone), but probably also because of general cultural changes caused by an increasing communication and exchange between Europe and the United States, which resulted in the new, syncopated dances (including jazz) and in heated debates about the status of popular culture. Around 1930, most of the larger Copenhagen concert societies had to close due to failing audiences while the DBC took up promoting concert broadcasts with live audiences. The extensive changes in musicians' job opportunities as cinema orchestras closed down almost overnight made it even more obvious that the DBC became the country's largest employer of musicians (around 250 full-time musicians at the time of Holm's retirement). While all this contributed to radiophonic centralization, there was also the opposite tendency as people with political ambitions of being a part of the radio circuit made local entrepreneurs support local musical life and sometimes even establish small symphonic orchestras (see Sneum 1948).

Importantly, Scannel and Cardiff mention that radio (in this case, the BBC) for the first time more or less mapped musical genres: 'Before broadcasting, music did not exist as a unified cultural field. It was scarcely meaningful to speak of music in general. What existed were particular musics' (Scannel and Cardiff 1991:182). Even though it might be somewhat overstated (publishers' lists did juxtapose several musical genres, and innumerable statements from before 1900 attest to a sensibility towards high and low culture), they are right that radio did a lot to unify the field. For the first time, it became possible to systematically compare the sound of serious music and light music next to each other within one framework. Even though different genres did bring their social and cultural connotations with them in the mediating processes thanks to listeners' previous experiences, radio did to some extent strip the genres of their connotations because they were 'reduced' to pure sound. Distracted listening contributed to this stripping as well. Scannell and Cardiff write that the consequence was that '[...] broadcasting universalized music as a socio-cultural category in a quite unprecedented manner. [...] broadcasters [...] found themselves responsible, in effect, for the standardization, classification and evaluation of the whole field of music' (Scannell and Cardiff:182).

The original listeners, the radio amateurs of the 1910s and 1920s, were the first to pick up on radio's ordering of international space. At first, energy was spent on finding something out there while surfing the radio waves. Like ornithologists, amateurs registered contact with other amateurs or stations on cards. Such contacts could be continents away. But as national broadcasting corporations became widespread in Europe, it became apparent that international cooperation was necessary, especially with regard to the distribution of the frequency space. In 1925, the IBU (the International Broadcasting Union) became a fact and after sorting out the most pressing technical problems, the organization turned to content as well. Concert transmissions became an important activity, and based on very complex logistics, the concert series *Nuits Nationales* (1926–1931) was developed. It was supplanted by *Concerts Européens* that ran 1931–1939 (Fickers and Lommers 2010:309–324). Apart from these early 'Eurovision' transmissions, bilateral music transmissions from restaurants, concert halls and opera houses could be heard continuously. Contrary to the centre/periphery structure at the national level, international radio supported an infrastructure, a network of relations among peers.

The move from radio amateurs (the technically fascinated) to radio aficionados (the musically fascinated) took place as radio technology and reception became more stable and the radio set became domesticated. Transmissions received via national broadcasting corporations were one aspect of radio's opening up of international space, and receiving broadcasts directly from foreign stations was another. 1930s radio sets mapped Europe either along a scale or in a circle. Some of the city names on the panel were well known but others like Königs Wusterhausen or Kalundborg (radio mast locations) would be completely unknown to most listeners. This produced an alternative map of European space, and newspapers and radio magazines carrying local radio programmes also carried pictures of foreign radio announcers and programmes for a wealth of European stations, helping listeners visiting exotic parts of Europe. In this way, the national broadcasting corporations can hardly be said to be monopolies.

Danish radio music broadcasts contributed to the construction of the nation while at the same time opening towards Europe. DBC programmes discussing the great masters of Danish culture were common. Most of them were authors, but as they had also written poems that had been set to music by other great Danes, the alliance of words and music helped fortify the rather traditional and romantic image of Danishness put forth by the DBC. Another point is that all music was played live and it was played by Danish musicians who were to become 'known from the radio'. They were contrasted with a few foreign ones – mainly conductors and soloists – who were presented as 'international' artists, that is, they were considered better than their Danish colleagues. It is of course difficult to differentiate between, say, Danish, German or Italian music if you do not know it beforehand. National traits are extremely elusive. Nevertheless, like today, when you look at the credits most of the music repertoire was foreign (German, British or North American). Far from all listeners realized this but the producers knew well that they contributed to the continuing internationalization of musical culture. The DBC lecture section supported this international outlook. They planned daily 20-minute instructions in foreign languages. Some days instruction was in German, French and English and occasionally there were even 30-minute lectures in one of those languages. Thus, even though Danishness was high on the agenda, it was complemented (not contrasted) with European-ness, thus pointing to the construction of a political balance where Denmark was a respected member of the European family.

In sum, the DBC helped the listeners make sense of the world – the vast space out there – it presented to them by structuring it in specific ways and by making unknown places known, partly through music, partly through words. In its programming practices, the DBC stressed sometimes the national, sometimes the international. To them it was apparently not a question of either/or. Both ideologies made sense, even if not at the same time.

Conclusion

The tri-partite structure of radio 'hereness', 'thereness' and 'between here and there' covers a trajectory from radio as part of personal and family life, typically in the home, over radio as a mediator between the local and personal on one hand and the global and public on the other, towards radio as a preliminary structuring of the world out there, be it just outside your house or international politics. By introducing this structure, I have sought to address the interiorizing and exteriorizing tendencies in mass media technologies mentioned by Born. It seems to be especially true for radio, as it may help listeners construct intimate spaces adjacent to shared ones. The three structures are conceived of as places and/or spaces for several reasons. First, because matters of geography are important to the, at that time, new mass medium (and vice versa); second, because space and spatiality are apt metaphors for other types of structuring: in transphonic sound and music, in the social;

third, because sound and music production in radio and in general become intertwined with the social and political in places and spaces, be they concrete or abstract. It is important to note that the three spaces might very well overlap, either because different listeners understand the situation differently or because one situation might suddenly turn into another, for example, if one's attention is drawn to the radio playing in the background or if the Town Hall carillon changed connotations from 'those Copenhageners' to 'us Danes' during the German occupation.

The myriad ways in which music and non-semantic sounds might become meaningful to listeners probably made music programmes the most versatile radio programmes for listeners. They offered sounds to wash to, to sigh to, to listen intensely to. But there are of course limits to music's polysemy. Music also came with its social and aesthetic values, making some programmes less versatile than others. Here, private and public spaces intertwine in sound. The analysis of the DBC music programmes showed that old and modern dance musics were by far the most broadcast genres, and the values related to those were those of light entertainment and relaxation – as Frith pointed out, such programming contributed to the creation of a middlebrow culture and the cultural space of the middle class. Nevertheless, questions of control over auditive space and the definitions of physical and mental places and space were constantly kept alive in the ongoing negotiations between listeners and radio, both at a formal level through the lobby work of listeners' associations and informally in the daily practices in the many homes.

References

Anon. (1927), 'Editorial', *Arbejder-Radio/Workers' Radio*, 1:2, p. 1.

Berland, Jody (1990), 'Radio Space and Industrial Time: Music Formats, Local Narratives and Technological Mediation', *Popular Music*, 9:2, pp. 179–192.

Björnberg, Alf (1998), *Skval och harmoni: Musik i radio och TV 1925–95/Noise and Harmony: Music on Radio and Television 1925–95*, Värnamo: Stiftelsen Etermedierne i Sverige.

Born, Georgina (2013), 'Introduction – Music, Sound and Space: Transformations of Public and Private Experience', in Georgina Born (ed.), *Music, Sound and Space: Transformations of Public and Private Experience*, Cambridge and New York: Cambridge University Press, pp. 1–70.

Briggs, Asa (1995), *History of Broadcasting in the United Kingdom*, Vol. II, Oxford: Oxford University Press.

Doyle, Peter (2005), *Echo and Reverb: Fabricating Space in Popular Music Recording 1900–1960*, Middletown: Wesleyan University Press.

Fickers, Andreas and Suzanne Lommers (2010), 'Eventing Europe: Broadcasting and the Mediated Performances of Europe', in Alexander Badenoch and Andreas Fickers (eds), *Materializing Europe: Transnational Infrastructures and the Project of Europe*, London: Palgrave McMillan, pp. 225–251.

Forman, Murray (2002), *The Hood Comes First: Race, Space, and Place in Rap and Hip-Hop*, Middletown: Wesleyan University Press.

Frith, Simon (1983/1988), 'The Pleasures of the Hearth – The Making of BBC Light Entertainment', in *Music for Pleasure: Essays in the Sociology of Pop*, Cambridge: Polity Press, pp. 24–44.

Führer, Karl Christian (1997), 'A Medium of Modernity? Broadcasting in Weimar Germany, 1923–1932', *The Journal of Modern History*, 69, pp. 722–753.

Hansen, Kristian Holt (1928), 'Kunsten at lytte/The Art of Listening', *Radiolytteren/The Radio Listener*, 31, p. 6.

Holm, Emil (1939), *Erindringer og Tidsbilleder fra midten af forrige Aarhundrede til vor Tid, bind 2/Memories and Period Pictures from the Middle of the Previous Century to Our Times*, Vol. 2, Copenhagen: Berlingske Forlag.

Kappel, Vagn (1948), *Musik i æteren/Music in the Ether*, Copenhagen: Jul. Gjellerups forlag.

Kurkela, Vesa (2010), 'Screaming Sopranos in Radio. Irritating and Pleasant Voices in Early Radio Broadcasting in Finland', in Vesa Kurkala, Markus Mantere and Heikki Uimonen (eds), *Music Breaks in: Essays on Music Radio and Radio Music in Finland*, Tampere: Department of Music Anthropology, University of Tampere, pp. 71–83.

Lacasse, Serge (2000), '"Listen to My Voice": The Evocative Power of Vocal Staging in Recorded Rock Music and Other Forms of Vocal Expression', Ph.D. thesis, Liverpool: University of Liverpool.

Lacey, Kate (2000), 'Towards a Periodization of Listening; Radio and Modern Life', *International Journal of Cultural Studies*, 3:2, pp. 279–288.

Larsen, Karl (1931), *Levende Musik, mekanisk Musik/Living Music, Mechanical Music*, Copenhagen: Levin & Munksgaard.

Lyytinen, Eino (1996), 'The Foundation of Yleisradio, the Finnish Broadcasting Company and the Early Years of Radio in Prewar Finland', in Rauno Endén (ed.), *Yleisradio 1926–1996: A History of Broadcasting in Finland*, Helsinki: Finnish Historical Society.

Matheson, Hilda (1933), *Broadcasting*, London: Thornton Butterworth.

McCracken, Allison (1999), '"God's Gift to Us Girls": Crooning, Gender, and the Re-creation of American Popular Song, 1928–1933', *American Music*, 17:4, pp. 365–395.

Michelsen, Morten (2012), 'Michael Jackson's Sound Stages', *Sound Effects*, 2:1, pp. 81–95.

ml (1928), 'Dansemusik i Radioen/Dance Music on the Radio', *Radiolytteren/The Radio Listener*, 4:2, p. 13.

Poulsen, Ib (2006), *Radiomontagen og dens rødder: Et studie i den danske radiomontage med vægt på dens radiofoniske genreforudsætninger/The Radio Feature and Its Roots: A Study of the Danish Radio Feature with Special Attention to Its Radiophonic Genre Background*, Frederiksberg: Forlaget Samfundslitteratur.

Sangild, Torben (2013), 'Jingler – radioens lydlige indpakning/Jingles – Radio's Sound Wrapping' *Seismograf/DMT*, theme issue on radio, http://seismograf.org/artikel/jingler-radioens-lydlige-indpakning. Accessed 15 December 2013.

Scannell, Paddy and David Cardiff (1991), *A Social History of British Broadcasting, volume one 1922–1939: Serving the Nation*, Oxford: Basil Blackwell.

Schaeffer, Pierre (1966), *Traité des objets musicaux, essai interdisciplines/Treatise on Musical Objects, Interdisciplinary Essays*, Paris: Seuil.

Sneum, Axel (1948), *Første Udsendelse fra Provinsen/The First Broadcast from the Provinces*, Aarhus: Self-published.

Uimonen, Heikki (2013), *Senses and Soundscapes* [power point presentation]. https://noppa.aalto.fi/noppa/kurssi/01247/materiaali/01247_senses_and_soundscapes.pdf. Accessed 10 November 2013.

Notes

1 These numbers appear when categorizing each music programme in the first week of November during the 15-year period. Although the DBC appears to be extreme in its use of non-art music, the tendency can be seen as well in other countries. According to Alf Björnberg, the balance between serious music and entertainment music in the Swedish Broadcasting Corporation during the years 1925–1940 was roughly 38/62 percent (1998:341). Eino Lyytinen does not quote any numbers, but in a discussion of the year 1927 he states that '[m]ost of the programmes consisted of opera and operetta, rhapsodies, marches and other light classical music) (1996:29). In Great Britain, the balance changed somewhat in the BBC from 3/4 to 2/3 of the music being light and dance music between 1927 and 1929 (Briggs 1995:34–35), and in Germany the Mitteldeutsche Rundfunk (MIRAG) broadcast 575 hours of serious music and 1.195 hours of entertainment music in 1927. The eight other German stations show similar figures (Führer 1997:750–751).

2 The programme was broadcast 22 May 1931, between 8:30 and 9:30 pm. The full title was *Danske Virksomheder. Et besøg paa et dansk Bryggeri. Hvorledes det danske Øl bliver til/ Danish Companies. A Visit to a Danish Brewery. How Danish Beer is Made.* At one point, the reporter (Aksel Dahlerup) even puts the microphone next to some of the machines so that the listener may listen to them. In this way, radio made present and maybe even created an awareness of specific soundscapes.

Part III

Sound

Chapter 9

Space and Place in Electroacoustic Music

James Andean

S ound plays a unique role in the human perception and conception of space and place. The capacity for sound to trigger this crucial dichotomy is carried over to the sonic arts, which are unique in their ability to include space and place in their creative toolkit. This is particularly true of a number of forms of electroacoustic tape music,[1] most notably acousmatic music (Emmerson and Smalley 2001:61) and soundscape composition (Truax 2002, 2008). With some exceptions (mostly with regard to soundscape composition), however, this capacity has received relatively little theoretical examination, often remaining a largely intuitive negotiation between composer and listener.

This chapter examines and contrasts some of the thinking around space and place from a number of theoretical perspectives, and their use and elaboration in electroacoustic music, in the hopes that each might perhaps be usefully informative with regard to the other. The creative use of space and place in the sonic arts has been quite fluid – as, indeed, are both our concepts and experiences of space and place, broadly speaking; as a result, rather than prescribe a limited definition of space and place and then examine sonic works through this limited lens, this chapter instead considers a number of sometimes contrasting or contradictory perspectives, and some of the shifting ways in which these are enacted in the aesthetic use and experience of sound.

Space and sound

Our sense of hearing is a remarkably rich source of information about the world around us. Each and every sound we hear offers several simultaneous layers of such information – for example, information about a given sounding object from our environment and, at the same time, information about that object's action or movement, or about action or movement that has been applied to that object.

Perhaps most critically of all, each and every sound we hear offers us information not only about the source of that sound, but also about the space surrounding that source. Sound waves from a sounding object radiate outwards; some of this sound reaches our ears directly, but much of it moves out into the environment, encountering surfaces, other objects, the ground, etc. Some energy is absorbed or transformed, while some is returned to the environment, to continue its series of environmental encounters, some of which will lead back to our ears, loaded with information about its voyage. We are extremely adept at decoding what sound has to tell us about its path: the size and shape of a room; the placement and characteristics of objects within the room; the materials of surrounding surfaces and objects; even details of temperature and humidity (Stocker 2013:2).

Each and every act of hearing receives these two layers of information, intertwined: information regarding a sounding object, and information about a space (Blesser and Salter 2007:11–26). Neither of these can be avoided: we cannot hear a space without sound, but nor can we hear sound without inferring a space. When we record sound, this duality is carried over to the recording: the act of recording transcribes not only the recorded sources, but also the recorded spaces. We can, of course, attempt to minimize the sense of sonic space surrounding a recorded sound, but we cannot nullify it completely. Recorded sound is therefore simultaneously a recording of a sounding source and a recording of a sounding space.

The dawn of sound recording opened up new possibilities in the creative use of sound. Many of these stemmed directly from the technical opportunities offered by new tools and technologies, beginning with the simple fact of the newly born capacity to store a sonic moment, to later be resurrected at will. From the end of the Second World War onwards, the swirling of all of these possibilities gave rise to an enormous outpouring of sonic creativity, including the birth over the following decades of a number of new compositional forms and genres predicated to varying degrees on the deployment of recorded sound.

One of the key aesthetic revolutions engendered by the creative use of recorded sound centred on the spatial component of our sonic experience. The capacity to record, manipulate and control space via recorded sound opened up new aesthetic potential, and brought space into the creative control of the composer and sound artist to a degree that had never before been possible (Harrison 1999). As a result, over the second half of the twentieth century, space grew to take a key position in the development and elaboration of an enormous number of modern musical genres (Zvonar 2004). This list includes all of the many genres of electroacoustic music, and particularly those that are primarily or entirely devoted to recorded sound, collectively referred to as 'tape music' (or 'music for fixed media').

Electroacoustic tape music uses recorded sound as its primary compositional material. As a result, the creative palette very quickly expanded to incorporate a much broader range of sonic materials: any and all sound sources that can be recorded can now be used as compositional material. This results in materials that not only serve a musical or sonic purpose, but that carry with them sonic imagery from the world in which they were recorded. This opens up a duality in a number of these genres, allowing for the use of sound simultaneously for musical purposes, and for symbolic or narrative purposes, based on our recognition or interpretation of recorded sound from our experience of the world around us (Andean 2010:107–115).

The spatial component of recorded sound described above is a key element of such sonic imagery. Just as recorded sound is simultaneously a recording of a sound source and of a space, an electroacoustic tape piece offers not only a sequence of sound events, but also a sequence of spaces, whether these were recorded together with the sounds heard, or crafted after the fact in the studio by the composer. Much as a sound can be employed by the composer for either its musical or its narrative properties, or for both simultaneously, sound can equally be used to deliver either an image of the *source* of the sound, or of the *space* in which the sound exists – or, once again, and most likely, both. In this way, in electroacoustic music, sound therefore serves as a double signifier: for both a particular sounding object and a particular space (Wishart 1996:140–159; Smalley 2007:38–39).

Space versus place

Spatial aspects of sonic imagery, however, are intimately bound to another, closely related, construct: place. While this dichotomy is extremely important in electroacoustic tape music, it is hardly unique to the sonic arts; space and place are widely discussed in a number of philosophical and cultural domains, most significantly perhaps in cultural geography. It is worth considering these perspectives on space and place, before considering their sonic applications.

'Space versus place' is often an attempt to distinguish between the objective and the subjective – between the objective quantity of 'space' and the subjective, culturally constructed notion of 'place'. This perspective is perhaps most closely associated with cultural geographer Yi-Fu Tuan: 'What begins as undifferentiated space becomes place as we get to know it better and endow it with value' (Tuan 1977:6). 'Space is transformed into place as it acquires definition and meaning [...]' (Tuan 1977:136). 'When space feels thoroughly familiar to us, it has become place' (Tuan 1977:73).

In other words, in Tuan's view, space becomes place once it has been 'lived in', or has otherwise acquired meaning or value. We find this perspective echoed elsewhere; narratologist Marie-Laure Ryan, for example, offers a similar elaboration:

> While space is an abstract collection of points separated by certain distances, place is a concrete environment with which people develop emotional bonds; while the points of space are interchangeable, place has its own unique character; while space is an empty container for discrete objects, place is a network of interrelated things; while space is open and infinite, place has boundaries; while space is anonymous, place involves a community and a lived experience; while space is timeless, place is shaped by history. In short, while space is a mathematical concept, place is a social concept.
>
> (Ryan 2012:108)

Space is thus viewed as quantitative, and place as qualitative. This perspective on place can also be found in the sonic arts. Composer Katharine Norman, for example, suggests that 'place – how we sense and make it – is a process', that it 'begins and ends with a relationship between the perceiver and the perceived', and 'requires our lived experience, and so requires a bodily presence "being in" an environment' (Norman 2012:258).

A number of other theorists have taken the dichotomy of space and place on board, sometimes with their own particular perspective. In the field of narratology, for instance, David Herman proposes that it is narrative that transforms space into place: 'stories can be used to turn *spaces* into *places* – to convert mere geographic locales into inhabited worlds [...] transforming abstract spaces into lived-in, experienced, and thus meaningful places' (Herman 2013:283). The place/space dichotomy is also closely related to Herman's contrasting of 'narrative simulation of place' versus 'narrative computation of place'; despite the fact that here Herman has labelled both as 'place', there is a close kinship between 'place' and Herman's 'narrative simulation', and between 'space' and Herman's 'narrative computation' (Herman 2013:289). Sociologist Anthony Giddens proposes that this distinction between space and place is not absolute, but is in fact a rather recent phenomenon:

> The advent of modernity increasingly tears space away from place [...] In conditions of modernity [...] [w]hat structures the locale is not simply that which is present on the scene; the 'visible form' of the locale conceals the distanciated relations which determine its nature.
>
> (Giddens 1990:18–19)

Giddens' stress on the role of the 'visible' in the creation of place is interesting here, making for a convenient contrast with perspectives that view space as a physical, acoustic construct.

It is worth noting, however, that both of these terms – 'space' and 'place' – tend to drift somewhat, depending on the theorist and the field in question. For example, the idea of a 'geographical region' is sometimes assumed to be endowed with specific cultural values, and therefore posited as 'place', while at other times it is considered a neutral quantity, and thereby placed in contradistinction with 'place', as 'space'. The notion of 'space' also tends to fluctuate somewhat – sometimes even within the writings of a single theorist – between a primarily geometrical construct and a much more fluid metaphor for psychological terrain. It is also important to note that there are a number of theorists who have objected to the space/place dichotomy, some on the grounds that either or both of these are treated as static entities, and some due to fundamental disagreements about the nature or existence of either (or both) of these concepts (Casey 1996:13–52; Ingold 2011:145–149).

Signs and symbols

In the establishment of both place and space, sound has the potential to play a particularly important role. This begins with sound's role as a signifier for, among other things, a given space or place. Here, the term 'signifier' comes to us from Saussure, who paired it with the 'signified' to form his notion of the 'sign' (Saussure 1959). It is Charles S. Peirce, however, who – in contrast to Saussure's more linguistic approach – offers a semiotic theory that better serves an application to sound. Peirce offers several relevant trichotomies, including 'icon', 'symbol' and 'index'; 'sign', 'object' and 'interpretant'; and his rather more abstract notions of 'Firstness', 'Secondness' and 'Thirdness' (Peirce 1955:104–115; Atkinson 2007:115–119; Monelle 1992:193–200).

Generally speaking, however, the use of the term 'symbol' in much writing on electroacoustic music – primarily with regard to the concept of 'sound symbol' (Young 1996:79–83; Wishart 1986:41–60; Emmerson 2007:8) – is closer to Peirce's 'icon' or 'index' than to a strictly Peircean definition of 'symbol':

One of the most powerful potentials of recognisable real-world sounds in electroacoustic music lies in the creation of symbols. The concept of the symbol has arisen in humans as a way of imbuing recognisable objects with associations that go beyond the immediate object [...] in order to convey ideas or feelings about aspects of our existence that are difficult to express in straightforward terms. Where conventional reasoning may tend to be finite in the way an idea is expressed, symbolic connotations are flexible, less bounded and elude precise definition. Recognisable sounds in electroacoustic music are symbolically potent because of their direct signification of objects and events, without the need for intermediary forms of signification, such as words.

(Young 1996:79–80)

Young's use of the term here is much closer to its use in Ogden and Richards' 'triangle of reference' than to its role in Peirce's triad (Ogden and Richards 1923:8–14; Monelle 2000:196).

It is useful here to refer to Denis Smalley's term 'source bonding': 'the *natural* tendency to relate sounds to supposed sources and causes, and to relate sounds to each other because they appear to have shared or associated origins' (Smalley 1997:110). Such references happen on any number of levels. The simplest is the direct use of sound as a signifier for an object: train sound = train. It is also common to use sound as a signifier for a sound-producing movement or action: the sound of something spinning, falling, bouncing, receding into the distance, etc. While such action signifiers may be equally tied to a producing object – it is a car that recedes into the distance; it is a ball that is bouncing – it is perfectly possible to use sound as a signifier for action, without clearly specifying the particular object that may be performing or experiencing such an action.

It is also possible for sound to act as a signifier for broader questions of context, environment, location and situatedness, and it is here that we find a particular relevance for questions of space and place. Field recordings can be used as signifiers on a number of levels: to signify broad categories of location – inside versus outside, for instance; or slightly more focused categories of location – a field, a busy street, the beach, the interior of a church; or to denote very specific locations – not just any street, but one particular street; not just any church, but one particular church. In electroacoustic music, the composer often makes these choices based on purely musical or sonic criteria, but this becomes arguably less likely as the reference becomes increasingly specific. A chiming clock may be used in a work generically for its musical properties; however, the more precise the symbol for 'clock' – the timbre of a specific size, shape or type of clock; the spatial imprint of the room around the clock – the stronger its impact as a symbol and reference. As the reference becomes more precise – a clock specifically chiming twelve for instance, or the use of a recognizable clock, for example, the chimes of Big Ben in London – it becomes increasingly probable that its use is thematically or narratively driven.

Electroacoustic soundmarks

The field of soundscape studies has offered some useful terminology here, including 'keynote sounds' – sounds from the sonic background, for example, wind in the trees; 'sound signals' – sounds in the foreground, or which provide important information, for example, footsteps in the grass or snapping twigs; and soundmarks – sounds that signify not just a generic class of sound signal or environment, but a very specific location – such as, in our example above, Big Ben (Truax 2008:106). The sound of a clock, mentioned above, can play a role in any of these three concepts, depending on the degree of foregrounding and relevance implied by its position in its surrounding sonic context: as a keynote sound, if blended in with a general soundscape of an interior living space; as a sound signal, if attention is particularly being drawn to the sound of a clock within this soundscape; or as a soundmark, if the clock in question is recognizably defined as not just any clock, but one specific clock (i.e. Big Ben).

All three of these levels – keynote sounds, sound signals and soundmarks – can play strong roles in the establishment of place in a work. There are, however, significant differences in the manner and extent to which each of these is accessed by composers across various genres of electroacoustic composition. For instance, it is only relatively rarely that composers who identify themselves with the acousmatic genre opt to include soundmarks in their works, while it is rather more common in soundscape composition, in part because recognition of context is often of key importance to soundscape works. Even here, however, such soundmarks are very often supported by extra-musical information – through explanatory programme notes, or even by naming the work after the location in question:

> [I]t is always clear what the soundscape composition is 'about', although with the absence of visual and other contextual cues, the composer may assist the listener with an explicit title and program notes. With highly clear and vivid sound materials, this information is probably unnecessary, but in other cases, a fair degree of ambiguity may exist in a soundscape recording and the listener may need to be oriented with an appropriate text.
>
> (Truax 2002:6)

To some extent, this reflects a shared challenge in deploying established soundmarks: 'The sound of an important church bell may be a significant "soundmark" for a location (Schafer 1977:10), but the mental image it generates is more likely to be broadly one of place and purpose [...]' (Naylor 2014:112). Soundmarks are heavily dependent upon personal knowledge of the soundmark in question, via familiarity with the location to which the soundmark is tied (Norman 2012:258; Andean 2012:26–31); while it is perhaps increasingly possible in our ever more connected mass-media environment to expect certain key locations to be familiar to most, this list is arguably, when it comes to sound, rather short.

The question remains, however: why is it more common for soundscape composers to reference soundmarks, while acousmatic composers often prefer to deploy keynote sounds and sound signals? The answer may lie in the above comment by Truax: if the intention in soundscape composition is for the work to clearly be 'about' something, then this surely applies to the specificities of place, considering the genre's emphasis on context. In contrast, consider, for example, acousmatic composer John Young's attitude to place in his work Five Versions of Reality, a work that includes sonic references to Paris, Prague, Helsinki, Christchurch and Corfu, and whose sections are subtitled for the places invoked:

> In the piece, sounds are not intended as some essential signifier of their 'place', but I mention the places in subtitles simply to connect them with an idea of location – a documented encounter with sound if you like. I could have used some more poetic titles, or perhaps something more literal: e.g. 'marina' for Corfu, but I wanted the sound rather than the label to evoke an atmosphere or a sense of the physical provenance.
>
> (Young 2013)

In other words, it is more important for Young that sound triggers an idea of 'place' as a general category (marina) than as a specific location (Corfu), although locations are nevertheless mentioned in the titles in order to trigger a general sense of 'place-ness'. When Young uses the recording of a marina in Corfu, he is not necessarily attempting to trigger an image of *that particular marina* in the mind of the listener; he is attempting to elicit the *listener's own*, perhaps remembered, image of *a* marina – or of boats, of water, of the seaside, etc. What is critical here is the personal nature of the image Young is attempting to invoke. It could be argued that there is a significant difference in intention here, between a more discursive approach (the composer is telling us something about Corfu), versus a more personal approach, achieved by being sufficiently ambiguous as to allow the listener's own memories and experience to swell up and create meaning. The work is personalized by the listener, and thereby made exponentially more powerful.

Sonic illusion

Sound, however, can do more than simply provide a signifier for a given place; sound also brings the listener into a direct relationship with the sounds heard. Humans use vision primarily in order to observe the world around us; while our hearing, of course, is also used to observe our environment, we also use it to place, situate and locate ourselves within that environment (Stocker 2013:2–5). Sound informs us about our own position in the space around us, and about our spatial relation to surrounding objects (including, unlike vision, the space and objects behind us) (Voegelin 2014:9–10). Sound not only offers an image of a particular space, it also has the capacity to place the listener *within* that space (Stocker 2013:2–4).

In part for this reason, sonic illusion is, at least potentially, a very different experience from visual illusion. It is unlikely that, while at the cinema, the viewer will be momentarily fooled into believing that the screen in front of them is in fact a window opening out onto whatever landscape or action is being viewed; there is, of course, the entertaining anecdote of alarmed spectators ducking at the approach of the train in the Lumière Brothers' early film, but this may well be apocryphal (Brownlow 1968:6). On the other hand, this is not an uncommon feature in sound projection, and increasingly so as technology advances – for instance, as loudspeakers become increasingly more accurate. One regularly finds instances at electroacoustic concerts where audiences confuse sounds within the composition for sounds from their surrounding physical environment, and vice versa; common examples include the sound of rain hitting the roof, sounds of traffic outside, distant police or ambulance sirens, and sounds of nearby human movement – shuffling or rustling, footsteps and so on.

When presenting a sound in an electroacoustic work, this sound can do more than simply act as a signifier for such a sound in the world, or for the thematic references we might connect with such a sound. For example, an electroacoustic soundscape has the capacity, thanks to the details of our hearing and our psychoacoustic processing of sound, to situate the listener within the presented soundscape: in other words, it is possible for the sonic illusion to be complete and successful, and, in fact, to move beyond illusion, to achieve fully embodied and situated experience – for the electroacoustic soundworld to be, for all intents and purposes, experienced as real.

This is true for both space and place: with the full resources of a large-scale electroacoustic concert apparatus, it is often possible to transform the acoustic space of the concert hall in which the listener is situated, into any number of other acoustic spaces. Of course, if one presents the illusion of an outside space, this is easily cognitively recognized by the listener to be false through recourse to their other senses (not to mention their common sense); on the other hand, if one presents the illusion of a space that is, for example, larger and more reverberant than the hall in which the listener is seated, this may in fact be fully accepted by the listener as simply being their current acoustic reality, not recognizing the presence of a sonic illusion. The same is true of the sounding objects involved: the illusion of a train passing through the middle of the hall is quickly and easily disproved (although potentially providing a pleasing frisson in the process), whereas more innocuous sounds may be readily, even unknowingly, accepted as real (Andean 2011:130).

Let us consider for a moment the characteristics of an electroacoustic soundscape that allow for this experience. First, we have the sound signal itself – for example, a bird singing. We recognize the source from our past experience of the world; while this is certainly enough for the sound to serve as a signifier, and for it to thereby deliver aspects of theme and narrative, it is not yet enough to enact illusion and direct experience. Next, we have the sound's location: again with the case of birdsong, it is reasonably likely that, given the opportunity, this sound would be presented above the listeners' heads, reinforcing the sense of a believable environment. Consider, on the other hand, a situation in which this birdsong is presented over loudspeakers underneath the audience seating; despite any other appropriate sound cues, the resulting sound image would be unlikely to relate effectively with most people's experience of birdsong, and may therefore be expected to result in a failure to access illusion, leading instead to the interpretation of this source and location according to symbolic, metaphoric or other culturally coded criteria.

After sound signal and sound location, we return to the characteristic that has the most power and potential in the creation of sonic illusion: space. We have an accurate recording of birdsong; we have located it above our heads. But so far, this is far from enough to convince our cognitive processing of the presence of this bird. For this, we need the full range of detailed spatial cues, which are our primary auditory tools for understanding the world around us, and our location therein. In this case, we would need more than simply finding the bird above our heads: we need the appropriate sense of distance, the dispersed reflections of the bird's singing off of surrounding trees or across open outdoor spaces, and so on. In other words, we need more than simply the signifier for 'a bird': in order to achieve illusion, we need a coherent acoustic context for our bird. (Of course, in our example, this will be complicated in concert presentation by the interaction between the acoustic cues embedded in the work, and those of the concert hall, whose reflections will work to impose a message of 'room-ness' onto the composed message of 'exterior-ness'.)

Electroacoustic space and place

Much as sound is critical to our understanding of space, it is often similarly important to the creation and negotiation of senses of place (Stocker 2013: 28); when sound is used compositionally, this dichotomy of space and place is carried over into the work:

[T]he work produces an affective geography [...] that maps the place, as a product of emotional bonds between people, between people and animals, between people and things, and between people and the landscape, created and lived, made appreciable in sound. [...] This sonic experience of home, of lived narrative territory, produces neither the analytical clarity of spatial theory nor that of discourses on belonging and identity. Instead, it provides an opaque and sensorial sense of a place that remains invisible and foreign, but in its sonic vicinity reminds us of what belonging is: the plurality of the particular. Images spell out the limits of the portrayed, sound constructs inexhaustibly the experience of the encounter, and that is what we take home.

(Voegelin 2014:34)

In the case of electroacoustic music, a dichotomy very similar to the above descriptions can be proposed. Sonic 'space' and sonic 'place' might be approached as a differentiation between 'acoustic' and 'location': sonic space draws up an understanding of a three-dimensional volume with certain parameters and characteristics; sonic place acts as a pointer to a specific locale, or to a slightly broader sense of context. Sonic place is then a culturally coded, loaded and constructed quality, moving beyond simple location and placement to aspects that carry a relation with the subject and with the listener. Space, on the other hand, is here a collection of acoustic cues that situate the listener in an environment. Birdsong and rustling leaves thereby create an immediate understanding of place, while the collection of acoustic information – reflection of birdsong off of surrounding trees and so on – creates space.

On the surface, the association of 'space' with 'acoustic' and 'place' with 'location' seems quite close to the proposals listed above, by Tuan and others; on closer examination, however, there are some key differences. To begin with, both sonic space and sonic place are *perceived* identities; they are both products of perception – neither can claim to be a neutral or objective unit. Both are entirely ecological (Gibson 1966:5; Clarke 2005:17–32); both exist not only *through* perception but *as* perception. Further, if we attempt to follow Tuan's dichotomy, can sonic place claim to be any more 'lived in' than sonic space? In fact, to some extent, here we find something of a reversal: where in cultural geography, the distinction is between an abstract phenomenon and a lived, embodied quantity, with sound we find the opposite – we find space to be 'lived in and embodied', and place to be a quasi-objective external unit. Sonic space *includes* the listener; it exists because the listener *experiences* it. Sonic place, on the other hand, points *outwards* and *away*, to *somewhere else*; it is a window or a reference (Norman 2012: 258). Sonic space is now a *personal* and *internal* quantity, while sonic place is now *impersonal* and *external*. Of course, whether place is experienced as 'impersonal' or not depends to a significant extent on whether you are hearing 'your' place, or the place of an 'other'. However, in electroacoustic music, even in the case of a sonic place with which the listener identifies, it remains to some extent 'external' – no longer through an act of personal removal, but of temporal removal: it is an act of memory. The listener is not actually currently situated in the place in question; it therefore serves either as an external marker for 'an other's place', or as an external marker for 'another time' – for place remembered (Young 2009, 2013).

At first glance, the concept of 'place' as 'humanized space' seems reasonable when applied to sound. However, once again, this assumes that we are dealing with the sound in question as a neutral entity. If we imagine a sonic space, and contrast it with an imagined sonic place, the space does indeed seem impersonal, unmarked by life and humanity, while it is precisely life and humanity that define and create place. However, this platonic ideal of a sonic space is a phantom: it does not exist – sonic space comes into being solely through the act of listening. There is no neutral sonic space; sonic space springs into being as an act of experience, and is thereby wholly and utterly human. What we find instead, therefore, is that sonic place is in a sense 'pre-humanized'; it comes already loaded with humanity – often with someone else's humanity – whereas space is humanized in the act of its perception, and thus of its creation.

Once again, we might propose that this is a vastly more personal engagement than that with a pre-charged, pre-loaded 'place'. To return to Peirce for a moment, these distinctions might be usefully described as embodying Peirce's trichotomy of Firstness, Secondness and Thirdness: the as-yet-unrealized potential of Firstness of an uncharacterized sonic space, that achieves Secondness through the act of perception, while a shared, generalized concept of 'place' might be viewed as a Thirdness (Peirce 1955:322; Monelle 1992:194). John Young, in discussing his work *Five Versions of Reality*, offers a personal twist on space and place in acousmatic composition:

> A notion of *place* is used [...] as a metaphor for a source of sounds outside the work: an invitation to reflect on contact with the physical world. *Space*, in the formal sense, I think of as a metaphor for a unity of content that might be regarded as a self-contained 'world' [...].
>
> (Young 2013)

Thus, rather than dwell on acoustic space, Young describes a broader, more conceptual notion of 'space' that draws close to narrative concepts such as Herman's 'storyworld' (Herman 2002:13), as well as to narratological approaches to space (Ryan 2012:107).

Something typically common to both space and place in an electroacoustic work is their compositional use as signifiers. A sonic place is, in part, employed by the composer as a sonic signifier for that particular place, or for that category of place, while a sonic space is equally used as a sonic signifier for that category of space – or, on occasion, for a single specific space. However, once again we find that perception steps in and makes a significant distinction: for the most part, space, as described above, is encountered first as direct experience, and only then proceeds outwards, through an interpretative act, to serve as signifier. Place, on the other hand, is often able to trigger direct experience only through its use of space; it is therefore much more likely to serve as signifier from the beginning, without access to the same degree of direct experience upon first encounter.

As a brief illustration, we might contrast two short, somewhat humorous sonic 'interludes' in Robert Normandeau's seminal work *Rumeurs (Place de Ransbeck)*. At 4'02", after a door creaks open, we are presented with a very clear sonic 'scene': a fly buzzing about, very close and in the foreground, while further away, loud boot-clad footsteps stomp about. While both of these act as clear signifiers for their sources – buzzing for 'fly', stomping for 'footsteps' – neither of these symbols, taken singly or together, is sufficient to present a clear image of place or space. However, there is a very clear spatial imprint surrounding the footsteps, painting a clear image of an interior space, of a room; this image is further clarified by the contrast in distance between the foregrounded fly and the more reverberant footsteps. (In the absence of this spatial imprint, one might expect a listener to assume an exterior scene, due to the presence of the flying insect.) Here, we clearly first *experience* the space, before interpreting the scene through the incorporation of the sound elements and the signified space. At 8'52", we find another humorous moment in the work: a passage that arguably serves as the climax of the piece is unceremoniously cut off by a flushing toilet. The toilet-as-symbol is undeniable; there can be no uncertainty regarding the place in question. However, in this instance there is little to no spatial information: the flushed toilet is presented 'dry', without reverberation, giving us little to no acoustic information regarding the setting in which it is located – a setting that is, in fact, typically quite reverberant, due to the tiling found in most such rooms. As a result, this is clearly an image of 'place', not 'space'. As a result, unlike the previous example, this moment is immediately perceived as signifier; the 'direct experience' component is limited, and largely irrelevant. In fact, it is precisely for the reasons described here that these two moments are so effective – the first, because it suddenly situates the listener 'within' the work; the second, through its immediacy as a simple, slapstick symbol.

These differences, exploited here by Normandeau, make this duality an extremely rich opportunity for the electroacoustic composer, as space and place are used sometimes singly, sometimes in tandem and sometimes in contradistinction. Cognitive acoustic processing grants us an experience of space, which situates us as listeners within a context, while place involves a process of cultural decoding, which references existing symbols 'out there' in the world, and offers access to a web of thematic and symbolic knowledge. Normandeau's ability to access each of these singly – and elsewhere in the piece, in combination and even in transformation – provides him with an effective rhetorical tool.

Space becomes place

It is possible, however, that sonic space and sonic place are more fluid concepts than they at first appear. Consider, for example, an image of 'church'. If a composer wishes to reference a church through sound, she or he might present a recording of ringing church bells. This is sufficient to trigger in the listener the recognition of a symbol for 'church'; however, it is unlikely that this in itself would achieve the illusion of being in the presence of actual church bells. On the other hand, the composer might present the same church bells in an acoustic context: for example, heard at a distance, with reflections off of surrounding hills. Now, with the appropriate surrounding acoustic information, if we close our eyes, perhaps we do indeed have the illusion of hearing church bells. However, as a symbol, this is now significantly different. In the first case, we recognized a Peircean index for 'church', and made our interpretations of the presence of this sound in the work accordingly. In this new case, however, these bells are situated and contextualized, and so now possibly serve less as an immediate symbol for 'church', and more as a symbol, for example, of 'a small village or rural landscape'. This transition from sound signal to keynote sound is achieved in this case by maintaining the sound source, but changing the spatial cues; the resulting changes to our associations and implications of the original symbol are significant.

On the other hand, space can be used by the composer not only as a set of acoustic markers to place a given sound source within a particular sound environment, but also as a culturally coded symbol for place. In the symbol for 'church' described above, the church emits a sound signal. The composer could instead select a different sound signal, completely unrelated to the symbol of 'church', but maintain the symbol for 'church' by placing this unrelated signal inside the church space. The heavy reverberance and long reverberation times of many church interiors are sufficiently recognizable that this space, in and of itself, can act as a symbol, and therefore can provide a sense not only of space, but also of place. Consider a recording of a voice speaking, perhaps describing the weather; under normal circumstances, this may serve as a symbol for 'a person', or for 'a social situation' or for the weather being described. The same recording, once given a reverberation that is recognizably familiar as that of a church interior, may now act as an entirely different symbol: the acoustic symbol for 'church' may well replace the symbols for 'person speaking', 'weather' or 'small-talk', which might now be interpreted as serving simply to trigger the symbol 'church'. In this case, we have achieved a transformation of 'space' into 'place', a distinction that rests primarily with the capacity of a given sonic space to act as a symbol in its own right.

This, of course, brings us full circle back to Tuan's dichotomy: 'When space feels thoroughly familiar to us, it has become place' (Tuan 1977:73). In other words, it is not the sound materials themselves that determine their role as space or as place; it is the listener's interpretation of those materials – and, most importantly, their familiarity with the materials in question. Acoustic properties are used primarily to define space; but if the listener links those properties to a particular location or context, they become place. In electroacoustic terms, this is in essence a question of source bond (Smalley 1997:110): source bonding transforms space into place – in the absence of source bond, a spatial image remains 'space'; but when such a spatial image is recognized and source bonds to a given context or location, as in the 'church' example outlined above, it is transformed into 'place'.

For the composer, this offers an example of one of the many tantalizing possibilities for space and place in electroacoustic music. Each may be deployed to great effect, and in a vast number of ways; or they may be deployed together, in an endless number of combinations; but, what's more, as we have seen here, space and place also offer the potential for transformation – not just from place to place and from space to space, but from space into place, and from place into space. Such transformational possibilities raise the compositional potential of notions of space and place in a manner that is somewhat unique in the history of music. For the listener, this interplay between space and place – both in juxtaposition and in transformation – offers not only an immediate and accessible aesthetic richness, taking full advantage of a side of the musical experience that was previously under-served, but also a fertile ground for us to explore and expand our concepts and notions of what space and place, both separately and together, might mean.

Conclusion

Sound is critical in establishing our senses of space and of place, and for this reason, electroacoustic composers are able to include these as part of their compositional toolkit.

This may serve simply to 'transport' the listener, but space and place may also act as symbols, opening up endless opportunities for sophisticated thematic development; simultaneously, sound's capacity to enact direct experience allows for a more immediate engagement with the work. Taken together, these possibilities offer a powerful compositional capacity for the aesthetic and conceptual exploration of space and place, which can now, thanks to the unique possibilities of recorded sound, be fully taken up as part of the composer's domain. This capacity is made particularly vital by the flexible, elastic and mutable properties of our concepts of space and place, as both cultural and sonic constructs. A key example of this mutability, as noted above, is that while certain instances or aspects of sonic space and place tend to support some of the common threads found in cultural geography, sociology, narratology and elsewhere, others appear to turn this version of the dichotomy on its head.

The aesthetic use of sound thereby offers a unique window into our cognitive and social expressions of these concepts, in essence providing a laboratory in which to explore space and place through active manipulation, rather than simply through passive response. In this way, not only can our understanding of space and place inform the sonic arts, but we can also hope that the sonic arts might help us to explore and to better understand cultural and cognitive concepts of space and place.

Most of all, the incorporation of space and place within the compositional palette offers a profound and expanded experience for the listener, by directly accessing our embodied, encultured and resonant experiences and histories of space and place and allowing these to inform and permeate our listening experience, in ways that can significantly strengthen and deepen our aesthetic experience of sonic works.

References

Andean, James (2010), 'The Musical–Narrative Dichotomy: *Sweet Anticipation* and Some Implications for Acousmatic Music', *Organised Sound*, 15:2, pp. 107–115.

—— (2011), 'Ecological Psychology and the Electroacoustic Concert Context', *Organised Sound*, 16:2, pp. 125–133.

—— (2012), 'Cultural Relativism in Acousmatic Music', *Musiikin Suunta*, 2, pp. 26–31.

Atkinson, Simon (2007), 'Interpretation and Musical Signification in Acousmatic Listening', *Organised Sound*, 12:2, pp. 113–122.

Blesser, Barry and Linda-Ruth Salter (2007), *Spaces Speak, Are You Listening?: Experiencing Aural Architecture*, Cambridge: MIT Press.

Brownlow, Kevin (1968), *The Parade's Gone By...*, Berkeley: University of California Press.

Casey, Edward S. (1996), 'How to Get from Space to Place in a Fairly Short Stretch of Time: Phenomenological Prolegomena', in Steven Feld and Keith H. Basso (eds), *Senses of Place*, Santa Fe: School of American Research Press, pp. 13–52.

Clarke, Eric (2005), *Ways of Listening: An Ecological Approach to the Perception of Musical Meaning*, New York: Oxford University Press.

Emmerson, Simon (2007), *Living Electronic Music*, Aldershot: Ashgate.

Emmerson, Simon and Denis Smalley (2001), 'Electro-Acoustic Music', in Stanley Sadie and John Tyrrell (eds), *The New Grove Dictionary of Music and Musicians*, New York: Grove, pp. 59–66.

Gibson, James J. (1966), *The Senses Considered as Perceptual Systems*, Boston: Houghton Mifflin.

Giddens, Anthony (1990), *The Consequences of Modernity*, Stanford: Stanford University Press.

Harrison, Jonty (1999), 'Imaginary Space', *eContact!*, 3:2, http://cec.sonus.ca/econtact/ACMA/ACMConference.htm. Accessed 9 November 2014.

Herman, David (2002), *Story Logic: Problems and Possibilities of Narrative*, Lincoln: University of Nebraska Press.

—— (2013), *Storytelling and the Sciences of Mind*, Cambridge: MIT Press.

Ingold, Tim (2011), *Being Alive: Essays on Movement, Knowledge and Description*, London: Routledge.

Landy, Leigh (2007), *Understanding the Art of Sound Organization*, Cambridge: MIT Press.

Monelle, Raymond (1992), *Linguistics and Semiotics in Music*, Chur: Harwood Academic Publishers.

—— (2000), *The Sense of Music*, Princeton: Princeton University Press.

Naylor, Steven (2014), 'Appropriation, Culture, and Meaning in Electroacoustic Music: A Composer's Perspective', *Organised Sound*, 19:2, pp. 110–116.

Norman, Katharine (2012), 'Listening Together, Making Place', *Organised Sound*, 17:3, pp. 257–265.

Normandeau, Robert (1987), *Rumeurs (Place de Ransbeck)*, Lieux inouïs [CD], Montreal: Empreintes Digitales.

Ogden, Charles Kay and Ivor Armstrong Richards (1923), *The Meaning of Meaning: A Study of the Influence of Language upon Thought and of the Science of Symbolism*, New York: Harcourt, Brace & World, Inc.

Peirce, Charles (1955), *Philosophical Writings of Peirce*, New York: Dover.

Ryan, Marie-Laure (2012), 'Space, Place and Story', in Stephan Füssel (ed.) *Medienkonvergenz – Transdisziplinär*, Berlin: de Gruyter, pp. 107–125.

Saussure, Ferdinand de (1959), *Course in General Linguistics*, New York: Philosophical Library.

Schafer, R. Murray (1977), *The Tuning of the World*, Toronto: McClelland and Stewart.

Smalley, Denis (1997), 'Spectromorphology: Explaining Sound Shapes', *Organised Sound*, 2:2, pp. 107–126.

—— (2007), 'Space-Form and the Acousmatic Image', *Organised Sound*, 12:1, pp. 35–58.

Stocker, Michael (2013), *Hear Where We Are: Sound, Ecology, and Sense of Place*, New York: Springer.

Truax, Barry (2002), 'Genres and Techniques of Soundscape Composition as Developed at Simon Fraser University', *Organised Sound*, 7:1, pp. 5–14.

—— (2008), 'Soundscape Composition as Global Music: Electroacoustic Music as Soundscape', *Organised Sound*, 13:2, pp. 103–109.

Tuan, Yi-Fu (1977), *Space and Place: The Perspective of Experience*, Minneapolis: University of Minnesota Press.

Voegelin, Salomé (2014), *Sonic Possible Worlds*, London: Bloomsbury Academic.

Wishart, Trevor (1986), 'Sound Symbols and Landscapes', in Simon Emmerson (ed.), *The Language of Electroacoustic Music*, London: Macmillan, pp. 41–60.

—————— (1996), *On Sonic Art*, Amsterdam: Harwood Academic Publishers.

Young, John (1996), 'Imagining the Source: The Interplay of Realism and Abstraction in Electroacoustic Music', *Contemporary Music Review*, 15:1–2, pp. 73–93.

—————— (2009), 'Narrative, Rhetoric and the Personal: Storytelling in Acousmatic Music', *2009 Electroacoustic Music Studies Conference: Heritage and Future*, Universidad Nacional de Tres de Febrero, Buenos Aires, Argentina, 22–25 June.

—————— (2013), 'Places, Spaces and Spectra', *InTime 2013 Symposium*, School of Art and Design, Coventry University, Coventry, 19–20 October.

Zvonar, Richard (2004), 'A History of Spatial Music', *eContact!*, 7:4, http://cec.sonus.ca/econtact/7_4/zvonar_spatialmusic.html. Accessed 17 August 2014.

Note

1 'Tape music' is used here in its broadest sense, as an umbrella term for electroacoustic compositions created in the studio and existing primarily in recorded form. While the term clearly references the tape medium on which such works would historically have been created, it also includes studio compositions created in the digital age, a discrepancy that has led to the alternative term 'music on a fixed medium' (Landy 2007:152).

Chapter 10

The Repeated Tone of Civilization

Jeffrey L. Benjamin

On a cold February day, standing beside a building foundation under construction, I engaged Dom in a conversation regarding the length of a piece of wood lying on the ground. From our standpoint on a knoll, it was lying obliquely, pointed slightly downhill so that, with foreshortening, its true length was difficult to discern (at least for me). I was convinced that it was a 'two by ten by twelve-footer' (two inches by ten inches by twelve feet); in Dom's opinion it was a ten footer. Discussions such as these are common in artisanal practice, and they are rarely heated or confrontational: the physical work is hard enough. More than anything they provide a handy excuse to briefly take a pause and rest, to lean upon something and take a break, and they often end with a good laugh and a return to work. In this instance, I was not belabouring my opinion regarding the length of this piece of wood, it could be settled quickly by picking it up or kneeling down to measure it, but when I said to Dom 'I think this is a twelve footer', he walked over to it, kicked it once and said in his gentle Dutch accent 'It doesn't sound like one' and then moved on to other business. Dom's message, that he could discern the length of a piece of wood by its sound, was not a boastful exaggeration. It was a clever and rather kind way of telling me that he had spent a lot of time building, and that the process of building was multi-sensory and these sensations had permeated his being. He could affix spatial dimensions through the sonic properties of materials, and this particular sound was a sound that he had likely heard thousands of times before, like the sound made by a particular bar of a xylophone when struck. He didn't need to measure it – *he didn't even need to look at it* – he could just walk over and tap it with his foot. I have never forgotten this moment of wry humour and wisdom, it certainly gave me reason to smile for the rest of the day, and it is to the memory of Dom – and as a tribute to all backwoods hippy builders – that I dedicate these thoughts.

A sonic archaeology of the self

In the following, I intend to present a line of historical and archaeological evidence for a serious consideration of the 'repeated sound' as an elemental component of industrial material and social formation. Rather than thinking about sound and industrial sonic forms as transitory by-products of industrial processes, I hope to convey their foundational and constitutive power. Repeated sounds are creative forces capable of delineating and erasing social boundaries as well as forming social identities. This is an interpretation of sound and music originating from discourse within the field of archaeoacoustics (Scarre and Lawson

2006, Rainio 2006, Reznikoff 2006). It is hoped that, placed within a discourse of social, cultural and artistic critique, this perspective may offer another layer of interdisciplinarity and depth. Discussions of industrial and urban sound and noise are frequently framed within environmental concerns such as noise pollution and sound abatement efforts (Smilor 1978; Bijsterveld 2001; Thompson 2002; Coates 2005). The history of industrialization itself is likewise often discussed in terms of exploitation and coercion. This political history of contention – sonic and otherwise – cannot be denied, but I would like to draw attention to the considerable amount of evidence that suggests that an understanding of industrializing processes can be deepened through an interpretive stance of affective sonic attachment.

The study of the history of industrialization poses a challenge of temporal and spatial proximity, that is: it is not over yet, and it is all around us. However, promising new disciplinary and theoretical constructs are emerging to meet this challenge, such as the nascent field of 'contemporary archaeology', which expands a range of inquiry initially framed by the processual investigation of industrial archaeology in the 1960s in England and the United States. Because of its omnipresence, it is difficult to gain the necessary distance to contemplate the social ramifications of the industrial sound-object, but thankfully the lulling effect of repetition and routine does not preclude contemplation and introspection. As suggested in the opening, the initial impetus for developing the thoughts in this chapter was borne of daily experience: the repeated day to dayness of working for 20 years as a carpenter in upstate New York and Manhattan, a city that also happens to have a repetitive form, a grid pattern. It is from this daily activity over the course of many years in the urban built environment – as an active participant in the creation and division of interior space – that the following observations have emerged. For this reason, it can also be thought of as an effort towards an archaeology of the self, a sonic 'auto-archaeology' (Harrison and Schofield 2009). A contemplation of the built environment, especially for one who has for years been actively engaged in its construction, is accompanied by a certain solemnity, eloquently summarized by Juhani Pallasmaa:

> Architecture emancipates us from the embrace of the present and allows us to experience the slow, healing flow of time. Buildings and cities are instruments and museums of time. They enable us to see and understand the passing of history, and to participate in time cycles that surpass individual life.
>
> (2005:52)

In support of an affective interpretation, I would like to extend a consideration of the repeated sound of industry into the 'habitus of listening' as theorized by Judith Becker (a modification of Pierre Bourdieu's notion of 'habitus') as: 'an inclination, a disposition to listen with a particular kind of focus [...] to move with certain stylized gestures' (Becker 2004:71). I will also bring forward specific historical accounts that attest to the seductive qualities of repeated industrial sonic forms, and following this, investigate the possible importance of trance as well as sonic and haptic entrainment in industrial social formation.

In the conclusion, I will present some thoughts on both the gravity and hope emerging from the preceding meditation.

Affect and sonority

Any discussion regarding the soundscape of industrial activity must first recognize and address the fact that industrial operations were locations of acquired hearing loss and that the social implications of this collective physical trauma are manifold and ongoing.

In his analysis of the sonic environment at a working drop forge in Lansing, Michigan, in 1971, Robert Lindberg calculated the average number of impact strikes from a single drop hammer at around twenty five thousand per day (Lindberg 1972:65). Given that there were two such working hammers in the shop, each with a hammer weighing around 3000 pounds, this doubled a listener's exposure to around fifty thousand strikes per day, with each strike's decibel level in excess of 130. An impact sound of this intensity is not simply perceived through the ears, it is *felt* in the chest and abdomen as a thud or a heavy force. In a detailed analysis, Lindberg demonstrated that the cumulative effect on the workers' hearing was demonstrable. Attempts to accurately reconstruct the complex soundscapes of such heavy industrial operations for experimental archaeology or heritage purposes would result in hearing loss for anyone exposed. For instance, at the Boott Cotton Mills exhibit at Lowell National Historic Park in Lowell, Massachusetts, visitors and operators wear hearing protection when a section of the looms is operated. In England, workers in cotton mills became adept at reading lips for the purposes of communication across distances due to the din of machinery that obviated spoken language. This fact is related in Kirkpatrick Sale's *Rebels Against The Future*: 'the noise of the looms was so deafening that workers developed a system of lipreading (called "mee-mawing") to communicate' (Sale 1995:46). Significantly, this practice did not stop in the workplace, it was perpetuated within the relatively calm and quiet locations of the home and community, even though vocalization and hearing were possible (Ludlam 2011: pers. comm.).

In a study of over 700 medical records from the Quincy Mining Company in Hancock, Michigan, from 1914 to 1916, I could not find a single entry mentioning loss of hearing as the primary complaint. In general, a worker was only considered injured if he was visibly bleeding, so the examinations detailed within the three medical records that were found to specifically address hearing loss were prompted by a complaint of bleeding from the ears or jaw (Adolphson 1916). This apparent lack of concern for hearing is particularly puzzling for a mining operation, since the sequence of underground operations was orchestrated largely through a system of bells. This points to a fundamental and underlying contradiction: an impossible working situation. Under normal working conditions, miners, as well as most other industrial workers, must remain acoustically aware in order to stay alive, simultaneously tuning out the deafening roar of machinery while listening for the barely audible whisper or tapping of an injured colleague, the clicking or groaning of an overburdened support column or a developing fissure in the rock above: the repeated sound-forms indicative of danger. For experienced miners, this is known as 'roof talk' (Bobick and Giardino 1976:53) and an intimate understanding of the language of the rock is crucial to life itself. Miners would often walk through the stopes, tapping the roof with an iron bar, a process known as 'sounding'. Studies akin to these texts that detail the consequences of this fundamental contradiction are few and far between, but the hazards and the unpleasantness of industrially produced sound as experienced by the wider American public (particularly during the Progressive Era of the early 1900s) have been given careful attention by several aforementioned scholars.

And yet, there is another side to the story. There is an attraction to the aesthetic quality of industrial sound and its repeated patterns that has frequently found expression in the documented recollections of those who lived and worked near mines, factories and assembly plants. An attentiveness to affective attachment to industrial sound may offer important clues regarding the advent of industrialization. As related by Mills, a particularly evocative passage portrays the refining operations of a mining district in Cornwall, England, in the early 1900s, referring to the sounds of the stamp mills as 'the music of the stamps':

> [...] once so well known to almost every Cornishman that, on leaving home, many of them lay awake at night, missing this rhythmic accompaniment to their slumber, and of such I have heard men say: 'when the stamps stopped we felt as if we had lost our best friend'.
>
> (Hamilton Jenkins 2004/1927:338 as quoted in Mills 2005:34)

A prime variable that allows the transformation of trauma-inducing impact noise into soothing, comforting music is physical distance. The geographical layout of early factories and company towns shows an intentional separation of management structures from the structures of fabrication. While many industrial configurations employ the panopticon (where management looks down on the workers from a glass-enclosed space, or from a house at a central location or the top of a hill), the *panauricon* is just as important to consider but less obvious. Certainly, from the point of view of management, the consistent, repetitive sound of the percussive, oscillatory machinery was an informative and reassuring presence. Augoyard and Torgue's definition of repetition as comprising 'phenomena of return, reprise, and enrichment by accumulation' (Augoyard and Torgue 2005:90) holds particular significance when contemplating the sonic experience of early industrialists, who often occupied an office space that was separated structurally or by distance from the sound sources. Sonic repetition projected a kind of safety, and for certain individuals, the repeated tapping of a steam hammer or a series of punch presses was akin to the soothing lull of crickets. A break in the repetition, or worse yet – silence – signified danger or alarm for those accustomed to the sound.

Schafer observes that the sonic component of the industrial revolution was characterized by 'low-information, high-redundancy sounds' (Schafer 1977:78), which, strung together, are perceived as a 'flat-line' sound: a drone, buzz or hum. While the capacity of such sounds to create a nuisance is borne out in every day experience, it is perhaps instructive to contemplate the possibility that such a sound could also indicate much more than safety, enrichment or comfort, but rather *salvation*.

In the fall of 2010, a dramatic event unfolded in Chile, where 33 miners were eventually released, one by one, from a collapsed section of the San Jose copper mine. The miners were trapped underground for over two months, almost 700 metres below the surface. For the first 17 days after the collapse, they spent their time in near total darkness, conserving their food and energy resources in the hope of being rescued. It is important to understand what those 33 miners were doing during the long days before the first bore hole reached them: *they were listening*. For days, before that moment, the miners could hear the exploratory boring drills moving closer to their location. Through attentive listening informed by artisanal knowledge and honed by necessity, they were prepared when the eighth boring drill reached them. They quickly taped a note to the bit reading: 'We are well in the shelter, the 33' (De la Jara and Gardner 2010). In correspondence, Dr Madeline Muntersbjørn of the University of Toledo suggested to me that the sound of the boring drills getting closer to the miners' location must have been the most beautiful music they had ever heard (Muntersbjørn 2011: pers. comm.). The rescue operation represents a very interesting reversal, where the machinery of mineral extraction is suddenly assigned a very different purpose. The very tools and processes whose initial design function was to remove underground resources became liberating devices in a dramatic transition from material exploitation to human salvation. Moreover, the miners' response, once they were discovered, was to sing. After the hole was widened and supplies were passed to them, they responded to their rescuers by singing the Chilean national anthem. The purpose of this story is to relate one particularly dramatic example where the repetitive, flat-line sound forms of industrial machinery acquire a victorious significance. However, as human beings now find themselves largely swaddled in industrially produced sound at all times, perhaps it is the omnipresence, the *ubiquity* of human-made sound that needs to be investigated more closely.

Repeated industrial sonic forms

In *Landscapes*, J. B. Jackson suggests that the grid layout of many American towns and cities as well as the country itself stems from a utopian agrarianism, a Jeffersonian ideal of decentralized uniformity. Jackson points out that Jefferson's National Survey of 1785, which still holds as the basis for the country's spatial division, 'made no provision for cities' (Jackson 1970:4). But cities emerged nonetheless, and they incorporated this wider grid layout into their design. I have often felt a sense of egalitarianism in the fact that urban dwellers all share the same sidewalks, horizontal space, if not the same elevators, vertical space. Brandon LaBelle offers an exuberant description of contemporary sidewalk experience, suggesting that it 'offers a generative stage for narratives [...] while bringing into relief new configurations, sudden excitement, arguments, and entire promiscuous and difficult economy at the heart of public life' (LaBelle 2010:90). While the planning of the city's layout – as a series of repeated forms – was perhaps born of utopian ideals, its perpetuation and maintenance stem from something different: a propensity, a predisposition. As this susceptibility to repetition pertains to sound, perhaps it is instructive to contemplate the historical fact that in the early American settlement of Jamestown, Virginia, as in most colonial communities, participation in all social affairs depended upon living within earshot of the village bell (Rath 2003:54), within the physical footprint of the bell tone sound-form.

Kierkegaard's *Repetition* can be seen as both a philosophical/poetic meditation as well as a record of a dawning modern sensibility, an industrial state of mind, expressing the true seductive power of repetition as well as a human longing for it. Suggesting that repetition is a mental state whose counterparts are recollection and hope, he states:

> It takes youthfulness to hope, youthfulness to recollect, but it takes courage to will repetition. He who will merely hope is cowardly; he who will merely recollect is voluptuous; he who wills repetition is a man, and the more emphatically he is able to realize it, the more profound a human being he is. But he who does not grasp that life is a repetition and that this is the beauty of life has pronounced his own verdict and deserves nothing better than what will happen to him anyway – he will perish. For hope is a beckoning fruit that does not satisfy; recollection is petty travel money that does not satisfy; but repetition is the daily bread that satisfies with blessing. [...] Who would want to be a tablet on which time writes something new every instant or to be a memorial volume of the past? Who could want to be susceptible to every fleeting thing, the novel, which always enervatingly diverts the soul anew?
>
> (Kierkegaard 1983 [1843]:132)

The narrative premise of *Repetition* stems from the desire of the pseudonymous author, Constantin Constantius, to return to Berlin to re-experience an evening of theatre, just as it had occurred a year before. As the evening unfolds, nothing is the same as he had anticipated, leading him to state despondently: 'There is no repetition at all' (Kierkegaard 1983 [1843]:169) – an observation that would be quite true in all cases without the concept of negligible variability and the curiously human propensity to group similar forms. However, upon returning home he discovers everything to be in the same place: 'My home had become dismal to me simply because it was a repetition of the wrong kind' (Kierkegaard 1983 [1843]).

Kierkegaard's 'will to repetition' seems odd to those of us who view this particular quality more akin to boredom and drudgery than beauty, but for anyone who has experienced Terry Riley's mesmerizing composition 'In C' (1964), where an ensemble of musicians repeat 53 cellular variations circling around the same note synchronously for 50 minutes or so, the concept of repetition becomes more complex. A composition that might be said to mimic the rhythmic tintinnabula of industrial operations, 'In C' (to isolate only one of many minimalist compositions), opens the door for scholars of industrial history to read descriptions of technical processes from trade journals and patents as musical scores, or at the very least as narrative accounts of organized sound. To provide one example, the following passage is a portion of patent number 731,727, awarded to William W. Word on 23 June 1903, describing his invention 'Process of Forging Rock Drills':

> Operation: The bar or blank 3 is placed in horizontal position with the end to be shaped inserted between the dies 2 and 5. The proper configuration is then imparted to it by setting the hammer 1 into operation, which after *repeated blows* and proper manipulation reduces the terminal approximately to the desired cruciform shape. The metal is thus displaced from the grooves 38, Fig. 8, and *driven by redundancy* into the recesses of the die which form the wings 39. This *redundancy* produces the curved contour (seen at 11) in the center with the shortened corners 16. [...] Power-hammer 7 is brought into operation against the adjacent ends of dollies 17 18, which *by repeated blows* gradually drives the *redundant* metal from the center outward, the dollies being at the same time progressively expanded by means of lever 29, so as to operate on successive portions of the *redundant* metal and gradually turn out the beveled portions 21 to become a part of the deficient side of the wings [...]

> (Word 1903: emphasis mine)

While most of us are not drill sharpener operators, we all use and operate a variety of mechanical devices on a daily basis, and the operation of each device was originally explained in a narrative within a patent just as above. Many aspects of our lives are, quite literally, scripted or scored.

To enter into the human-built environment is to enter into fields of repeated forms: walls of alternating brick and stone, windows evenly placed, cobble stones on the street, patterns on fabric, endless grids, equally spaced lines on the sidewalk and the notebook, identically sized pieces of paper within identically proportioned binders, the examples are endless. As children, as soon as we are able to walk, we learn to contend with repetition: to alter our newly discovered gait to accommodate the regular expansion joints in the sidewalks. Human beings live their entire lives within structured fields of repeated forms, and also their sonic counterparts, their echoes. Sonic repetition can be contemplated without a quality of immediacy or exigency, as if every contemporary sound has only happened 'just now'. Moreover, any theoretical reinforcements of the enduring nature of sound will help to establish its place in history, for it is not just the producers or perceivers of sounds that warrant remembering, but also the sounds themselves. Conventional thinking suggests that the only way to preserve a past sound is through electronic capture. This point was made fully clear to me during a recent visit to a local history museum, but examples of this kind of sonic confusion are ubiquitous. In this particular instance, a sound artist installed an art piece within an historic house with the purpose of presenting sounds from the region's past. Each room contained a sound amplification speaker, and all of the different speakers simultaneously piped in a cacophony of recorded sounds from disparate sources, in the process completely obliterating and making inaudible the subtle squeaks and groans, the echoes, the reverberations, the sonifacts of the historic structure itself.

Repetition and trance in industrial social formation

In a broad survey of historical accounts of early industrial settings, an interesting phenomenon emerges: the nostalgic recollection of industrial sound, sometimes taking the form of a poem or song. In many historical texts, sound is often mentioned to add ambiance, to provide a background, setting or dramatic embellishment. Many of these accounts attest to the calming effects of rhythmic mechanical sound. Closely related to the passage from Mills' study mentioned earlier, the author of a history of the Champion copper mill in Freda, Michigan concludes with a description of the final moments of its operations:

> [...] residents came out on their porches and saluted and wept as the old mill ground to a halt, and an eerie silence crept over the town site. [...] Many residents still remember the sound of the crusher which used to be very loud, but also comforting, as it put them to sleep at night.
>
> (Monette 1989:105–106, 111–112)

In a similar account, Lucy Larcom, a textile worker at the mills in Lowell, Massachusetts, recalls the reassuring quality of the sounds she experienced, writing in her journal: 'I found that I enjoyed even the familiar unremitting clatter of the mill, because it indicated that something was going on' (Larcom, as quoted in Smith 2012:54). In *The Tuning of the World*, Schafer includes a particularly relevant passage from D. H. Lawrence: 'As they worked in the fields, from beyond the now familiar embankment came the rhythmic run of the winding engines, startling at first, but afterwards a narcotic to the brain' (Lawrence, as quoted in Schaefer 1977:74). The spoken word, *the repeated vocal sound-form*, the chatter and gossip of mineral extraction, also had a similar effect, albeit for different reasons. Often congregating in bars in the Keeweenaw Peninsula of upper Michigan, miners and prospectors would share information and stories about the location and procurement of different ore bodies: 'There was a fascination in the mysticism of the terms of the jargon. You could work yourself into a trance-like spell by merely uttering the sound of enough of them' (Jamison 1939:213).

The perpetuation of industrial rhythms and patterns can be seen as a vehicle through which innate 'tropismatic' (Veblen 1964/1914:38) or automatic impulses of motion are given their expression. In *The Instinct of Workmanship*, Thorstein Veblen obliquely addresses this propensity for repetitive motion. In a fascinating chapter entitled 'The Savage State of the Industrial Arts', Veblen suggests that industrial processes are akin to 'ritual observances' (Veblen 1964/1914:105). Emerging from a small Minnesota farming community, Veblen's clear distaste for the new phenomenon of industrial activity is an important testimony to the rather foreign and alien quality of factory work for those newly exposed to it. In support of this are the following observations of a witness to the operations of a Ford Motor Company assembly line:

[...] I always think about a visit I once paid to one of Ford's assembling plants every time anyone mentions a Ford car to me. Every employee seemed to be restricted to a well-defined jerk, twist, spasm, or quiver. [...] I never thought it possible that human beings could be reduced to such perfect automats (sic).

I looked constantly for the wire or belt concealed about their bodies which kept them in motion with such marvelous clock-like precision. I failed to discover how motive power is transmitted to these people and as it don't seem reasonable that human beings would willingly consent to being simplified into jerks, I assume that their wives wind them up while asleep.

(Hounshell 1984:321)

In *Music and Memory*, Bob Snyder discusses two forms of memory: *explicit* and *implicit*, indicating that implicit memories 'are memories of muscular acts ("motor" memories), which have no specific language component. Such memories are essentially the same as skills: how to do things' (Snyder 2001:73). Classical discussions of memory from Aristotle, recapitulated by Paul Ricouer and Frances Yates, present a close parallel in *mneme* and *anamnesis*, the former being ingrained, instinctive, unconscious, automatic, and the latter representing recollection, recall, specific memories: those which can be prompted and coaxed out of hiding by conscious effort (Ricouer 2004:19; Yates 2001/1966:192). The phenomena of repetition and sonic rhythm are clearly aided by, and perhaps even a function of, the first form of memory: the unconscious, automatic, trance-inducing. One important point needs to be made, however. Jankowsky notes, as observed by Rouget, that 'there are no formal qualities (rhythms, modes, tempos, frequency, instrumentation, etc.) of music that appear necessary for trance' (Jankowsky 2007:188) and furthermore makes the case for an origin of trance that is largely a function of cultural conditioning rather than a strictly natural or biological process. I would agree with Jankowsky, as the earlier passage of Jamison relating the trance-inducing power of mining jargon suggests, that trance is a function of vulnerability and *belief*, but I would also suggest that within a wider social construct of belonging (and this is borne out by the experience of myself and others of my acquaintance) 'the right kind' of sonic repetition has demonstrably mesmerizing qualities. A description of trance offered by Becker states:

Trance is practiced within a communal framework, is usually accompanied by music and often involves strenuous activity on the part of the trancer. Institutionalized, religious trancing takes place within a context of sensual overstimulation; the trancer is bombarded with arresting sights and sounds.

(Becker 2004:1)

A study by Martin Clayton, Rebecca Sager and Udo Will of entrainment within biological systems proposes that human behaviour is 'cyclical, oscillatory or rhythmical', and 'the temporal patterns of individuals who are in interaction become mutually entrained to one another, that is, that they get in synchrony of phase and period' (Clayton, Sager and Will 2004:10). LaBelle also discusses the power of entrainment in the everyday urban environment, relating a definition of entrainment from Tia DeNora as 'the alignment or integration of bodily features with some recurrent features in the environment' (DeNora 2000:77–78, as quoted in LaBelle 2010:90). The role of sound in the creation and perpetuation of rhythmic patterns cannot be dismissed, and the ability of a sound to project and maintain rhythmic patterns across the soundscape provides a compelling reason to consider its influence upon the creation of industrial social forms. The intensity of the nostalgia, the sense of loss expressed in the following poem, suggests that industrialized individuals at the Quincy Mine location, in Hancock Michigan, placed more value on sounds of copper being extracted from the ground more than the copper itself:

> We miss the sounds of the Quincy Mine:
> The sounds of the hoist wheels singing:
> The bellow's blow and the blasts below
> And the locomotive ringing…
> No whistle's roar;
> No falling ore;
> No 'lectric signals jangling.
> We miss the sounds of the Quincy Mine;
> Old sounds, oft repeated.
>
> (Malmgren, as quoted in Lankton 1982:174)

Because of its early use in bell casting, it can be tentatively posited that the rush to mine copper in the Keweenaw peninsula of upper Michigan had a significant sonic component. While the conductive properties of copper are well known, the initial copper rush began in 1843, well before the advent of electricity. This has led one historian to view the rush as 'premature, absurd and paradoxical' (Murdoch 1964:6). In general, the use of copper for pots and pans as well as sheathing for shipbuilding is frequently cited (Murdoch 1964:5), and certainly was used for these purposes, but a very interesting historical reference that directly ties the ore mined in the Keweenaw to a specific use states that the unique qualities of this ore resulted in a finished metal that was particularly well suited for the production of bells (which, in turn, produce sound). Historian Arthur W. Thurner cites a report from 1849 stating

> this mix of copper and silver found at the Cliff and nearby Copper Falls Mine had been "used in Boston for making church bells, and has proved to be of excellent quality". So began the widespread use of copper from Michigan in the developing industrialism of

the late nineteenth century. Thousands from all over the country, as well as from Europe, were attracted to the Keweenaw.

(Thurner 1994:45)

From this passage, one could hypothesize that the sound-form of the repeated musical tone – as produced by quality bell metal cast into bells – served to form a part of the initial impulse for a substantial human migration in the mid-1800s.

Conclusion

In *Noise: The Political Economy of Music*, Jacques Attali offers a critique of sonic repetition that is largely concerned with the mass reproduction of recordings. It is worth contrasting with Kierkegaard's appraisal of repetition as 'the daily bread that satisfies with blessing', the 'actuality and the earnestness of existence' (Kierkegaard 1983 [1843]:132–133). Attali suggests that reproduction signifies 'the death of the original' (Attali 2011 [1977]:89), and continues to hypothesize: 'if our societies seem unpredictable, if the future is difficult to discern, it is perhaps quite simply because *nothing happens, except for the artificially created pseudoevents and chance violence that accompany the emplacement of repetitive society*' (Attali 2011/1977:90, italics in original). In his desire to move away from repetition, essentially equating it with death, Attali seems to crave the 'every fleeting thing, the novel', which seems so threatening, so unnerving to Kierkegaard, while admitting that 'once the repetitive world is left behind, we enter a realm of fantastic insecurity' (Attali 2011/1977:146). Offering a sombre conclusion, he implores:

> Bringing an end to repetition, transforming the world into an art form and life into a shifting pleasure. Will a sacrifice be necessary? Hurry up with it, because – if we are still within earshot – the World, by repeating itself, is dissolving into Noise and Violence.
>
> (Attali 2011 [1977]:148)

As it turns out, this close connection between sonic repetition and death has recently manifested itself in a particularly sinister manner, as the 'drone'. This word, once reserved for repeated sound impulses exceeding 20 per second (Schafer 1977:78), also in music as 'a constant layer of stable pitch in a sound ensemble with no variation in intensity' (Augoyard and Torgue 2005:40), has now come to signify a semi-secret airborne weapon of the state. The appropriation of tangible and sonic forms for armaments is nothing new, however, as it is observed that during the French revolution, over a hundred thousand bells from sixty thousand church steeples were cast into cannons, and that 'the confiscation of bells in times of war was a long-standing tradition in Europe' (Siegert 2013:106). I am sure that most of us can agree with Kierkegaard, that this kind of repetition is a 'repetition of the wrong kind'.

Since repetition seems inevitable, the task is distinguishing a salutary kind: 'We repeated ourselves into this culture. We may be able to repeat ourselves out' (Fink 2005:22). Innumerable accounts attest to the fact that people are viscerally drawn to repeated prehistoric sound-forms: the enduring sounds of nature that persist into the present day. Lamenting his inability to repeat the so-desired previous experience of an evening at the theatre, Kierkegaard's Constantius seeks solace, a return home, to the source of all sounds, all speech, all music: water:

> You did not deny me what men want to deny me by making eternity just as busy and even more appalling than time. Then I lay by your side and vanished from myself in the immensity of the sky above and forgot myself in your soothing murmur! You, my happier self, you fleeting life that lives in the brook running past my father's farm, where I lie stretched out as if my body were an abandoned hiking stick, but I am rescued and released in the plaintive purling!

(Kierkegaard 1983 [1843]:166)

Conflict, coercion and exploitation – common features of political and agonistic explanatory models of industrialization – are familiar, partible, manageable and do not challenge existing social forms. An attentiveness to positive affective responses to industrial sonic forms as a counterpoint to the dominant transcript is akin to the discovery of social 'dark matter'. Like Ariadne's gift of a ball of string, or 'clue', to Theseus, the archaeological record of industry has formed an archive, a line of evidence, which, in its retracing, may offer the possibility of egress. Moreover, an archaeological awareness of the sounds of industrialization may assist in a recognition of the hopeful prospect of emergent and heraldic sonic forms.

References

Adolphson, Rudolph (1916), *Medical Record*, Quincy Mining Company Collection, Box 002, File 552, Michigan: MTU Archives and CCHC, MTU.

Attali, Jacques (2011 [1977]), *Noise: The Political Economy of Music*, Trans. Brian Massumi, Minneapolis: University of Minnesota Press.

Augoyard, Jean Francois and Henry Torgue (2005), *Sonic Experience: A Guide to Everyday Sounds*, Montreal: McGill University Press.

Becker, Judith (2004), *Deep Listeners: Music, Emotion and Trancing*, Bloomington and Indianapolis: Indiana University Press.

Benjamin, Jeffrey L. (2013), *Sound as Artifact*, Master's Thesis, Michigan Technological University.

——— (2014a), 'The Industrial Sonifact and the Soundscape of the Anthropocene', *Journal of Contemporary Archaeology*, 1:1, pp. 119–123.

——— (2014b), 'Listening to Industrial Silence: Sound as Artifact', in Hilary Orange (ed.), *Reanimating Industrial Spaces*, Walnut Creek: Left Coast Press.

Bobick, Thomas and Dennis Giardino (1976), *The Noise Environment of the Underground Coal Mine*, Washington: Mining Enforcement and Safety Administration, U.S. Department of the Interior.

Bourdieu, Pierre (1977), *Outline of a Theory of Practice*, Translated from French by Richard Nice, Cambridge: Cambridge University Press.

Buckley, Ann (ed.) (1998), *Hearing the Past: Essays in Historical Ethnomusicology and the Archaeology of Sound*, Liege: Etudes et Recherches Archeologiques de l'Universite de Liege.

Clayton, Martin, Rebecca Sager and Udo Will (2004), 'In Time with the Music: The Concept of Entrainment and Its Significance for Ethnomusicology', *ESEM Counterpoint*, 1, pp. 1–82.

Coates, Peter A. (2005), 'The Strange Stillness of the Past: Towards an Environmental History of Sound and Noise', *Environmental History*, 10:4, pp. 636–665.

De la Jara, Antonio and Simon Gardner (2010), 'Trapped Chile Miners Alive but Long Rescue Ahead', *Reuters* (2010), 22 August. Archived from the original on 25 September 2010. Accessed 6 August 2014.

Deetz, James (1967), *Invitation to Archaeology*, Garden City: Natural History Press.

DeNora, Tia (2000), *Music in Everyday Life*, Cambridge: Cambridge University Press.

Domanska, Ewa (2006), 'The Material Presence of the Past', *History and Theory*, 45, pp. 337–348.

Fink, Robert (2005), *Repeating Ourselves: American Minimal Music as Cultural Practice*, Berkeley: University of California Press.

Harrison, Rodney and John Schofield (2009), 'Archaeo-ethnography, Auto-archaeology: Introducing Archaeologies of the Contemporary Past', *Archaeologies*, 5:2, pp. 185–209.

Hobart, Henry (1991), *Copper Country Journal: The Diary of Schoolmaster Henry Hobart, 1863-1864*, Detroit: Wayne State University Press.

Hounshell, David A. (1984), *From the American System to Mass Production, 1800–1932*, Baltimore: Johns Hopkins.

Jackson, John B. (1970), *Landscapes*, Amherst: University of Massachusetts Press.

Jamison, James K. (1939), *This Ontonogan Country: The Story of an American Frontier*, Ontonogan: The Ontonogan Herald Company.

Jankowsky, Richard C. (2007), 'Music, Spirit Possession and the In-Between: Ethnomusicological Inquiry and the Challenge of Trance', *Ethnomusicology*, 16:2, pp. 185–208.

Kierkegaard, Søren (1983 [1843]), *Repetition*, Trans. Howard and Edna Hong, Princeton: Princeton University Press.

LaBelle, Brandon (2010), *Acoustic Territories: Sound Culture and Everyday Life*, London: Continuum.

Lindberg, Robert F. (1972), *Drop Forge Impact Noise: Temporary and Permanent Effects on Hearing Thresholds*, Ph.D. thesis, Lansing: Department of Audiology and Speech Sciences, Michigan State University.

Malmgren, Ruth (1982), 'Shut Down', in Larry D. Lankton and Charles K. Hyde (eds), *Old Reliable: An Illustrated History of the Quincy Mining Company*, Hancock: The Quincy Mine Hoist Association, Inc.

Mills, Steve (2005), *Applying Auditory Archaeology to Historic Landscape Characterisation: A Pilot Project in the Former Mining Landscape of Geevor and Levant Mines, West Penwith, Cornwall. A Report for English Heritage*, Cardiff: Cardiff School of History and Archaeology.

Monette, Clarence (1989), *Freda, Michigan: End of the Road*, Lake Linden: Self-published.

Muntersbjørn, Madeline (2011), email communication, 20 February.

Murdoch, Angus (1964), *Boom Copper: The Story of the First U.S. Mining Boom*, Calumet: Roy W. Drier and Louis G. Koepel.

Pallasmaa, Juhani (2005), *The Eyes of the Skin: Architecture and the Senses*, Chichester: John Wiley & Sons, Ltd.

Poincaré, Henri (1963), *Mathematics and Science: Last Essays*, New York: Dover Publications.

Rainio, Riitta (2006), 'Jingle Bells, Bells and Bell Pendants – Listening to the Iron Age Finland', *ICTM Study Group on Folk Musical Instruments: Proceedings from the 16th International Meeting*, pp. 117–125.

Rath, Richard C. (2003), *How Early America Sounded*, Ithaca: Cornell University Press.

Reznikoff, Iegor (2006), 'The Evidence of the Use of Sound Resonance from Palaeolithic to Medieval Times', in Chris Scarre and Graeme Lawson (eds), *Archaeoacoustics*, Cambridge: McDonald Institute for Archaeological Research, pp. 77–84.

Ricouer, Paul (2006 [2004]), *Memory, History, Forgetting*, Trans. Kathleen Blamey and David Pellauer, Chicago: University of Chicago Press.

Sale, Kirkpatrick (1995), *Rebels Against the Future: The Luddites and Their War on the Industrial Revolution*, Reading Massachusetts: Addison-Wesley.

Scarre, Chris and Graeme Lawson (eds) (2006), *Archaeoacoustics*, Cambridge: McDonald Institute for Archaeological Research.

Schaefer, R. Murray (1977), *The Tuning of the World*, Toronto: McClelland and Stewart.

Schaeffer, Pierre (2012 [1952]), *In Search of a Concrete Music*, Trans. Christine North and John Dack, Berkeley: University of California Press.

Siegert, Bernhard (2013), 'Mineral Sound or Missing Fundamental: Cultural History as Signal Analysis', in Alexandra Hui, Julia Kursell and Myles W. Jackson (eds), *Music, Sound and the Laboratory From 1750–1980, Osiris 28, A Research Journal Devoted to the History of Science and Its Cultural Influences*, Providence: University of Rhode Island.

Smilor, Raymond Wesley (1978), 'Confronting the Industrial Environment: The Noise Problem in America, 1893–1932', PhD Dissertation. University of Texas at Austin.

Smith, Mark M. (2012), 'The Garden in the Machine: Listening to Early American Industrialization', in Trevor Pinch and Karin Bijsterveld (eds), *The Oxford Handbook of Sound Studies*, Oxford: Oxford University Press, pp. 39–57.

Snyder, Bob (2001), *Music and Memory*, Cambridge: MIT Press.

Thompson, Emily (2002), *The Soundscape of Modernity: Architectural Acoustics and The Culture of Listening in America, 1900–1933*, Cambridge: MIT Press.

Thurner, Arthur W. (1994), *Strangers and Sojourners: A History of Michigan's Keweenaw Peninsula*, Detroit: Wayne State University Press.

Trower, Shelley (2012), *Senses of Vibration: A History of the Pleasure and Pain of Sound*, New York: Continuum.

Veblen, Thorstein (1964[1914]), *The Instinct of Workmanship*, New York: Dover.

Witmore, Christopher L. (2006), 'Vision, Media, Noise and the Percolation of Time', *Journal of Material Culture*, 11:3, pp. 267–292.

Yates, Frances (2001 [1966]), *The Art of Memory*, Chicago: University of Chicago Press.

Chapter 11

Hearing the Music

Claudia Gorbman

I am indebted to the scholar Tania Modleski for the title of my 1987 book on film music (Gorbman 1987). It is she who came up with the line from John Keats's 'Ode on a Grecian Urn': 'Heard melodies are sweet, but those unheard/Are sweeter; therefore, ye soft pipes, play on'. Keats bestowed a literary pedigree on my study of what was then a mostly unheralded musical form, and it seemed to express perfectly a basic, unchanging truth about the place of music in the filmic experience.

Keats's ode apostrophizes a Grecian urn, musing on the poet's relationship to art, mortality and time. The 'unheard melodies' in the poem are images of music-making painted on the ancient vessel. They are literally silent, and wholly unlike cinema they are frozen and static (or rather, ec-static), 'for ever young'. My use of the phrase 'unheard melodies' of course wrenched it from the poem's context. What does it mean to say that film music goes unheard, or more accurately, went largely unheard in the era of that book? Further, what does it mean for those who wrote about film music to assert that it *should* go unheard? In hindsight, *Unheard Melodies* is a distinctly twentieth-century work, inadequate to so much that is seen and heard in the digital age. Two related conditions that have massively changed, even before the arrival of digital technology, are the aesthetics of film music composition and mixing, and the degree to which music on screen is unheard. By the mid-1980s, pop music soundtracks not only rendered music emphatically heard, but they changed moviegoers' relationship to film music forever.

Thus, two issues are at stake here: the long-held *aesthetic*, the idea that musical scoring in film should not be heard but should go about its work unnoticed; and second, the *psychological* matter of whether and when audiences hear background music in films. This chapter considers these two issues and concludes by briefly offering unusual models from films of Paul Thomas Anderson.

Aesthetics

As soon as dramatic sound films acquired musical scores in the early 1930s, composers and critics vigorously debated the 'place' of music (henceforth recorded) in the new audiovisual hierarchy imposed by its coexistence with recorded dialogue and sound effects. While Korngold (whose status as a kind of genius specially invited from the concert world to compose for films at Warners set him apart) seemed to conceive of dialogue and even the image as mere settings for his music, and while more adventuresome film-makers, mostly in

Europe, envisioned all manner of possibilities for music-image relations, a general consensus rapidly arose in Hollywood advocating music's 'invisibility'. Nothing should impede the film-goer's focus on the primary narrative elements of visuals and dialogue. Music should be transparent; it should be the discreet waiter serving your soup from behind, allowing primacy to the food and the conversation.

Where did this aesthetic come from? In part, the technical limitations of early soundtracks. Anyone who has had the occasion to see a silent film with musical accompaniment knows that much of the thrill involves the live presence of the music. Especially in the movie-palace era of the 1920s, film was a theatrical experience, allowing for give and take between audience and musicians. When film adopted recorded sound, audiences traded in liveness for the privilege of hearing synchronized dialogue. In very short order, the cinema became vococentric, organized around the speaking voice.[1]

The felt necessity to relegate music to 'unheard' status then arises from the coronation of the speaking voice in film. With less than ideal technical conditions of sound recording and reproduction, music literally competed for space and intelligibility on the soundtrack. The clear transmission of speech won over everything else, at the very least until Dolby and multitrack sound allowed for greater separation and definition of soundtrack elements. Leonid Sabaneev cautioned composers in 1935: 'It should always be remembered, as a first principle of the aesthetics of music in the cinema, that logic requires music to give way to dialog':

> The dialog, which has replaced the caption, naturally occupies the first place, if only for the fact that it explains the meaning of the picture on the screen and music should therefore give way to it [...] As everyone knows, it is difficult to listen to music and speech at the same time; usually one of them is lost – either the music, or the meaning and beauty of the words.
>
> (Sabaneev, in Cooke 2010:44)

Apart from the technical problem of audibility, there was the concern that not only might music compete with dialogue but also, somehow, with the image itself. According to Hermann Closson, who wrote in the pages of *Modern Music*:

> The music must always be appreciably secondary to the screened image [...] It sometimes happens in the movies that the music suddenly asserts its rights, taking one away from the visual images into a blind world of sound. This of course is not permissible. The sound film relegates music to the inferior role of accompaniment, a sort of running bass that contributes merely a kind of emotional atmosphere.
>
> (Closson 1930:18, cited in Steiner 1989)

More generally, there was the issue of music versus 'the drama'. Composer Herbert Stothart wrote, 'If an audience is conscious of music where it should be conscious only of drama, then the musician has gone wrong' (Stothart 1939:143)

'Nobody goes to a movie theater to hear music', said Franz Waxman. We might surmise that there prevailed a fear of losing track of cinema's essence, as an art of moving pictures. But this was not necessarily the case at all, since for a few years at least, people did go to the movie theatre to hear/see synchronized dialogue. What some of these warnings about wayward music suggest is rather the fear of audiences being seduced, abducted by music, being 'taken away into a blind world of sound'. There is some ambiguity about Waxman's statement that no one goes to the movies to hear music. What is it that spectators went to see or hear, once the novelty of talking pictures had abated? Certainly, the appeal of moving pictures telling stories lay at the core of cinema; beyond that it can only be remarked that movies without music are almost as rare as movies without dialogue. But the music had to be tamed and subdued in its new relationship to talking images.

Music's subservience clearly meant different things for different writers. For Maurice Jaubert (1937) in France, music should bring a new element to the film, 'make physically perceptible to us the inner rhythm of the image' – although by no means should it 'detach' itself from the action. For others, it must underline, explicate, illustrate or dynamically match the action, and avoid standing out or conveying contradictory meanings or feelings that might cause confusion. Rules arose in order to carry out this aesthetic. Composers made certain to set background music in a different pitch register than voices to allow for maximum intelligibility of dialogue; sound mixers lowered the music's volume to 'give way' to dialogue, or they simply eliminated music from dialogue scenes altogether. Problems of how to start and stop music cues in the most unnoticeable ways were worked out. Composers and soundmen developed musical means to 'bring out' mood, and convey information such as settings and the feelings of characters, which might not otherwise be explicit.

There were rules governing the use of pre-existing music too, although these rules were more flexible. Max Steiner spoke out against the use of recognizable music, writing in 1937:

> It is my conviction that familiar music, however popular, does not aid the underlying score of a dramatic picture. I am [...] opposed to the use of thematic material that might cause the audience to wonder and whisper and try to recall the title of a particular composition, thereby missing the gist and significance of a whole scene which might be the key to the entire story.
>
> (Steiner, in Cooke 2010:60)

Underlying these rules of thumb was the notion of the engrossed or distracted film-goer. Music's function, like the functions of classical editing and camerawork and the invisible fourth wall, should be to wed the film-goer to the narrative, to enhance the suspension of disbelief. This is what 'unheard' meant: unnoticed as a distraction.

In sum, the cinema pushed to clarify narrative, to restabilize the apparatus of storytelling in the new audiovisual regime of synchronized sound and to minimize the potentially disruptive influences of music. This essentially meant changing the public's habits of music listening into a kind of music non-listening.

Given the language these composers and critics used – 'No one goes to the movie theater to hear music' – it is surprising how big and *operatic* film scoring actually was during Hollywood's classical studio years.[2] Dialogue underscoring as a kind of *Sprechgesang*, the use of stingers, along with Mickey Mousing and other widespread illustration practices, wedded the score extravagantly to visual and emotional movements on screen. It seems striking today that to those writing in the 1930s and 1940s such music was unobtrusive. How can this be? The answer lies in the history of conventions. Once given practices became the norm – even excessive devices such as Mickey Mousing – audiences were less likely to attend to them. It is the interactions between conventions and the historical conditions of audio-viewership that appear to change the paradigms of what goes heard and unheard.

All the same, in contemporary films where just about anything goes, from popular songs with lyrics to ethnic musics to idiosyncratic choices in sound mixing and audio-video editing, the 'servant of the image' (Maurice Jaubert) or 'servant of the story' position still persists. Maureen Crowe, co-founder and president of Hollywood's Guild of Music Supervisors, asserted in a recent interview, 'The main purpose [of music, by which she now

Figure 1: *Mildred Pierce* (Michael Curtiz, 1945). Mildred (Joan Crawford)'s horror at her cold-hearted daughter is emphasized by Max Steiner's loud orchestral stinger in the score.

means songs] is to serve the story, just like wardrobe and set design. If it doesn't serve the story – if it's forced into something – inevitably it doesn't work' (Chagollan 2013:13).

'Serving the story' may be the slippery phrase here. Is there any music that cannot be construed as serving the story? I have long claimed that *any* music placed onto a soundtrack will do *something*. Take a scene in, say, *Mildred Pierce* where the mother and daughter argue, and imagine it not with Steiner's romantic underscoring but with atonal music. The 'eerie' association with which Hollywood encodes it could work just fine, to express the mother's anguish about the alienation forming between her daughter and herself. Or substitute scoring with a song on the soundtrack –Cyrus's 'Wrecking Ball' or the Beatles' 'Yellow Submarine': very odd choices to be sure, but with each song we would instantly set about deriving meaning from the juxtaposition of music and visuals, determining how it serves the story.

The advocacy of unobtrusive, unheard music in the 1930s and beyond was based on the notion that perception in narrative cinema must be channelled on characters and actions. Narrative elements – setting, dialogue, acting, sound, lighting – must help to convey the story transparently. And perhaps in the early years of imperfect sound recording and mixing, this model of the single-focused spectator made sense. However, various kinds of distraction, encouraging multiple levels of spectatorship, were already in place by the end of the 1930s. One example would be extranarrative in-jokes about actors; the Cary Grant character in *His Girl Friday* refers to one Archie Leach. The entire genre of the movie musical addresses a kind of dual spectator, in its alternation between story and numbers. Above all, most postclassical cinema dismantles or at least mitigates the model of the spectator as unable to focus on more than one central phenomenon at a time.

Perception

Thus we move from considering the aesthetic imperative to make music the servant of the image, to exploring whether in the act of watching/hearing films, music is indeed noticed or not noticed. In the 1940s, Aaron Copland said of background scoring:

> Since it's music behind, or underneath, the [spoken] word, the audience is really not going to hear it, possibly won't even be aware of its existence; yet it undoubtedly works on the subconscious mind.
>
> (Copland, in 'Our New Music' [1941], Cooke 2010:87)

A brief note about vocabulary here. Even Copland would agree that the issue is not whether film music is heard; it is heard by anyone who is not deaf, as the sounds fall on the ears and register in the brain. In *Unheard Melodies*, I erroneously used the terms *conscious* and *unconscious* for the kind of hearing involved, and perhaps Copland's 'subconscious' is a little better than my 'unconscious'; but it is more appropriate to think in terms of active and passive hearing. More simply still, music either is or is not *noticed*. It is in that sense that I henceforth use the term 'heard'.

Is it even possible to explore the extent to which film music is actually heard? This is a perplexing question in terms of method. What film-going population are we talking about, and does it include music-lovers as well as the tone-deaf or merely musically untrained? Second, how can one determine empirically who notices music while watching a scene in the middle of a movie? If you ask a group of viewers after a screening whether they noticed the music in scene x, normally their short-term memory will fail them. If you tell subjects in advance what your purpose is, you are loading the dice and have already ruined your experiment. Similarly, you cannot show a film excerpt to subjects and ask about their response, since they have been prompted to attend to the music. We must approach the heardness or unheardness of film music with humility and circumspection. I base my findings on wholly unscientific data – film reviews, and the minor and arbitrary evidence gleaned from my own students in film courses. There is still less to rely on to understand how audiences in the past heard or didn't hear music; all that remains is film reviews and film criticism, and on a few occasions, studio audience research from test screenings. With film classes I can at least attend to audible responses of students during specific moments in a screening, and on unsolicited comments they may make immediately afterward.

Audio-viewing is determined historically, as well as generically and socially. Today's university students as a rule do not notice the excessively dramatic brassy jazzy music that accompanies an extreme long shot of Jean-Paul Belmondo running across a field after he shoots the motorcycle cop in Godard's *Breathless*/À *bout de souffle*, even though in 1959 it was appreciated as a camp reference to American B pictures. Students do, however, notice the insistent romantic scoring in a 1940s American melodrama like *Mildred Pierce*, which passed as 'inaudible' at the time. In other words, the interactions between conventions and the historical conditions of audio-viewership have retroactively changed the paradigms of what goes heard and unheard.

Unheard Melodies maintained, as a linchpin of its use of psychoanalytic theory, that classical film music is unheard. I compared cinema to hypnosis, since both induce a kind of trance (in the willing subject at least). I wrote:

> The trusting subject (trusting the hypnotist, the system of cinematic narrative) removes defenses to accessing unconscious fantasies. The hypnotist has his/her induction methods: soothing voice, repetition, rhythm, suggestion of pleasantly enveloping imagery, and focusing the subject's attention on one thing to the exclusion of others. Narrative cinema has its own 'induction methods'– including the harmonic, rhythmic, melodic suggestiveness and channeling effects of music. Film music lowers thresholds of belief.
>
> (Gorbman 1987:5–6)

I continued that film music relaxes the censor, and allows us no longer to find the diegetic action as unbelievable, however violent or intimate it may be. Music that is noticed – that calls attention to itself and swings away from the trance-inducing effect and toward the censor, the reality principle – disturbs this immersion.

I further asserted that 'most fiction films relegate music to the viewer's sensory background, that area least susceptible to rigorous judgment and most susceptible to affective manipulation' (Gorbman 1987:12). If we notice the music, the game is up.

Quite similarly to the 1930s critics and composers, the implicit model of the film-goer in this description is again a unitary subject, a film-goer incapable of shuttling back and forth between being *in* the story, in the trance, identifying with it and/or the characters, and being *outside* it at the same time. I echoed the idea that the great pleasure of classical cinema is that all of its elements, from camera positioning and editing to music, conspire to put a story on a silver platter for us. But it is clear now that this 'for-me-ness' need not exclude the pleasures of being outside the narrative at the same time. The far more accurate model of the film-goer at least since the 1960s is not a unitary subject but a multitasker, perfectly able to experience the film on multiple levels. Spectatorship itself has changed; postclassical spectators are used to multitasking, receiving films both inside and outside simultaneously.

This is not the occasion to trace the historical evolution of conventions of unobtrusive scoring (many have done so), but we know what would have been 'noticeable' in given eras and what passed as serviceable background music. It is well known that some composers and directors resisted the classical aesthetic. One notable case was Hanns Eisler, whose famous treatise written with T. W. Adorno, *Composing for the Films*, denounced the aesthetic of subservience, essentially claiming that this mode of scoring makes film-goers into passive idiots. Eisler's Brechtian aesthetic is especially strongly felt in his non-Hollywood film scores. Today we are still jolted by the music in his score for *Night and Fog/Nuit et brouillard* (1955), Resnais' documentary about the Holocaust: how original and moving it is to hear not low, minor-key, ominous orchestral sounds 'interpreting' the footage of crowded cattle-car trains leaving for the death camps, but instead, a flute playing a winsome solo. The flute contributes to the horrific images in an unconventional way, the way poetry makes us work harder than does prose.

Jean-Luc Godard's films are emblematic of the impulse to jettison the classical code. Godard unmasked (and continues to unmask) the arbitrariness of cinematic conventions through violations of editing rules, parody and irony, citation and allusion, language play, inconsistencies of character and sudden shifts of genre or tone. He likewise set about to violate the rules that made music the servant of the image and to give it a modernist place of honour. *My Life to Live/Vivre sa vie* (1962) first showed his penchant for interrupting musical lines in mid-phrase. Sometimes 'nondiegetic music', in Godard's questionably diegetic films, is mixed too loud, drowning out dialogue, in a direct affront to the mandate to make the speaking voice intelligible at all costs. Further disturbing the sanctity of the division between diegetic and nondiegetic, in *Hail Mary/Je vous salue Marie* (1985) the 'underscoring' consists of a string quartet – Beethoven, of all things, in a film about bank robbers; to complicate things further, the film periodically shows the actual members of the string quartet rehearsing their Beethoven. Godard playfully dismantles the conventions of music for specific genres: in *Pierrot le fou*, Karina and Belmondo break out into song as if they're in a musical, though the resulting 'number' does not behave like any musical seen up to 1965. The snippets of musical quotations frequently heard in his films cause us to wonder what they are and why they are placed there, creating precisely the distraction Max Steiner feared. Anyone familiar with Godard's work is aware of his films' prodigious play with music, his effort to open music to conscious hearing.

In Hollywood, too, music has evolved since the heyday of the classical model of music as servant. The introduction of the nondiegetic popular song in the 1960s challenged the notion that film-goers are unable to listen to a song's lyrics and musical logic at the same time as attend to the narrative onscreen. As late as 1987, I wrote that:

> songs with lyrics threaten to upset the aesthetic balance between music and narrative cinematic representation. The common solution movies take is not to declare songs off limits – for they can give pleasures of their own – but to defer significant action and dialogue during their performance.
>
> (Gorbman 1987:20)

This proved incorrect. The increasing tendency for films to include recognizable music of all kinds has assumed (and likely created) greater ability in the film-goer to be both in the story and outside it, and to appreciate how this music behaves.

The wide range of styles and formats of music in postclassical film raises a new question. In this constantly evolving film-musical environment – where my students do not especially notice Godardian tricks with the diegesis, or once-novel ironic genre play, or the quotation of pre-existing music – what does it take to refresh the heardness of scoring? How do you make music heard in the era when we've heard everything?

Paul Thomas Anderson

In the lineage of those auteurs who make scoring audible, a family that would have Godard, Kubrick and Tarantino as key ancestors, Paul Thomas Anderson must figure prominently. By his third feature, *Magnolia* (1999), he clearly discovered the freedoms allowed by unconventional uses of music. Among many examples, the film self-consciously blares Richard Strauss's *Also sprach Zarathustra*, or 'the *2001* theme' – in other words, a twice-familiar quotation – to introduce the stage appearance of Tom Cruise as the self-help sex guru. Most famously, *Magnolia* has a striking instance of what Jane Feuer's book on the Hollywood musical calls the passed-along song (Feuer 1982:16), a musical number that is sung in continuity by successive characters in different spaces. René Clair may have invented the device in 1931 in *Sous les toits de Paris/Under the Roofs of Paris*, in a sequence where characters in their separate flats sing or hum the title song. Another well-known example occurs at the beginning of *Meet Me in St Louis* (1944), when various members of the Smith family sing that title song in and around their home. The passed-along song that appears in *Magnolia* is Aimee Mann's 'Wise Up', heard as each of the dozen main characters sings along with a phrase or two. Anderson does not fret about the narrative placement of Mann's voice with which the various characters sing; could each of them have a radio on, or tape players precisely synchronized? The film takes total liberty with narrative space and causality, playing on the 'magical' departure from reality found in the musical.

The facts that *Magnolia* is not a musical, that this altered passed-along song expresses resignation rather than happiness and that it occurs entirely outside the context of genre expectations, make this sequence emphatically heard. The song at this point in the story shows each character reaching bottom of his or her individual torment – the refrain says, 'It's not going to stop, 'til you wise up' – and the auteur is exercising the right to unite them all at this moment that is both in diegetic narrative time and outside it. When Jason Robards, whose character Earl is so near death that he is no longer talking, suddenly sings too, we know that just as in musicals, this song has violated diegetic possibility. *Magnolia* was roundly praised and criticized, both as an astounding masterpiece and/or as a sprawling mess of a film, and this song is almost universally mentioned in the reviews and essays it spawned. In other words, the song couldn't help being noticed.[3]

In Anderson's next film, *Punch-Drunk Love* (2002), Adam Sandler plays Barry Egan, who owns a wholesale business in novelty toilet accessories. The movie draws us into the subjectivity of Barry, an outwardly self-effacing everyman but one who is highly anxious and prone to outbursts of violence. In one long sequence in his warehouse, he is barely coping with several serious distractions all at once. A phone-sex worker named Georgia, whom he called anonymously the previous evening, is in a nightmarish turn of events phoning him back and demanding money, increasingly hostile and threatening with each call. He makes a call to his bank to cancel his credit card so Georgia cannot access his funds. One of his eight sisters enters his workplace unannounced, accompanied by Lena, a woman he has seen before and to whom he is attracted. There are also the usual demands of his workplace, too numerous to itemize here.

The prolonged sequence has highly intrusive scoring (by John Brion). We may take as proof of its heardness the fact that several students in my course walked out of the film, saying they could not stand the soundtrack. It consists of a kind of concrete music, with electronic sounds, percussion both regular and irregular – a chime, snare drums, timpani, other varieties of drums, electronic growls, scrapings, a marimba sound. The sequence violates the usual relationship of music to the spoken voice. The pitch and rhythm of the score mix almost indiscriminately with dialogue and diegetic sounds such as phones ringing. As for the sound mix, the scoring threatens to drown out speech, so we must strain to hear the actors' words. Narrative surprises occur, such as a cargo loader vehicle crashing and spilling boxes, visible outside Barry's glass-walled office, and his sister marching back to Barry's office with an angry, purposeful expression. All the while, this half-music, half-random concrete sound obfuscates rather than clarifies. Visually, the use of a Steadicam for extremely long takes reinforces the subjective sense that Barry has no escape from the pressures assailing him from all sides.

Figure 2: *Punch-Drunk Love* (Paul Thomas Anderson, 2002). Barry (Adam Sandler) poses next to a small harmonium at his desk, his nervousness heightened by Jon Brion's chaotic score.

The scoring in *Punch-Drunk Love* is clearly subjective. In fact, while the content of some chatting between Barry and Lena about work and Hawaii is perfectly benign, only the noisy, fragmented scoring tells us that it is monstrously difficult for Barry to sustain his end of their conversation. The musical noise becomes an internal manifestation of his effort to focus and act casual while so much is threatening him. Few movies show such audacity in putting us inside the head of an angst-filled character in a comedy, which normally demands detachment.

Anderson's fifth film, *There Will Be Blood* (2007), was his *Citizen Kane* (Orson Welles, 1941), as a tale of a bigger-than-life American capitalist at the turn of the last century. What Welles did for the newspaper tycoon, Anderson does with his portrait of the oilman Daniel Plainview (Daniel Day-Lewis). The film shows the rise in Daniel's fortunes, his single-minded dedication to exploiting land and people, and ultimately his lonely isolation in Anderson's version of Kane's Xanadu. Two musical phenomena in *There Will Be Blood* deserve special mention: the overbearing loudness of some scoring, and a striking use of pre-existing music.

Intrusive scoring

The music, by Jonny Greenwood of Radiohead, befits the film's obsessive realism of setting, costume and language. It behaves rather unobtrusively: strings, close dissonance and mostly thin musical textures serve to underline Daniel's backbreaking years of prospecting, planning and tragedies and loss in the unforgiving western landscapes. (Although a bit of

Figure 3: *There Will Be Blood* (Paul Thomas Anderson, 2007). Jonny Greenwood's atonal sounds pulsate at the well explosion.

Arvo Pärt creeps in too, generally the music has been 'serving' the story well.) But then, in a highly dramatic sequence, an oil well catastrophically explodes with no warning. The destruction of the well rig and the subsequent fire seriously injures Daniel's young son who happened to be on the platform; the boy is rendered permanently deaf from the explosion's force. Once the wounded boy has been hurriedly carried to safety, Daniel simply abandons him, running out to lead the men to deal with the infernal oil well. As day turns to night, we witness the destruction of the rig, but emphatically not the destruction of Daniel's fortunes.

The scoring here nearly drowns out the dialogue, upsetting the conventional sound hierarchy. This music consists of a rhythmic throbbing of percussion and atonal strings. It is a kind of industrial mix, in which mechanical sounds and unidentifiable bass-register tonalities figure prominently. Daniel reacts to the catastrophe by realizing how vast the oil field underground is and knowing that he owns all the land. 'No one else can get to it!' he shouts over the sounds of roaring fire, crashing beams and discordant music. The shot silhouetting Daniel and his deputy against the night blaze evokes the devil himself in the dance of death, aided and abetted by the cacophonous soundtrack.

Pre-existing music

Earlier in *There Will Be Blood*, Daniel moves in on a godforsaken town on a prairie, importing work crews to construct oil rigs. When the first well is complete and ready to operate, he gathers the townspeople to witness its inauguration. It is a happy ceremony for a new era

Figure 4: Daniel (Daniel Day-Lewis) inaugurates a well before the western community.

that will, he promises, bring prosperity and a better life to the residents. In a theatrical gesture before the ragtag gathering, Daniel instructs his boy to start the well pump. The music that strikes up nondiegetically on the soundtrack is the final movement of Brahms' D major violin concerto. It does not function to give us access to Daniel's consciousness, as scoring does in *Punch Drunk Love*. Nor is it appropriate to the film's setting; it hails from the right era, but not at all from the right cultural milieu. It is fittingly exultant, but there is a jarring clash of style between image and music. Perhaps this sensation of strangeness has to do with the concerto's gorgeous quality: the clean, bright, high-fidelity recording and the evocation of high European culture contrast with the unremittingly naturalistic New World dust and grime on the screen.

The mismatch in styles points to a wilful auteur signature: Paul Thomas Anderson is putting a soundtrack to this moment, and not subtly either – the music again drowns out dialogue and other sounds. The narrative moment is fraught, because the local minister is being upstaged, the townsfolk have signed onto an oil-drilling enterprise that will in truth destroy their frontier town and Daniel Plainview is conning everyone into believing he is a benevolent capitalist and family man. Is the magnificent violin concerto lying, somehow, in cahoots with the protagonist's false promises? Or is this just a case in point that any music you put on a soundtrack will do *something*?

That is not all. At the very end of *There Will Be Blood*, Daniel has alienated his now-adult son forever; he is a rich old oil baron, alone and mad. The final scene takes place in the bowling alley of his mansion. Eli the preacher comes to visit him, and the conversation that ensues, baring the base motives and abjection of both characters, ends in Daniel's unhinged killing of Eli. The manservant, having heard some commotion, comes downstairs and asks his master if everything is all right. Daniel, exhausted, sits in the wreckage and utters the final words: as if talking about the meal the man had served him, he says, 'I'm finished'.

With that, the beautiful Brahms violin concerto returns! It is utterly unmotivated. Yet at the end of this harrowing scene it provides a flourish of beauty, completely outside meaning. Daniel's 'I'm finished' might signify in a number of ways. He is finished with the visit that has just been paid him, he has finished the food the servant had brought, he is finished as a man. He has self-destructed in all his greed, competitiveness and inhumanity – which paradoxically makes him so very human. The Brahms is *heard*, perhaps as Anderson's musical 'I'm finished'.

Conclusion

This chapter began with the idea of background music, the functional music designed to occupy the rear of consciousness, in order then to consider what people tend to hear and not hear of movie music. It should be emphasized that generalizations, often unfair ones, are necessary in order to think about the phenomenon of heardness. Of course, millions of movie-goers have indeed noticed 'background' music, as we know from the market for movie soundtrack albums that has flourished especially since the 1950s.[4] And there are entire genres and cycles – think of the Star Wars movies and the theme songs for James Bond films – that make a spectacle of music, so that we cannot help but recognize those tunes. Thus, both the degree of film-goers' orientation to music and repeat experiences with given films allow for great variation in the consequent tendency to attend or not to film music.

Be that as it may, in light of this discussion it is possible to come to some basic conclusions in answer to the question of what it takes to make music heard in a film now. We may sum up three primary routes to increasing music's heardness: (1) defying current formal and stylistic convention, (2) introducing technical 'errors' of recording, mixing, or editing, and (3) introducing recognizable pre-existing music. Paul Thomas Anderson's sophisticated awareness of the powers of music moves it from background to foreground. His films invite us to richly feel the physicality and texture of music as it mixes with images, and to marvel at the strong poetic potential for meaning in the mix.

References

Anderson, Paul Thomas (1999), *Magnolia*, USA: New Line Cinema.
—— (2002), *Punch-Drunk Love*, USA: New Line Cinema.
—— (2007), *There Will Be Blood*, USA: Miramax, Paramount Vantage.
Antheil, George (1936), 'On the Hollywood Front', *Modern Music*, 13:4, pp. 46–49.

Chagollan, Steve (2013), 'Add a Song, Make a Movie', *New York Times*, 3 March 2013, Entertainment section, p. 13.

Chion, Michel (1999), *The Voice in Cinema*, Trans. Claudia Gorbman, New York: Columbia University Press.

Clair, René (1930), *Under the Roofs of Paris/Sous les toits de Paris*, France: Films Sonores Tobis.

Closson, Hermann (1930), 'The Case against *Gebrauchsmusik*', *Modern Music*, 7:2, pp. 15–19.

Cooke, Mervyn (2010), *The Hollywood Film Music Reader*, New York: Oxford University Press.

Curtiz, Michael (1945), *Mildred Pierce*, USA: Warner Bros.

Feuer, Jane (1982), *The Hollywood Musical*, Bloomington: Indiana University Press.

Godard, Jean-Luc (1960), *Breathless/À bout de souffle*, France: France: Société Nouvelle de Cinématographie (SNC).

—— (1962), *My Life to Live/Vivre sa vie: film en douze tableaux*, France: Les Films de la Pléiade.

—— (1985), *Hail Mary/Je vous salue Marie*, France: Sara Films.

—— (1965), *Pierrot le fou*, France: Société Nouvelle de Cinématographie (SNC).

Gorbman, Claudia (1987), *Unheard Melodies: Narrative Film Music*, Bloomington: Indiana University Press.

Jaubert, Maurice (1937), 'Music on the Screen', in Charles Davy (ed.), *Footnotes to the Film*, New York: Oxford University Press, pp. 101–115.

London, Kurt (1936), *Film Music: A Summary of the Characteristic Features of Its History, Aesthetics, Technique, and Possible Developments*, Trans. Eric S. Bensinger, London: Faber & Faber.

Minnelli, Vincente (1944), *Meet Me in St. Louis*, USA: Metro Goldwyn Mayer.

Resnais, Alain (1955), *Night and Fog/Nuit et brouillard*, France: Argos Films.

Sabaneev, Leonid (1935), *Music for the Films: A Handbook for Composers and Conductors*, Trans. S. W. Pring, London: Pitman. Excerpted in Mervyn Cooke (2010), pp. 38–47.

Smith, Jeff (1998), *The Sounds of Commerce: Marketing Popular Film Music*, New York: Columbia University Press.

Steiner, Fred (1989), 'What Were Musicians Saying about Movie Music during the First Decade of Sound? A Symposium of Selected Writings', in Clifford McCarty (ed.), *Film Music I*, Los Angeles: The Film Music Society, pp. 81–107.

Steiner, Max (1937), 'Scoring the Film', in Mervyn Cooke (2010), pp. 55–68.

Stothart, Herbert (1939), 'Film Music', in Stephen Watts (ed.), *Behind the Screen*, London: Barker, pp. 139–144.

Notes

1 For the sound film's vococentrism, see the works of Michel Chion, for example, Chion (1999:1–13).

2 Composers and critics frequently invoked the comparison of film to opera during the 1930s. George Antheil (1936) wrote in his film music column, for example: 'Picture music is, quite simply, a kind of modern opera'.

3 Janet Maslin wrote in the *New York Times*, 'But when that group sing-along arrives, *Magnolia* begins to self-destruct spectacularly' (17 December 1999). For his part, Roger Ebert wrote

in the *Chicago Sun-Times*, '*Magnolia* is the kind of film I instinctively respond to. Leave logic at the door. Do not expect subdued taste and restraint, but instead a kind of operatic ecstasy' (7 January 2000). I vote with Ebert: the passed-along song creates a complicated kind of grace, musical comfort and community.

4   On the other hand, this market did not take off significantly until dynamic interaction of two media industries – popular music and film – made popular songs profitable in the 1950s. Jeff Smith's now classic study *The Sounds of Commerce* (1998) documents the economic, institutional and formal evolution of film music trends in that period.

List of Contributors

James Andean is a musician and sound artist. He is active as both a composer and a performer in a range of fields, including electroacoustic composition and performance, improvisation, sound installation and sound recording. He is a founding member of the improvisation and new music quartet Rank Ensemble; the interdisciplinary improvisation ensemble the Tuesday Group; and is one-half of the audiovisual performance art duo Plucié/DesAndes. He has performed throughout Europe and North America, and his works have been performed around the world. He is a Lecturer at the Music, Technology and Innovation Research Centre of De Montfort University.

Jeff Benjamin is an artist and writer living in New York, USA. He has a Masters degree in Industrial Archaeology from Michigan Technological University, and is currently a Ph.D. student in archaeology at Columbia University.

Johannes Brusila is Professor of Musicology at Åbo Akademi University in Turku, Finland. Previously he has also worked as Director of the Sibelius Museum and as freelance journalist at the Finnish Broadcasting Corporation. His writings include 'Local Music, Not from Here' – The Discourse of World Music Examined through Three Zimbabwean Case Studies: The Bhundu Boys, Virginia Mukwesha and Sunduza, and publications and co-edited volumes on the music culture of the Swedish-speaking minority of Finland, on music industry and on various ethnomusicological subjects.

Sara Cohen is a Professor at the School of Music, University of Liverpool, and Director of the Institute of Popular Music. She has a DPhil in Social Anthropology from Oxford University and is author of Rock Culture in Liverpool: Popular Music in the Making (1991, Oxford University Press) and Decline, Renewal and the City in Popular Music Culture: Beyond the Beatles (2007, Ashgate).

Jez Collins works at Birmingham City University in the Centre for Media and Cultural Research, where he researches popular music, cultural heritage and public history and activist archiving in online communities. Collins is interested in the role popular music plays in the manifestation of individual and collective memory and identity. Collins is the founder of the Birmingham Music Archive and co-executive producer of the film *Made in Birmingham: Reggae Punk Bhangra*. He is a co-Director of Un-Convention, a trustee of the UK National Jazz Archive and an advisory board member of the Community Archives and Heritage Group as well as Birmingham Civic Society's Heritage Committee.

Jelena Gligorijević completed her MA in Popular Music Studies at Liverpool's Institute of Popular Music (IPM), after which she continued with her studies at Turku University's (UTU) musicology department. She is currently a member of two Finnish doctoral programmes – one in Popular Culture Studies (PPCS) coordinated by UTU (2012–2014), and the other in Music Research (MUTO) coordinated by Helsinki's Sibelius Academy (2015). Her Ph.D. project is concerned with two major Serbian music festivals whose conceptual differences provide fruitful ground for an analysis of the multi-layered relationships between culture, politics and national identity in post-Milošević Serbia. She has published in the fields of classical music theory, music education, popular music studies, gender and queer studies, focusing in particular on issues of identity, place and music.

Claudia Gorbman is Emeritus Professor of Film Studies at the University of Washington Tacoma (USA). She taught at UW Tacoma since it was founded in 1990; before that she taught for 15 years at Indiana University. She is the author of *Unheard Melodies: Narrative Film Music* (Indiana and BFI, 1987). She has translated and edited five books by Michel Chion: *Audio-Vision: Sound on Screen* (Columbia UP, 1994), *The Voice in Cinema* (Columbia, 1999), *Kubrick's Cinema Odyssey* (BFI, 2001), *Film, A Sound Art* (Columbia, 2009), and *Words on Screen* (Columbia, 2016). With John Richardson and Carol Vernallis she co-edited *The Oxford Handbook of New Audiovisual Aesthetics* (NY: Oxford, 2012). She writes about film sound, film music and French film.

Yrjö Heinonen, Ph.D., is Senior Lecturer in Musicology (University of Turku, Finland) and Adjunct Professor in Contemporary Culture Studies (University of Jyväskylä, Finland). Since 1985, Heinonen has worked in several teaching and research posts at the universities of Jyväskylä and Turku. His doctoral dissertation (1995) explored the songwriting and recording practices of the Beatles as a compositional process. During 1997–2001, he led the BEATLES 2000 Research Project and acted as the Editor-in-Chief of the *Beatlestudies* series (1–3). During 2002–2007, he conducted a research project called 'Historicity, Autobiographicality, and Nostalgia in Contemporary Finnish Popular Music'. Since then, his work has dealt with various musical genres, often applying approaches from both cultural history and cultural anthropology to contemporary cultural and media studies.

Bruce Johnson, formerly a Professor in English, is now Adjunct Professor, Communications, University of Technology Sydney, Visiting Professor, Music, University of Glasgow, and Docent and Visiting Professor, Cultural History, University of Turku. His current research lies in music, acoustic cultural history and the emergence of modernity. A jazz musician, broadcaster, record producer and arts policy advisor to Australian state and federal governments, he was prime mover in the establishment of the government-funded Australian Jazz Archive, and co-founder of the International Institute for Popular Culture based in Turku. His publications include *The Oxford Companion to Australian Jazz; Dark Side of the Tune: Music and Violence* (with Martin Cloonan); *Earogenous Zones: Cinema, Sexuality and Music* (ed.); *They Do Things Differently There: Essays on Cultural History* (ed. with Harri Kiiskinen).

Lars Kaijser is Associate Professor at Department of Ethnology, History of Religion and Gender Studies, Stockholm University. His research focuses on middlemen working in the commercial, cultural and voluntary sectors. His doctoral dissertation was on the work of country shopkeepers (1999). In addition, he has studied Beatles tourism in Liverpool, concert organizers in rural Sweden and how different social networks organize and use 1970s Swedish music in today's practices.

Kaarina Kilpiö (Doctor of Social Sciences) currently works as University Lecturer at Sibelius Academy of the University of the Arts, Helsinki. Her research interests include the study of different (mainly historical) uses of music and sound technologies. In addition to numerous articles about advertising music, background music and Finns as music listeners, she has published a 2005 dissertation *Kulutuksen sävel. Suomalaisen mainoselokuvan musiikki 1950-luvulta 1970-luvulle* (with an English summary 'Consumer Tunes. Music in Finnish advertising films from 1950s to 1970s') and the 2015 book on cassette culture in Finland, *Koko kansan kasetti.* She has also co-edited several volumes, including *Kuultava menneisyys*, an anthology of Finnish soundscape history.

Paul Long is Professor of Media and Cultural History and Director of the Birmingham Centre for Media and Cultural Research at Birmingham City University, Birmingham, UK. He is the author of *Only in The Common People: The Aesthetics of Class in Post-War Britain* (Cambridge Scholars Publishing, 2008). Alongside work on history, archives and heritage, his writing on popular music includes studies of songwriting (with Simon Barber), BBC4's Britannia series (with Tim Wall) as well as the role of student unions in the UK live circuit. He recently completed research into community engagements with culture as part of the AHRC-funded project 'Cultural Intermediation and the Creative Economy'.

Morten Michelsen is Associate Professor in Musicology in the Department of Arts and Cultural Studies at the University of Copenhagen. He has focused on popular music and published a book on US and UK rock criticism (*Rock Criticism from the Beginning*, 2005), a book on Danish rock culture (*Rock in Denmark*, 2013) and shorter analyses of the music of Björk, Bowie, Metallica and Michael Jackson, with a focus on the sound parameter. Michelsen is also engaged in the establishment of the research field of sound studies in Denmark and Europe. Currently, he is Chair of the European Sound Studies Association

ESSA and member/head of a series of research projects concerned with sound and radio. His special focus here is interbellum music-radio relations.

John Richardson is Professor and Chair of Musicology at the University of Turku in Finland and a specialist in cultural musicology, research on avant-garde music, popular music studies and audiovisual studies. His publications include the edited volumes *The Oxford Handbook of New Audiovisual Aesthetics* (eds. Richardson, Gorbman and Vernallis 2013) and *The Oxford Handbook of Sound and Image in Digital Media* (eds. Vernallis, Herzog and Richardson 2013), *Essays on Sound and Vision* (eds. Richardson and Hawkins; Gaudeamus 2007), and the monographs *An Eye for Music: Popular Music and the Audiovisual Surreal* (Oxford University Press, 2011) and *Singing Archaeology: Philip Glass's Akhnaten* (1999). Richardson's work is widely known and cited, he has given keynote presentations in several countries and held honorary positions including Chair of the Finnish Society for Musicology and Director of the International Institute for Popular Culture (IIPC).

Index

Note: Usual procedure has been followed in indexing scholars and publications dilated upon at greater length than simple citation in the main text, but not in passing or parenthetical source citations.

Bold numbers denote reference to illustrations.